Open Heritage

Birkhäuser
Basel

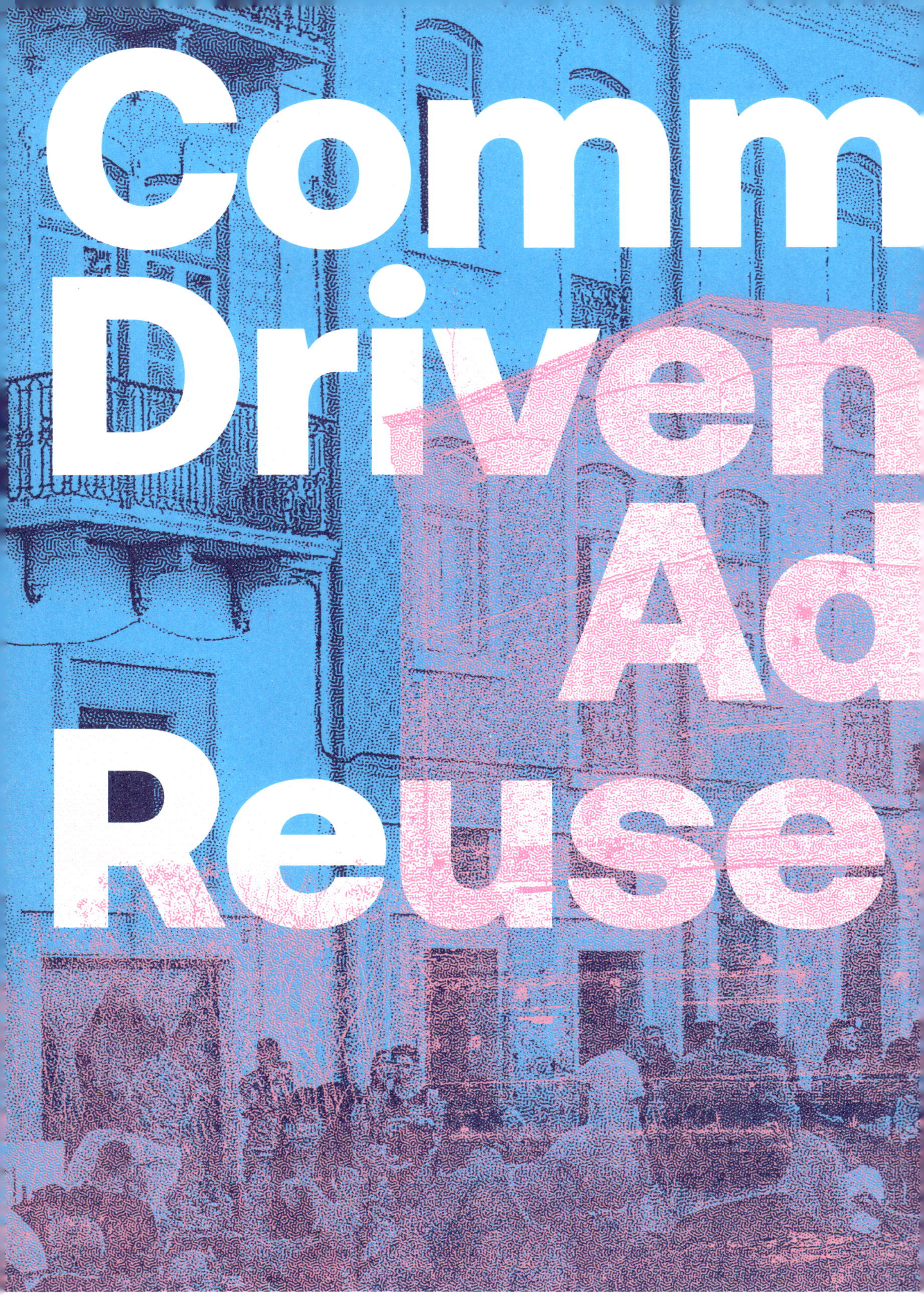
Comm
Driven
Ad
Reuse

unity–
ptive

in Euro
Best P

pe:
actice

Table of Contents

Introduction

Heike Oevermann,
Hanna Szemző,
Levente Polyák,
Harald A. Mieg

How to bring new meanings and purposes to heritage sites that are overlooked, situated in marginal areas, or underused for other reasons? How to approach local communities and involve them in meaningful ways? The practical responses to such questions often involve complex processes. This book explores these challenges while addressing several core themes: reducing the neglect and waste of built resources; broadening the access to and beneficiaries of refurbished heritage sites; and building institutionalised and political support for the multi-vocality that should define local heritage(s) throughout the countries and regions of Europe.

The contributors to this book are all researchers involved in the OpenHeritage project, and began work on this publication with the ambition of sharing some of the in-depth case studies explored in the project, the results of its experiments, and the theoretical considerations and methodological innovations arrived at. They have diverse backgrounds that have allowed the development of complex and nuanced viewpoints in the course of this work. The project also shaped their conviction that reusing heritage sites requires openness on several levels: an open definition of what constitutes heritage; who can be involved in its maintenance; and finally, an open process of reuse, capable of flexibly adapting to current and future challenges. The book shows that people are key to identifying, understanding, conserving, and adaptively reusing heritage sites and places.

What is the OpenHeritage project?

The OpenHeritage project (Grant Agreement No. 776766) was a four-year European project, funded by the Horizon 2020 programme, that brought together actors from diverse academic backgrounds and practitioners with various roles in heritage, planning, and adaptive reuse from 11 countries. The project identified and tested challenging and pioneering practices of adaptive heritage reuse (AHR) in socially or geographically marginal contexts throughout Europe. It also explored best practices in policy, governance, funding, and management for the adaptive reuse of heritage in Europe, and presented the lessons learned, focusing on socially and financially sustainable models of heritage management. Through six Cooperative Heritage Labs (Fig. 1, 2, 3), it worked with communities, local businesses, local and municipal administrations; tried out new forms of engagement techniques; employed crowdfunding and crowdsourcing mechanisms to create active heritage communities; and contributed to both research and policy development, by analysing 16 Observatory Cases. The project also devised various models and a 'toolbox' of practical measures for inclusive management of AHR projects, creating a flexible, adaptable framework that is applicable under different institutional circumstances.

Such inclusive approaches align with the broadened and refined concept of adaptive reuse laid down in the European Council's Work Plan for Culture 2015–2018. Among other aspects of cultural policy, this outlines the European Union's approach to cultural heritage sites, emphasising accessible and inclusive culture, an enhanced role for the creative economy, and the promotion of cultural diversity, with improved access to different forms of cultural and linguistic expression. Furthermore, it allows the update of the functions of cultural heritage assets in line with changing societal needs. Previously, heritage has primarily served to stimulate local economic development through its integration into 'the experience economy' (Harrison, 2010, pp. 84–88), i.e., the service industries, tourism, and travel. In contrast, open-heritage-inspired reuse through participatory methods opens up development pathways that are more community-oriented and less dependent on tourism or cultural industries per se.

Lastly, even if it is not always evident, the project work was strongly inspired by the concept of the governance of commons, i.e., the innovative governance idea focusing on the community management of shared resources (Iaione, 2015; Ostrom, 1990). For cultural heritage, this creates a new approach to managing sites in mutual ownership. This approach puts forward clear-cut mechanisms of responsibility and involvement, provides accessible solutions for resolving disputes, allows modification of the common rules, and assumes that members have the interest and capacity to maintain the common heritage through a commoning process. The applicability of these ideas has been greatly improved by the advances in internet-based co-management practices.

Fig. 1
Bicycle tour in the Centocelle Park

Fig. 2
Workshop in Scugnizzo Liberato

Fig. 3
Sunderland High Street West

1

2

3

About this book

The book is divided into two parts to highlight both the practical experience gained in the project and the theoretical lessons learned from it. The first part – *Cases, Labs, Tools: Enabling Collaboration* – presents nine cases from Portugal to Ukraine, and Northern England to Southern Italy, and provides short texts on how collaboration can be supported in governance, financing, and regional integration. The cases also summarise the main findings and provide orientation for the practical field. The second part – *Theory, Definition, and Context* – embeds the findings of the cases within the academic discours on heritage management, focusing on the aspects of heritage-making and planning, AHR, and transferability. Beyond the traditional understanding of listed heritage – and its counterpart, the discourse of authorised heritage – these chapters discuss how the potential of heritage places can be realised through sustainable and inclusive heritage reuse.

Starting points

Three starting points shaped both the OpenHeritage project and this book. Firstly, the geographical focus lies in Europe, and thus the political aspects discussed here are related to Europe's politics. The book applies the European Commission's definition of cultural heritage as: 'a rich and diverse mosaic of cultural and creative expressions, our inheritance from previous generations of Europeans and our legacy for those to come' (European Commission, 2023). This definition is sufficiently open and flexible to accommodate a variety of meanings, and supports our emphasis on giving local communities an important role in defining, shaping, reusing, and maintaining built heritage assets. By applying the term 'heritage community' (Council of Europe, 2005), this commits to involving various groups attached to heritage sites but also acknowledges that affected parties can reside beyond the locality. The concept of heritage communities implies building attachment and fostering engagement. Our understanding is in line with the findings that heritage conservation efforts based on grassroots community engagement have much better long-term prospects, since the community is more likely to remain motivated and engaged with the initiative over time (Harrison, 2013; Macdonald, 2013; Perkin, 2010).

Secondly, the practices of alternative financing and adjoining new governance arrangements and juridical instruments provide input for this book. The financial crisis of 2008 and its shockwaves in real estate markets were major drivers of developments in this sector. A whole range of new financial and institutional models have been developed by civil society initiatives, activists, financial and legal innovators, public authorities, private investors, public–private and private–public partnerships, as well as by current and prospective residents of innovative housing initiatives and civic consortia. Derived from various authors, the book presents case studies and discusses innovative approaches to finance projects that enable collaboration.

Thirdly, the cases and labs use new and evolving concepts and tools with regard to governance and actor-relational planning. Rather than governing a demarcated area, governance is focused on places that elude fixed territorial borders. Its point of departure is the consideration of the holistic added values and framing of places of cooperating actors (stake- and shareholders) from business, the public sector, and civic society. Instead of relying solely on a traditional vertical (top-down or bottom-up) concept of 'government', the governance frameworks in OpenHeritage integrate organisational approaches inspired by networks and (re-)framing processes (Rydin, 2010). Governance, therefore, is also horizontal, exploring mutual arrangements and win-win engagements between stakeholders and communities. In an interdisciplinary logic, the book links the fields of heritage conservation and management with recent experiments in territorial development, community finance, citizen participation, and shared administration (Polyák et al., 2021). Durable and resilient relations can be established when community-led and bottom-up initiatives are matched with government action, especially if participation in decision-making is extended to participation in governance, management, and maintenance.

To summarise: based on the results of the project, this book introduces the open heritage approach, which is both novel and is conceptualised here. Abandoned or underused listed and potential sites of cultural heritage provide major opportunities for local communities to overcome social, economic, and environmental challenges, and to utilise such sites as cornerstones of local development, as will be highlighted in the following chapters.

List of References

Council of Europe. (2005). *Framework convention on the value of cultural heritage for society* (CETS No. 199). Council of Europe. https://www.coe.int/en/web/culture-and-heritage/faro-convention

European Commission. (2023). Cultural heritage. European Commission. http://ec.europa.eu/culture/policy/culture-policies/cultural-heritage_en

Harrison, R. (2010). *Understanding the politics of heritage*. Manchester University Press.

Harrison, R. (2013). *Heritage: Critical approaches*. Routledge.

Iaione, C. (2015). Governing the urban commons. *Italian Journal of Public Law*, 7(1), 170–221.

Macdonald, S. (2013). *Memorylands: Heritage and identity in Europe today*. Routledge.

Ostrom, E. (1990). *Governing the commons: The evolution of institutions for collective action*. Cambridge University Press.

Perkin, C. (2010). Beyond the rhetoric: Negotiating the politics and realising the potential of community-driven heritage engagement. *International Journal of Heritage Studies*, *16*(1–2), 107–122.

Polyák, L., Bod, S., & Bródy, L. S. (2021). *The power of civic ecosystems: How community spaces and their networks make our cities more cooperative, fair and resilient*. Cooperative City Books.

Rydin, Y. (2010). *Governing for sustainable urban development*. Routledge.

Part 1
Enabling Collaboration: Cases, Labs, Tools

Café
Estúdio

The three sections on enabling collaboration – A. Policies and Governance, B. Financing Projects, and C. Supporting Regional Integration – show that the impact of any model applied for community-driven multi-stakeholder adaptive reuse will be strongly influenced by the local and national regulatory-institutional environment.

This Part 1 of the book introduces nine case studies: Cascina Roccafranca (Turin, Italy), High Street West (Sunderland, UK), London CLT (UK), Färgfabriken (Stockholm, Sweden), Stará Tržnica (Bratislava, Slovakia), Jam Factory (Lviv, Ukraine), Largo Residências (Lisbon, Portugal), Praga Lab (Warsaw, Poland), and Broei (Ghent, Belgium). Some concern listed heritage buildings, and all are built heritage sites that are adaptively reused through community-driven processes. Eight were part of the cases examined in OpenHeritage, while the Broei case was included following a consortium visit to the site.

Policies and Governance: the specific legal framework that regulates the applicability of inclusive reuse is of particular importance regarding open heritage's room for manoeuvre. Heritage cultures and institutions vary between – and even within – countries.

Financing Projects: most built heritage sites in EU countries are reused or accommodate changing functions through market mechanisms; but there is great variation in whether the historical or architectural character of sites considered as 'heritage' are viewed as either adding value or impeding development. Local narratives and developments of economically and socially successful projects create a more fertile context for future adaptive reuse proposals. A further challenge is the potential scarcity, within the construction industry, of the traditional skills necessary for such projects. Financial incentives (tax concessions or grants) to reuse heritage are also highly variable, as are the opportunities for combining public heritage funding with other sources and with new and innovative funding mechanisms.

Supporting Regional Integration: as the OpenHeritage project has shown, local democratic traditions are important in achieving participatory engagement, which depends upon: a project's local embeddedness; local authorities' willingness to engage; and whether citizens identify with and feel connected to local heritage – whether officially defined as such or not, tangible or intangible.

A

Enabling Collaboration: Policies and Governance

By Levente Polyák, Daniela Patti, Loes Veldpaus

The OpenHeritage project was conceived to explore a more inclusive, sustainable, and community-based concept of adaptive heritage reuse (AHR), a concept that is discussed in greater detail in Part 2 of this book. The project built on hands-on good practices (Observatory Cases) and ongoing processes (Cooperative Heritage Labs), as well as their policy contexts. Researchers emphasised the uniqueness of all cases, often based on individual initiatives, idiosyncratic constellations of actors, and personal engagement; and also revealed clear patterns across the cases, particularly in some of the key factors facilitating or hindering success (Veldpaus et al., 2019). All of the Observatory Cases and Cooperative Heritage Labs were contextualised through policy analysis of their broader contexts, particularly the enabling or hindering policies and the governance structures that define the modalities of cooperation and decision-making between the various actors involved in developing them (Polyák et al., 2019).

Adaptive heritage reuse at the crossroads of policies

There is a wide variety of policies potentially relevant for the community-driven adaptive reuse of heritage assets, which need to be taken into account for an integrated approach. The structural factors include horizontal and vertical policy integration, e.g., across heritage and planning policies, and between tiers of governance (Veldpaus et al., 2020). Moreover, AHR also becomes easier when heritage is seen as 'useful' to broader policy aims such as sustainability or regeneration. This can extend to a wide range of policies dealing with place, including those on environmental sustainability, participation, health and wellbeing, socio-economic development, housing, culture, and tourism. Finally, it is helpful to rethink building codes, regulations on changes of use (including temporary uses), and zoning laws, as well as tendering, funding, and procurement criteria, and fee/tax levies or waivers. Such policies often focus on new-build or archetypal restoration projects, with no regard for the 'hybrid' needs of AHR.

The policies used in the OpenHeritage Observatory Cases and Cooperative Heritage Labs, to enable community-driven adaptive heritage reuse, range from heritage protection (withholding demolition permits), urban planning (zoning to allow experimental uses), and real estate policies (providing access to properties or innovative financial mechanisms to renovate endangered heritage buildings), to housing (requiring a proportion of affordable housing), and social and cultural policies (funding activities or encouraging local cooperation).

Cascina Roccafranca

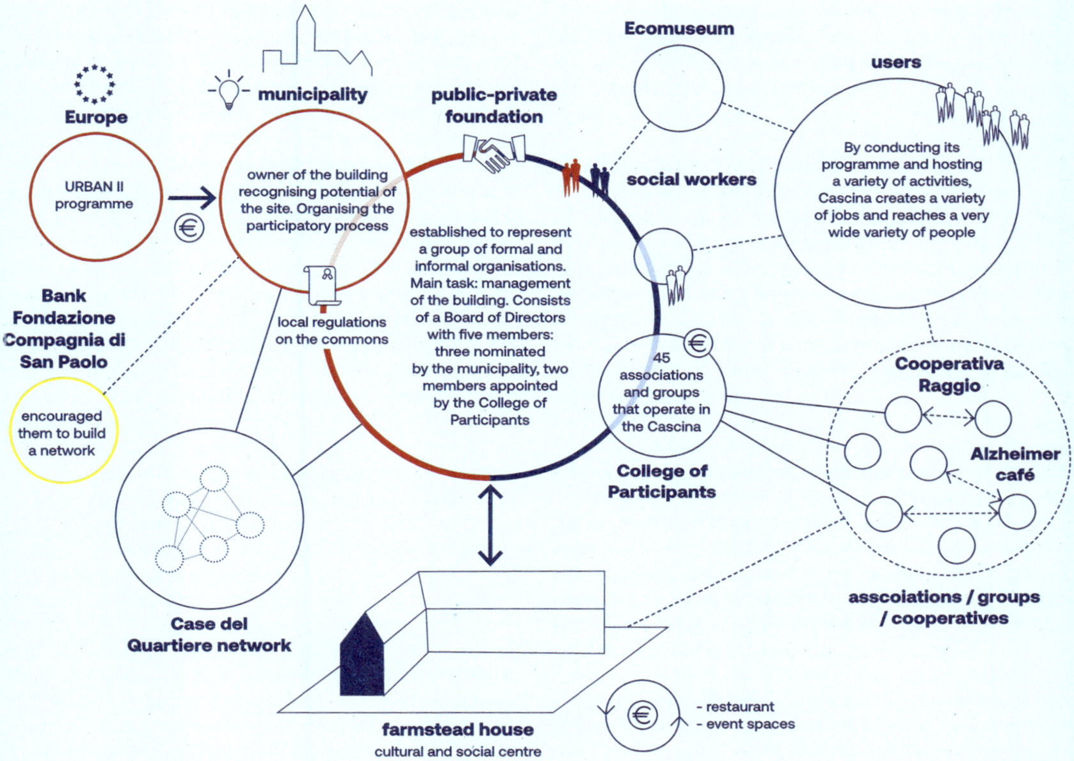

- Business actor
- Civic actor
- Institutional actor
- Initiator (s)
- Contract / specific legislation
- Money (rent, investment, ...)
- Collaboration / agreement

The lineweights indicate the importance of the actor or relationship.

Fig. 1
Governance structure of Cascina Roccafranca

Policies and governance in the OpenHeritage cases

This chapter focuses on three case studies that intertwine decision-making structures with specific policies. If public policies or third-sector strategies can support initiatives in securing land or buildings, raising funds to purchase properties, or for renovation or structural collaboration at the local level, they can also shape collaboration at the local level by encouraging more inclusive modes of governance, allowing for horizontal decision-making and co-management structures (Fig. 1).

Cascina Roccafranca in Turin has a strong public policy dimension (Fig. 2). While its current form is the result of a series of public policies, it has also decisively contributed to shaping the city's commons regulation and related policies. A former farmstead transformed into a community venue in Turin's Mirafiori district, Cascina Roccafranca is a public facility managed collaboratively by the municipality and various civil society organisations. The partnership here is based on a decision-making structure that involves both municipal departments and representatives of NGOs, thus creating a balance between institutional and community interests and ensuring both municipal support and greater outreach to local citizens and communities.

Cascina Roccafranca has been a testing ground for Turin's commons regulation that, through its Pacts of Collaboration (tailored agreements between the municipality and various organisations / individuals), allows citizen groups or civil society organisations to care for and co-manage public or private properties defined as commons. These properties are often regarded as heritage for their important role in local narratives or social infrastructure, and their reuse is often initiated by the surrounding community.

Public-civic cooperation around commons is facilitated by a municipal working group that connects 'representatives of sectoral departments of the city administration, including those in charge of green areas, social services, real estate management' (Polyák, 2022) and representatives from the local district. Cascina Roccafranca's governance model exemplifies the potentials of the commons framework, and has provided a blueprint for various other initiatives in Turin that subsequently founded Rete delle Case del Quartiere, a network of similar community centres mostly in vulnerable and peripheral areas of the city.

The Sunderland High Street Lab helped us implement some of the key concepts of OpenHeritage (Fig. 3). The three 18th-century buildings, originally built as merchant townhouses but soon turned into shops, are now listed as Grade 2 heritage buildings. They were acquired and renovated by the Tyne and Wear Building Preservation Trust (TWBPT) in order to reverse the decline of Sunderland's city centre. Collaboration with local groups and organisations generated new activities and increased footfall, and TWBPT was a key stakeholder in the project to regenerate the wider area.

Public policies played an important role in this work. The buildings, located within the Old Sunderland conservation area, which was designated by the national heritage protection body Historic England as 'Heritage at Risk', became a catalyst project of the Sunderland Heritage Action Zone (HAZ). The HAZ policy tool was newly introduced by Historic England to prompt the creation of local partnerships and 'focus heritage expertise and funding towards marginalised areas', as detailed in the chapter on Sunderland. The HAZ also acts as a governance model, facilitating cooperation between different partners and stakeholders in the area. TWBPT is now involved in discussions on establishing a more permanent governance structure for the area, and building on the current collaborations towards collective maintenance, finance, and governance.

Sunderland City Council, another key stakeholder in the HAZ, played a crucial role in protecting the buildings – first preventing their demolition, then purchasing the properties and immediately transferring ownership to TWBPT for a symbolic price of £1. This required TWBPT to develop a viable business plan for the buildings' regeneration, initially through a mix of grants for capital works and temporary/future uses, and later also through crowdfunding and loans. Key in this was the collaboration with Pop Recs, a local café and music shop that now operates in two of the three buildings. The trust model is a key element of the Sunderland High Street Lab. Building preservation trusts (BPTs) typically acquire ownership (or long-term lease) of buildings, and raise funds from various organisations (including Historic England, the National Lottery Heritage Fund, and the Architectural Heritage Fund) to renovate them for sustainable uses. Any revenues are used to repay loans and support further projects. Heritage trusts take various forms (including heritage trust networks), and have proven to be an efficient vehicle for restoration (especially where local government steps away from direct involvement), and can also facilitate cooperation between public, private, and third-sector organisations.

Community land trusts (CLTs) are another version of the trust model. London CLT is one of the first urban community land trusts in the UK, and thus exercises significant influence on new CLTs both in the UK and on the European continent. CLTs are usually created to counter gentrification or the financialisation of housing assets, through community ownership. By owning land or leasing it from public owners, community land trusts can control rental and purchase prices and keep properties affordable in the long run. Depending on the particular CLT, homes may be rented or purchased from the Trust but cannot be resold for above-inflation profit. In the case of London CLT, housing prices are based on the median income within the local borough.

Horizontal governance is a key feature of CLTs. To ensure better integration within a neighbourhood, CLTs often involve residents, together with experts willing to support the project, in their decision-making. This involvement means that the individual interests of homeowners need to be harmonised with (rather than dominating) those of the community.

Fig. 2
Visit at Cascina Roccafranca

Fig. 3
High Street Sunderland, Heritage Open Days

2

3

Enabling policies are important for creating CLTs. As the CLT model is based on accessible, affordable land, initiatives to establish new CLTs rely on a great diversity of public property owners (municipalities, public railway companies, etc.) or charities to donate or lease land. This is possible when public actors or charities have a long-term strategy for affordable housing or a development focus on a certain area that allows them to provide land for purposes that match these long-term goals.

In some cases, the CLTs' quest for affordable land is supported by complementary policies. In the case of London CLT, Section 106 planning obligations attached to the former St Clements hospital site stipulated an affordable housing allocation of 30%. Such mechanisms can ensure the future diversity of a neighbourhood in transition as well as the adaptive reuse of its heritage assets.

While the policy sphere is particularly pronounced in defining the modalities of decision-making and co-governance in these three cases, policies are key to most of the Observatory Cases and Cooperative Heritage Labs presented in this book and the OpenHeritage database (Baudier & Erzberger, 2020). The rent-to-investment scheme of Stará Tržnica in Bratislava has created a financial mechanism that ensures the renovation of the Old Market Hall while also allowing the association managing the building to experiment with new uses and activities to make better use of it. In Lisbon, the BIP/ZIP funding scheme supports development in vulnerable neighbourhoods and encourages local initiatives to collaborate towards shared goals. In Naples, commons regulation provides a set of policies designed to create open community venues with horizontal co-governance structures, enabling citizen initiatives to utilise empty buildings such as the Scugnizzo Liberato, Ex Asilo Filangieri, and Ex OPG.

Supporting community-driven governance

Policy has important implications for adaptive heritage reuse. The OpenHeritage Policy Briefs present a series of recommendations designed to support policymaking in enabling community-driven AHR processes (Veldpaus et al., 2022), Mechanisms to support partnerships between different authorities as well as local stakeholders (Policy Brief #02: Veldpaus et al., 2022) can mobilise a diversity of skills and competences while ensuring more horizontal decision-making processes and outreach to a broader community. A diversity of funding sources, including grants, loans, equity, guarantees, or community investment (Policy Brief #03: Veldpaus et al., 2022), can enable AHR initiatives to build a sustainable financial trajectory. A long-term territorial vision (Policy Brief #05: Veldpaus et al., 2022) for an area helps different approaches, policies, and projects coalesce into a coherent strategy with better-defined local impact.

While these policy recommendations focus on local and regional administrations, they also have a strong EU dimension (Policy Brief #04: Veldpaus et al., 2022). AHR has been an important focus of European heritage and cultural policies, especially since the European Year of Cultural Heritage in 2018. Within the EU policy landscape, AHR is already central to EU cultural- and heritage-themed programmes and is included to some extent in agendas on economic, urban, and regional development. Particularly in the context of the European Green Deal and the New European Bauhaus, AHR is also becoming important more broadly in improving the quality of the built environment and architecture, as well as greening and circular economies, material sustainability, recycling, and waste reduction. AHR is not, however, reflected in how the majority of EU subsidies are spent within the European territories. Given that innovation, inclusion, and sustainability are already criteria for funding research (Horizon Europe), innovation (European Capital of Innovation Awards), and urban (URBACT, European Urban Initiative) programmes, it is time to rethink how the EU's investment funds and Structural Funds can be utilised to finance territorial development.

List of References

Baudier, M., & Erzberger, J. (2020). *OpenHeritage database*. OpenHeritage. https://db.openheritage.eu/#~

Polyák, L., Patti, D., Nasya, B., Fava, F., Cannella, F., Caudo, G., Tönkő, A., Szemző, H., Mérai, D., Kulikov, V., Cwik, A., Schulbaum, O., Nadesan, N., Tomescu, A., Skoklina, I., van Knippenberg, K., & Boonstra, B. (2019). *Observatory cases report (OpenHeritage Deliverable 2.2)*. OpenHeritage. https://openheritage.eu/wp-content/uploads/2020/01/D2.2_Observatory_Cases_Report.pdf

Polyák, L. (2022, 26 September). Turin's Tavolo Tecnico: Inter-departmental cooperation for the commons. *Cooperative City Magazine*. https://cooperativecity.org/2022/09/26/turins-tavolo-tecnico-inter-departmental-cooperation-for-the-commons/ Accessed on 3 March 2023

Veldpaus, L., Fava, F., & Brodowicz, D. (2019). *Mapping of current heritage re-use policies and regulations in Europe: Complex policy overview of adaptive heritage re-use (OpenHeritage Deliverable 1.2)*. OpenHeritage. https://openheritage.eu/wp-content/uploads/2020/01/D1.2_Mapping_current_policies_regulations.pdf

Veldpaus, L., Krajewska, O., Miah, J., & Szemző, H. (2020). *Adaptive heritage reuse: Learning from policy and governance frameworks across Europe (Policy Brief #01)*. OpenHeritage. https://openheritage.eu/wp-content/uploads/2020/12/Open-Heritage-policy-brief-01-pages.pdf

Veldpaus, L., et al. (Eds.), (2022). *Policy brief package (Policy Briefs #01–05). OpenHeritage*. https://openheritage.eu/wp-content/uploads/2022/09/Open-Heritage-policy-brief-package-all.pdf

Cascina Roccafranca: Co-Governing the Commons in Turin

By Levente Polyák and Andrea Giuliano

Cascina Roccafranca is a multi-functional community centre located in a former farmstead in Mirafiori, a former industrial area on the outskirts of Turin. After 30 years of vacancy, Cascina Roccafranca was purchased by the Municipality of Turin and repurposed with the support of Urban II, the European Union's programme to regenerate troubled urban districts. Today, it is a public asset managed collaboratively by public and civic actors, and provides a wide range of social and cultural activities. This management approach offers a valuable model for policies on citizen empowerment and public-civic cooperation connected to the regeneration of neglected areas and buildings. Since 2012, Cascina Roccafranca has been a key member of the Case del Quartiere, a network of similar community centres in Turin that was formalised in 2017, and today collaborates with the City Council in the management and regeneration of urban commons.

The farmhouse and its renovation

Cascina (farmstead) Roccafranca was built in the 17th century to serve as a farmhouse for the Compagnia dell'Immacolata Concezione religious confraternity. In 1689, the farmhouse was sold to Count Lorenzo Ballard. In 1840 the next owner, Baroness Chionio, enlarged the farmhouse and modified its original structure. From 1957, the agricultural land connected to Cascina Roccafranca was progressively reduced and taken over by the Fiat Mirafiori establishment and workers' residences. In the 1970s, Cascina Roccafranca ultimately lost its function and its buildings were abandoned. The building became an urban void, degraded by time and marginalisation. However, with its 2,500 m² floor space and 2,000 m² courtyard, it retained a significant place in local memory.

Cascina Roccafranca is located in Mirafiori Nord, a neighbourhood on the south-western outskirts of Turin, six kilometres from the city centre, covering an area of more than 3 km² (Fig. 3). Its population grew exponentially in the 1950s with the establishment of the Fiat automobile factories and the subsequent construction of public housing estates in the area. With Fiat's departure and the closure of many of its production facilities, the area experienced an economic crisis and growing unemployment starting in the 1990s.

Today, Mirafiori Nord has about 25,000 inhabitants, 30% of whom are over 65. The area has struggled with severe social and economic problems: unemployment, homelessness, crime, poverty, low levels of education and training, decaying

Fig. 1
Cascina Roccafranca in Turin. Map

Timeline	1600—2017
1600s	Cascina Roccafranca was built by the Compagnia dell'Immacolata Concezione
1689	Cascina was sold to Count Lorenzo Ballard
1734	Cascina Roccafranca became an independent estate
1840	Baroness Chionio bought and enlarged the building
1957	Cascina Roccafranca's agricultural lot was halved
1970s	The estate's agricultural function ceased due to the area's industrialisation
1999	The municipality launched a social forum (*tavoli sociali*) to discuss the regeneration of the Mirafiori area
2001	Mirafiori Nord was selected as a target area under the European Union's Urban II programme
2002	The Municipality of Turin bought Cascina Roccafranca with Urban II funds
2004	The renovation of the buildings started
2006	The Cascina Roccafranca Foundation was established
2007	Cascina Roccafranca opened
2012	Coordinamento Case del Quartiere was formed
2014	The Case del Quartiere network was awarded a national 'Che Fare?' grant
2015	Manifesto delle Case del Quartiere was published
2016	Turin City Council approved the Regulation on Urban Commons
2017	Network Case del Quartiere was established

buildings and public spaces, as well as high levels of air and noise pollution. On the other hand, the area has significant green and open spaces and a history of strong community involvement.

In 2001, Turin was selected for the European Union's URBAN II programme, receiving 16 million euros to regenerate the Mirafiori Nord area. This intervention took into consideration various types of innovative actions: public space renovation, ecological renewal, economic interventions for employment and trading, and cultural and social action. In 2002, the Municipality of Turin used Urban II funds to purchase Cascina Roccafranca and transform it into a space for public services.

When it was selected for regeneration, the site's infrastructure was dilapidated, covered by vegetation, and affected by structural problems. The building was already zoned for service provision, and so no changes of land use regulations were needed. The building also lacked heritage protection, meaning that there were no restrictions concerning its reuse, and so the architectural project was free to change its physical aspects.

Regeneration work commenced in 2004. During the redevelopment, in 2006, the management of the building was assigned to Fondazione Cascina Roccafranca, a foundation established to represent a group of formal and informal organisations that aimed to redevelop the building and to transform it into a multi-purpose neighbourhood centre. The redeveloped Cascina Roccafranca opened in 2007.

While the complex was entirely rebuilt in accordance with current safety and environmental norms, its new design evokes the original historical appearance, maintaining architectural features important for the identity and recognisability of the place, such as door and window fixtures and brickwork. The participatory planning process around the conception of *Cascina Roccafranca* fed many ideas into planning the new venue. The idea of total accessibility, with no barriers or thresholds of control, as in a public living room, came from this process; so did the idea of architectural transparency, which allows people to see what is happening inside the building (Fig. 3).

"This building is 'transparent', to facilitate the idea of sharing and of publicness. In the past there have been similar activities in the district, but they were not concentrated in a space instead carried out in rented spaces often in former classrooms or basements – never in a beautifully designed space."
Stefania Ieluzzi

Cascina Roccafranca is today divided into five parts that refer to the pre-existing spaces in the ancient Cascina. The canopy, originally used as storage, now forms the main entrance, featuring an entrance hall, the reception, a play area, and an incubator space. The stall is the best-preserved part of the old farmhouse, now hosting a cafeteria, multi-media rooms, artistic workshops, and classrooms. The villa, completely rebuilt following its original structure, is now used for adminis-

2

3

4

Fig. 2
Event at Cascina Roccafranca

Fig. 3
The entrance of Cascina Roccafranca in Turin

Fig. 4
Theatre rehearsal at Cascina Roccafranca

Tavoli Sociali

In 1997 – 98, the Turin municipality launched Progetto Speciale Periferie, a programme to requalify its urban peripheries. The programme created a series of *tavoli sociali* (social roundtables), working groups composed of various formal and non-formal organisations present in the area of intervention (such as associations, informal groups, social workers, and school teachers), plus a variety of people working, living, and managing activities in the neighbourhood. The roundtables were coordinated by municipal workers specifically selected for this task. The Tavolo Sociale di Mirafiori Nord was composed of about 60–70 people, representing associations, social workers, health services, and children's organisations. These discussions gave birth to the idea of Cascina Roccafranca as a community venue.

trative offices and the area's Ecomuseum. The barn hosts a restaurant and a large room used for meetings, gatherings, and parties. The internal courtyard connects all parts of the building and is used as a venue for summer events.

Social roundtables for community involvement

The redevelopment of Cascina Roccafranca was informed by the communities living in the Mirafiori area. At the end of the 1990s, the Municipality of Turin sought to develop a plan of interventions that would improve the environment and relaunch economic activities in Mirafiori Nord. For a year and a half, a group of formal and non-formal organisations composed of social, educational, and healthcare workers, religious organisations, associations, local committees, and schools came together in a social forum to discuss the possibilities for innovation in their area. This highlighted the need for a community meeting space and suggested Cascina Roccafranca as a suitable venue.

The participatory planning process revealed that residents of Mirafiori Nord lacked a suitable space for intergenerational encounters; one that could respond to a wide range of needs and interests but also be sufficiently fluid to regularly accept new proposals. Cascina Roccafranca was envisioned as a multi-purpose space for socialisation, civic engagement, and cultural activities; to promote ethical lifestyles and to support the dignity and diversity of ethnic, religious, gender, or physically challenged minorities.

"For us, a challenge was to imagine a space that could be used on the same day by users of different ages.
Space is shared, and everybody needs to feel at home, but at the same time it has to be adapted to everybody's needs."
Stefania de Masi

In 15 years of work, Cascina Roccafranca has adapted to new needs that were not envisioned during the planning phase. For example, with the economic crisis of 2007, Cascina Roccafranca became a support facility for local residents facing unemployment or poverty, as well as a centre for integration of the local migrant community. Although officially closed for several months during the COVID-19 pandemic, the entire building was reconfigured as a food distribution centre focusing on families with children, older people living alone, and people with physical disabilities. Additionally, they organised community activities (workshops, meetings, and games), and counselling for psychological issues and victims of domestic violence.

Cascina Roccafranca targets a variety of groups and interests. About 90% of its activities are directly organised by associations and independent groups that use the venue. The social workers employed by Cascina Roccafranca are also involved in planning events and meetings, but much of their work is dedicated to supporting groups in organising activities, especially younger or more disadvantaged groups that lack experience. The programming closely follows the needs of the community, and therefore many events and activities are proposed by the users of Cascina Roccafranca.

> "We imagine this place, and this project, as a container with spaces to fill. As operators, we monitor if activities correspond to the framework that we defined, the strategic goals we decided upon, the working conditions. But we expect the groups and associations to fill this space with activities."
> Renato Bergamin

Cascina Roccafranca hosts around 200 cultural programmes each year. These activities include music, theatre, conferences, book readings and presentations, language courses, cabaret, and dance courses (also for persons with disabilities). Events that are free of charge for participants can be held in the Cascina's spaces at no cost (Fig. 4).

The complex also hosts regular educational activities, such as an after-school programme run by volunteers; summer activities such as games, workshops, and excursions for groups of children (aged 0–13); and support activities for children with physical or mental challenges. Cascina Roccafranca regularly collaborates with two cooperatives promoting the integration of people with mental disorders: Mente Locale uses creative methods to address depression and eating disorders; Alzheimer Café organises informative meetings with educators and specialist doctors and physiologists.

Building a network for the commons

Mirafiori Nord and Cascina Roccafranca have been at the centre of a series of urban policies and funding programmes that enabled the Turin municipality to design and implement a long-term regeneration strategy (Pinson, 2002). In the late 1990s, in the midst of growing discussion about the problems of urban peripheries across Italy, but in the absence of any national policy addressing the issue, the Turin municipality launched the Progetto Speciale Periferie (PSP – Special Periphery Project). The capacities developed in PSP further enabled the municipality to mobilise resources from other funding sources. Since the early 2000s, the municipality's careful use of URBAN II (2000–2006) and Urban Innovative Actions (2017–2020) resources allowed the city to articulate a coherent vision for the territory.

The URBAN II programme's €10.7 million funding included €6.2 million for infrastructure and urban rehabilitation, €2.5 million for training and economic development, €1.4 million for social development and integration, and €0.6 million for technical assistance. The intervention in Mirafiori included infrastructure development, economic development, and training, as well as cultural and social activities. Renato Bergamin, the founder of Cascina Roccafranca, was responsible for some of these cultural and social activities, and one of the actions funded by URBAN II was dedicated to the adaptive

Progetto Speciale Periferie

Launched in 1997 by the Turin Municipality, PSP aimed to help the municipal administration to develop skills and capacities necessary to work with larger urban regeneration programmes. PSP focused on Turin's crisis areas in the peripheries, according to an incremental logic that facilitated local development and the active participation of local citizens. The programme linked the territorial logic of the 'neighbourhood' with a wider urban strategy of rethinking the city according to a polycentric model and building new centralities and identities at the peripheries.

Case del Quartiere

Turin's eight *Case del Quartiere* (Neighbourhood Houses) are community spaces that offer citizens opportunities to meet through cultural events, social encounters, and self-produced workshops. They are managed by local teams that collect proposals from external organisations (associations, third sector organisations, social enterprises, committees, groups, individual citizens) to develop a rich programme of activities using the spaces of the Houses.

reuse of the Cascina Roccafranca and its transformation into a community venue.

As part of the PSP, participatory planning processes in several neighbourhoods resulted in an ambition to create spaces to host initiatives, and give a structure and continuity to participation. The spaces created through these processes, despite having different trajectories, also shared many similarities. At some point, these spaces began to connect to each other and identify themselves as *Case del Quartiere* (Neighbourhood Houses). Cascina Roccafranca was more developed than other Houses, and was hence defined as a model for the Case del Quartiere.

> "We realised that different single programmes of urban regeneration in different neighbourhoods with different stories, different characteristics, different financial tools, and different operational tools shared the same goal of creating a space for informal socialisation and service provision."
> Giovanni Ferrero

The Case del Quartiere are spread across Turin, and their rootedness in different neighbourhoods makes them an important partner for the municipality. In May 2012, the eight Neighbourhood Houses in Turin established an informal coordination platform to favour the organisation of common projects. Its first milestone was winning the national grant *Che Fare?* (What shall we do?) in 2014, which provided economic resources for regular meetings. Following the publication of a manifesto in 2015 (Retecasedelquartiere, 2018), the Coordination of the Neighbourhood Houses was eventually transformed in 2017 into a formal Rete delle Case del Quartiere (Network of Neighbourhood Houses), in the form of an *Associazione di Promozione Sociale* (Association for Social Promotion).

The Case del Quartiere model, based on an experimental cooperation between the Turin Municipality and local civic actors, has opened a new way for public-civic cooperation. The network's experience contributed to the design of Turin's version of the Regulation of the Urban Commons, approved in January 2016.

The Regulation of the Urban Commons in Turin provides tools for formal collaboration between citizens and the city administration in running community venues. Specifically, by signing the Pact of Collaboration, the municipality and active citizens (such as informal groups, associations, NGOs, or individuals) agree to share responsibility for managing various urban spaces. Enabled by the Regulation, the municipality gathers proposals submitted by citizens and opens public consultations to identify urban common assets to include in collaboration pacts.

Shared responsibility and self-sustainability

The buildings of *Cascina Roccafranca* are owned by the Turin Municipality, which assigned the venue to the Cascina Roccafranca Foundation that manages it jointly with the municipality and district representatives. As a public asset, *Cascina Roccafranca's* use is limited to social and cultural purposes, preventing commercial activities.

Cascina Roccafranca is managed by the *Fondazione Atipica in Partecipazione Cascina Roccafranca* (Cascina Roccafranca Atypical Participation Foundation), legally established in 2006. This foundation works with a model between public and private law: in some aspects it depends on public procedures, and for others it acts as a private organisation. As a legal entity, *Cascina Roccafranca* must adhere to public procedures for subcontracting, procuring goods or services, and regulations on corruption prevention and privacy. At the same time, it is a flexible entity and can hire external contractors and freelancers if it needs specific expertise.

"This structure of governance created a positive form of co-responsibility between public and private actors: the administration gave up some of its powers, and on the other hand, the private associations' mindset shifted from an idea of claiming something from the administration to a perspective in which they co-manage it."
Renato Bergamin

The foundation's governance structure consists of a Board of Directors with five members: three are nominated by the municipality (the councillor for integration policies, the President of the District, and one member appointed by the district) and two members are appointed by the College of Participants (45 associations and groups that operate in the *Cascina*). The College of Participants meets every six months and nominates its representatives who attend the Board of Directors. The Board meets monthly to decide on some activities and current challenges.

The foundation is autonomous in its financial management and produces its own financial report, besides its institutional report, to the municipality. It differs from classical foundations as it relies on more than material assets (funds, buildings, etc.), instead adopting a form of joint management by the public administration and various informal groups. The foundation works with more than 80 associations and informal groups, as well as 20 individuals who promote activities at the venue.

The Turin municipality is not only a founding member of the Fondazione Cascina Roccafranca but also contributes to the foundation's work in a variety of ways: it provides the building free of charge, employs some of the staff, and covers some of the maintenance and utility costs.

Besides the seven employees that are directly paid by the municipality, Cascina Roccafranca's yearly expenses amount to around €200–250,000, constituting salaries for the foundation's seven own employees (50%); another 10% is paid out in taxes and other charges, while around 40% is spent on safety compliance and organising services and events (Fig. 5).

Social impact

In 2019, Cascina worked with 125 partners and hosted 656 activities, with 78% organised by regular partners and 38% of the events free of charge. In the same year, 324 volunteers contributed to the venue with over 11,000 hours of work, equivalent to eight full-time employees. In 2019, Cascina registered over 165,000 single entries, with more than 4,500 people enrolled for courses and other activities.

"This structure of governance created a positive form of co-responsibility between public and private actors: the administration gave up some of its powers, and on the other hand, the private associations' mindset shifted from an idea of claiming something from the administration to a perspective in which they co-manage it."

Renato Bergamin

Fig. 5
Restaurant with outdoor tables at Cascina Roccafranca

Cascina Roccafranca's yearly revenues amount to about €250,000. The foundation format simplifies Cascina's management and enables it to generate revenues through its spaces and activities, such as the rents paid by the café and restaurant. Further revenue is also generated through fundraising and sponsorships.

"We aim at reaching maximum self-sustainability. When we started in 2007 we could only cover 33% of our costs on our own; now we cover 66%. Besides our income from commercial activities and space rental, we do fundraising with public and private foundations and develop economic partnerships with the private sector on joint projects."
Stefania de Masi

Cascina Roccafranca's economy goes beyond the foundation's own revenues and expenses. According to data from 2019, Cascina Roccafranca's partners (mostly users of its spaces) have generated over €1 million of economic value.

The COVID-19 pandemic presented financial challenges for Cascina Roccafranca. All employees on site had access to the government's Wages Guarantee Fund to substitute the lost incomes of their organisation and to pay them salaries. Under this system, employees worked only at a rate of 20%, being officially unemployed for the remaining 80%. Fortunately, the organisations working in Cascina received economic help from the Turin Municipality as well, in the form of support for food distribution activities, and a tax discount on some of their economic resources. Ultimately, the financial loss was estimated at around €50,000.

By conducting its programme and hosting a variety of activities, Cascina creates a variety of jobs. According to data from 2019, all the organisations on the site together employed around 217 people, with hours equivalent to 35 full-time employees. Some of the activities in Cascina Roccafranca are provided by social cooperatives, selected through inclusive procurement that aims at creating positive social impact through the choice of partners or service providers. Cooperativa Raggio, the cooperative managing the restaurant and the cafeteria, gives work to 25 people.

Despite the well-founded ambition of Cascina Roccafranca to become self-sustaining, the foundation continues to depend partially on public subsidies and private grants. While this dependence exposes Cascina to changing political or funding priorities, its economic activities are also vulnerable to unforeseeable events.

List of References

Cascina Roccafranca (2023). *Social impact study of the Cascina Roccafranca.* http://www.cascinaroccafranca.it/valutazione-di-impatto-sociale/

Città di Torino (2020). *Regulation of the urban commons.* http://www.comune.torino.it/benicomuni/cosa_sono/index.shtml

European Commission (2002, 17 January). *Urban II programme: European Union contributes Euro 10.7 million to urban regeneration in the 'Mirafiori Nord' suburban area of Turin, Italy* [press release]. European Commission. https://ec.europa.eu/commission/presscorner/detail/en/IP_02_83

Fioretti, C. (2009, October). Buone pratiche in Italia. *Planum.*

Guercio, S., Robiglio, M., & Toussaint, I. (2004). Periferie partecipate. Cinque casi di riqualificazione urbana a Torino. *Ciudades, 8*(1).

Iaione, C. (2016). The Co-City: Sharing, collaborating, cooperating, and commoning in the city. *American Journal of Economics and Sociology, 75*(2).

Maldera, D. (2015). It happens in Turin. From Cascina Roccafranca to the 'Case del Quartiere Network'. *Tafter Journal, 83.* https://www.tafterjournal.it/2015/07/15/it-happens-in-turin-from-cascina-roccafranca-to-the-case-del-quartiere-network/

Patti, D., & Polyák, L. (2017). *Funding the cooperative city: Community finance and the economy of civic spaces.* Cooperative City Books.

Pinson, G. (2002). Political government and governance: Strategic planning and the reshaping of political capacity in Turin. *International Journal of Urban and Regional Research, 26*(3), 477–493.

Retecasedelquartiere. (2018). *Rete delle Case del Quartiere: Il Manifesto.* Retecasedelquartiere.org. http://www.retecasedelquartiere.org/manifesto/

Case related websites:
Social impact study of the Cascina Roccafranca. http://www.cascinaroccafranca.it/valutazione-di-impatto-sociale/

The case study is based on interviews with: Renato Bergamin, director of the Cascina Roccafranca Foundation; Stefania de Masi, project manager at Cascina Roccafranca; Giovanni Ferrero, project manager of Co-City; Stefania Ialuzzi, project manager at Cascina Roccafranca; Marialessandra Sabarino, president of the Rete delle Case del Quartiere.

Gathering a Family Around the Coffee Machine: The People at the Heart of the Sunderland Cooperative Heritage Lab

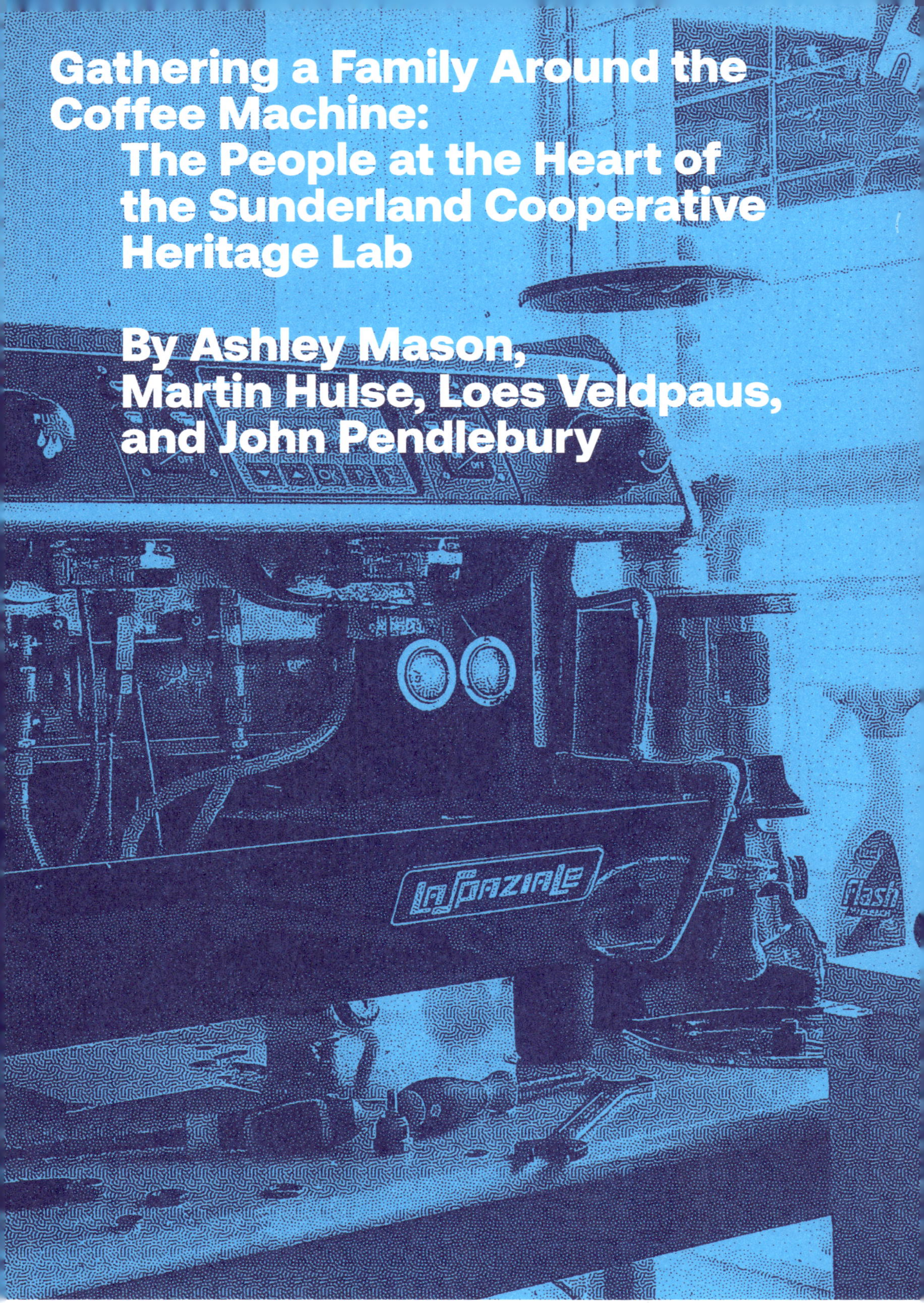

By Ashley Mason, Martin Hulse, Loes Veldpaus, and John Pendlebury

On 1 June 2013, popular local indie band Frankie and the Heartstrings took over the former tourist information office in Sunderland city centre, North East England, to promote their new album and protest the disappearance of record shops from UK high streets. Intended as a two-week, temporary publicity exercise, Pop Recs swiftly became a pillar of the local community, offering much-needed space for cultural activities, including yoga classes, photography exhibitions, and gigs by both local upcoming artists and more established UK musicians. In 2015, Pop Recs' music venue, independent coffee shop, and community hub moved to its next location, on the west side of the city centre, continuing to provide invaluable support for the people of Sunderland through music and much more.

Meanwhile, the Tyne and Wear Building Preservation Trust (TWBPT) – an organisation engaged in the restoration of heritage properties across North East England – was wondering where it might find the magic that would help to steer a vision for three dilapidated properties at 170 to 175 High Street West, towards the East End of Sunderland. Following an impasse in which the Sunderland City Council refused permission to demolish the buildings, the council finally agreed their purchase from the previous owner. Once the site of the first Binns store in Sunderland (before the drapery became a famous department store both in Sunderland and across the north of England), but subsequently abandoned to squatters, copper thieves, pigeons, fire, and the elements for more than a decade, these buildings certainly needed a vision for their future reuse. Former occupier Henry Binns had also unwisely removed the entire first floor and supporting walls of number 172; as such, without sufficient structural support for the roof throughout the preceding 150 years, the building was slowly collapsing in on itself. With immediate emergency repairs and subsequent extensive restoration works required, it was clear from the beginning that this project would not be viable without support, trust, and a true partnership of people working together. And so, the buildings were acquired by TWBPT for the symbolic fee of one pound from the council in order to help rescue them, with early community consultation indicating a desired cultural and community-centered future for the spaces. Thus, the seeds were sown for a cooperative relationship between TWBPT and Pop Recs, in addition to many others.

Fig. 1
High Street, Sunderland. Map

Timeline	2015—2022
2015	Community outreach undertaken by TWBPT and Sunderland City Council to determine local needs and visions for 170–175 High Street West; search begins for anchor tenant
2016	Collaboration commences between Pop Recs and TWBPT
2017	Historic England's Heritage Action Zone (HAZ) in Sunderland established
2018	TWBPT purchases 170–175 High Street West from Sunderland City Council for symbolic £1; OpenHeritage project begins
2019	Immediate repairs and restoration works to 170–175 High Street West undertaken; meanwhile it begins to be used in 170 High Street West by Pop Recs, including Heritage Open Days 2019 with *Rebel Women* exhibition
2020	COVID-19 pandemic impacts plans; alternative financing opportunities tested through crowdfunding campaigns
2021	Major construction works are completed; the ground floors of 170 and 172–175 High Street West open; Heritage Open Days 2021 takes place with *Local Edible Heritage* exhibition; commemorative blue plaque installed at 172 High Street West
2022	Upper floors of 170–175 High Street West continue to be restored; 177 High Street West acquired by TWBPT and restoration works begin to roof and shell; Making Space / Keeping Space event begins looking at the project's impact and legacy

Heritage Action Zone (HAZ)

The HAZ was a newly developed policy tool for Historic England to focus heritage expertise and funding towards marginalised areas; to work with the communities in these deprived areas; to enable long-term engagement and the building of trust; as well as to promote meanwhile uses and stimulate people to see opportunities in rescuing heritage properties. It came with some funding, but more important was the shift in focus by Historic England from 'Grade 1' and 'Grade 2*' listed buildings to marginalised places and people. Equally crucial was that the HAZ partnership was led by the local planning authority, which meant that it was committed to and invested in making the adaptive reuse projects within the HAZ a success. The High Street West project buildings were key in the local planning authority's application to Historic England for HAZ funding and, reciprocally, the HAZ was crucial in returning the buildings to use.

Taking risks

Beyond economic repair, the buildings were nevertheless of considerable and continued historic value due to their notable former Quaker occupants, as well as their prominent location at a key gateway into Sunderland city centre. The buildings are located within the Old Sunderland conservation area, all of which is designated by Historic England as Heritage at Risk, thereby connecting them to wider strategies as well as funding opportunities that would support their rescue and thus the regeneration and conservation of this neglected part of Sunderland. The project consequently became the catalyst for a Historic England Heritage Action Zone (HAZ). The HAZ partnership, which began in 2017 and continued until early autumn 2022, was formed of Sunderland City Council, Historic England, TWBPT, Sunderland Culture, Sunderland Heritage Forum, and the Churches Conservation Trust.

Without this and invaluable heritage funding from the Architectural Heritage Fund, repair and reuse of the badly damaged project buildings would not have been feasible. It is thus, as Historic England Historic Places Adviser Jules Brown notes, 'a really important example of how partnership can work for historic buildings [where] no player in this project could have worked alone [... and where] most importantly, working in partnership allows people to make bold decisions' (InvestSundUK, 2022). It is this trust between actors that is essential in enabling projects to take risks beyond what would otherwise be possible.

Following footsteps

Nothing ever arises in isolation. Visiting other projects, similar to what we (all those connected to the Sunderland Cooperative Heritage Lab between 2018 and 2022) imagined High Street West could become, was so much more important than initially anticipated. At the Granby Four Streets project in Liverpool, for example, we saw their winter garden set within two terraced houses in the middle of the street. The project was conceived with the Assemble collective and in 2015 became the first architectural entry to win the UK's Turner Prize for art. We also heard from the residents, about their fight against demolition, and gained an understanding of the moments, organisation, and governance models involved in bringing the project to fruition. This and other project visits to Berlin and London provided inspiration, in both the material and design senses, and in demonstrating what is possible, especially if everyone involved works together towards shared goals. Hopefully, we are now passing on that same message and inspiration to other projects that are following in our footsteps, as we have followed in others.

It was through community consultation that Pop Recs' name was first mentioned. For co-founder and then director Dave Harper, it was the highest compliment. Indeed, Pop Recs CIC (Community Interest Company) had the magic that TWBPT was seeking, which would transform this adaptive heritage reuse project. It may have been a relatively small operation in business terms, but its reach and impacts within Sunderland's communities and far beyond are immeasurable. In the words of Dave Harper, Pop Recs could 'circumnavigate a lot of the bureaucracy that prevents creative people in Sunderland getting to the point where they've got a product and are doing something; [Pop Recs] could be the antidote to that [...] and try to support people, because we didn't have that support when we were younger, [...] When I was growing up, the support would have been greatly welcomed'. (TWBPT, 2019b)

The people of the East End consulted during the early stages of the project did not want the buildings to be converted into affordable housing (although this is equally needed within the area); instead, they wanted something with a community focus. And so, with Pop Recs fully on board, the process began of transforming number 170 to make it suitable and safe for meanwhile use, working with Sunderland College apprentices to patch the building back together through the establishment of the Living Classroom project. The first concert at the venue opened as scheduled at 7:30 pm, despite the electricity only being reconnected (thanks to an electrician, standing in a hole in the road) 15 minutes earlier. Only Pop Recs could do that: everyone could feel that they had the ability to develop a vision for the site, and to see it through.

2

Acknowledging the overlooked

While more extensive works began to repair Pop Recs' intended home at 172–175 High Street West, reconnection of electricity to number 170 meant that more people could begin to gather around a kindly donated coffee machine (Fig. 2). Gatherings drew from far-reaching communities, re-welcoming those already part of the family through Pop Recs' pre-existing socio-cultural initiatives (from gigs to exhibitions), but also new additions. Indeed, support and collaboration among many different actors (including national organisations such as the Arts Council, and local cultural organisations such as Sunderland Culture and We Make Culture) has helped to build strong partnerships through cultural community outreach throughout the duration of the project. As part of a variety of activities and events organised as meanwhile uses at number 170 for Heritage Open Days 2019, the Rebel Women of Sunderland project was born and shared with the community. It included an exhibition, a Mini Manifestoes workshop for children, and a lecture on Marion Phillips (Sunderland's first female member of parliament). Led by Laura Brewis from Sunderland Culture, and funded through the Great Place scheme, it was an immensely rewarding collaboration between Sunderland Culture, OpenHeritage, and the HAZ, with local illustrator Kathryn Robertson and author Jessica Andrews commissioned to illustrate and tell the stories of Sunderland's inspirational yet previously overlooked women.

For Laura Brewis, also founder and director of We Make Culture, it was 'fantastic to profile these untold stories of women from Sunderland, and I think it'll go on and on'. (TWBPT, 2019b) Since its first showing, the project has indeed been extended, re-exhibited, and shared both locally and nationally. The con-

Fig. 2
The coffee machine

Fig. 3
Rescuing Heritage at Risk

tributions made by the city's women have continued to be acknowledged, with a blue plaque installed on the facade of the former Binns store at number 172 recognising the role played by Sunderland's Quaker women in opposing the slave trade. The recognition of overlooked heritage, too, was furthered through Heritage Open Days 2021 and the Local Edible Heritage project, where this time food (rather than coffee) was a means of bringing everyone back together, following a period of global precarity and uncertainty.

Taking care

Sometimes, events outside our control reminded us of what was important. The adverse effects of the COVID-19 pandemic, in addition to energy and cost of living crises, on both finance and community engagement could be keenly felt at times during the project's journey. Obvious and immediate detrimental impacts of the pandemic were seen in lengthy delays and rising material costs that hampered the progress of on-site construction works considerably throughout 2020 and into 2021. But more significant were the longer-term impacts on both the individuals affiliated with the project and the wider public supporting it, in terms of the limits placed on their access and participation. During periods of social distancing measures introduced by the UK Government, collective resilience was fostered through numerous mutual aid initiatives that enabled people to voluntarily support each other in solidarity. Post-pandemic, many of these initiatives are still vital and in ever-increasing use. Yet, these measures also kept communities spatially separated and forced many interactions to migrate to online spaces, thus somewhat dampening the project's community-nurturing momentum. Online tools were an invaluable means of maintaining connections and were widely implemented by both the tenants and ourselves, but they could not entirely replace the more serendipitous opportunities of being somewhere in-person and chatting over coffee. From the moment that restrictions were eased, the project has been able to grow and flourish.

3

It is difficult to comprehend just how close the buildings once were to collapse (Fig. 3). Now, with the light pooling in from the skylight above, the double-height venue space of Pop Recs is an undeniably special setting for musical and community activities. Saved by a steel support structure, it is a truly communal space for people to gather and share their lives and stories, through food, music, and more. Plans for Pop Recs' relocation next door progressed swiftly in 2019, working carefully and closely with key members of the council's regeneration and conservation teams, as well as the lead architect and contractor; indeed, the council was key in its support of a restoration that, while sympathetic and respectful of the historic importance of the properties (number 172 is Grade II listed), was still open to their creative, adaptive reuse. Certain elements were subsequently maintained, including wallpaper fragments, stairs to nowhere, and the bow in the roofline of 172 that speaks of its near-collapse (Fig. 4). The process was not easy, and funding paths were not always straightforward, resulting in a softer and step-by-step approach based on need and luck. Much of the funding was obtained through mobilising TWBPT's collaboration with Pop Recs, and the importance of this partnership was recently recognised in its shortlisting for the North East Culture Awards 2022. Different options to financially support the works were also explored, including through the 'Buy a Brick for Sunderland' crowdfunding campaign. Beyond stimulating funding, these mechanisms sought to generate buy-in from the local community, understanding that the more people that are emotionally invested in a place, the more support it will receive from those communities going forward, and therefore the more sustainable it will be. The ground floor spaces were the first to be completed and were tested in July 2021 for the Summer Streets Festival – a local music festival organised annually by musician Ross Millard, who played an instrumental role in connecting Pop Recs to TWBPT and is also a member of Frankie and the Heartstrings. Following the official opening of Pop Recs in autumn 2021, more of the upper floor spaces across the buildings have gradually been brought into use, with the remaining rooms to follow when the time is right.

Growing the family

The project is perhaps a story of adaptive heritage reuse, of salvaging buildings, but it is more so a tale of collaboration, community, and cultivating local pride (Fig. 5). Pop Recs' new venue space has a capacity beyond that of their previous locations, bringing more people around (and onto) their stage through the care, vision, and dedication of co-founder and director (and Frankie and the Heartstrings guitarist) Michael McKnight. Midnight Pizza Crü – a pandemic success story – is now fully part of the menu of Pop Recs' meat-free kitchen, with founder Dan Shannon coming on board as an equally dedicated director of Pop Recs in autumn 2021. The directorial team has since further expanded, with Naomi Griffin joining in mid 2022. Pop Recs has hosted the Young Musicians Project run by We Make Culture, and continues to host the Teenage Market run by Washington Mind, attentively recognising the lack of support and opportunity for youth within the area and providing a space for them to thrive. The increased turnover for Pop Recs has been remarkable. By reinvesting any profits made from sales and larger events, Pop Recs can provide a low-cost (often 'pay what you can') venue for many social activities, including for Little Pops, long-term residents Stitch and Bitch, King Ink, Sunderland Book Club, Sunderland Shorts Film Festival, and many others. In 2023, Pop Recs is also celebrating its ten-year anniversary with a series of what will undoubtedly be poignant gigs, including by the band of its founders, Frankie and the Heartstrings.

In early 2020, Sunshine Co-operative – a sustainable food company that had previously operated online, delivering food boxes – joined the family to occupy the ground floor of 170. The company has a community room, hosts a stall as part of the Teenage Market, and is beginning to transform its external

4

5

Fig. 4
170–175 High Street West

Fig. 5
In loving memory of Dave Harper

space into a food-growing garden. It is also part of the Sunderland Community-Led Local Development Programme. Washington Mind, a local mental health charity that already offered sessions to young people at Pop Recs' previous location, now occupies an upper-storey office above Pop Recs, offering sessions to support Sunderland's youth. Global Teacher CIC, which provides off-grid access to education for marginalised communities, has moved into the upper floors of 170 and has since established a further CIC called Good Habits, a sustainable non-profit focused around wellbeing. Through gathering like-minded and mutually supportive cultural organisations across the tenancies of the restored buildings, the current, forthcoming, and wider High Street West family will hopefully continue to gather around the coffee machine. The buildings are but a backdrop, a space to allow things to happen. As this collection of wonderful groups shows, it is the people who really matter.

Facilitating possible futures

Not only is the family of users within 170–175 High Street West increasing, but the family of buildings has since expanded to include 177, with discussions over the fate of 176 ongoing. While works to the shell of 177 are under way, the interiors will be refurbished in due course ready for new occupants. The entire High Street West project has evolved through genuine cooperative effort, and its future will depend on that same type of partnership working towards mutual benefit – ideally with a governance structure developed to facilitate collaboration between partners, as well as to support the collective maintenance of the buildings. This could be between the tenants and owners of the buildings, or possibly through a wider local land-trust including even more land and buildings in the area. Adding additional buildings to the complex – and thus the family of cultural users – along High Street West will consolidate the occupation of this location as a cultural hub for the community; indeed, perhaps for a new or extended community, should the proposed 'Living Arts Hub' development happen on a vacant adjacent site (a feasibility study was led by a resident steering group established by local housing charity Back on the Map; developer TOWN and social enterprise Create Streets have since been leading the 'Living Arts Hub' development and are now working with the local authority to develop a masterplan for the Sunniside area as a whole). The restored buildings are thus becoming a catalyst for the further regeneration of the area; as such, a strong area partnership, building upon the foundations of the HAZ, will remain crucial. It is key that the relationships nurtured over the preceding years do not dissipate, and that those collaborations continue and be strengthened by follow-on work, as creating truly meaningful impact within a place and within a community is undoubtedly only possible with long-term commitment.

Significant sums have been invested in these buildings, money which is unlikely to be recouped if assessing the project solely in narrow monetary terms. The value of the properties remains low, due to land-value depression in the area; never-

"This is a really important example of how partnership can work for historic buildings [where] no player in this project could have worked alone [... and where] most importantly, working in partnership allows people to make bold decisions."

Jules Brown

theless, this can be a great advantage. For the project's ultimate value lies not in its financial metrics (although the resident businesses now provide significant economic benefits); rather, its value lies in its commitment to local people – whether that is the capacity to bring joy and to change the narrative of a previously neglected area of the city, or to make people aware of the area's rich heritage once more. Indeed, spinning tales acknowledging the area's overlooked histories or telling of the area's possible futures, together with the people who are spending time in the East End of Sunderland, remains important. We hope this chapter captures only the very beginnings of a tale that will continue for many years to come.

Dave's vision

The story of the Sunderland Cooperative Heritage Lab has been tough in places, but most especially when Pop Recs founder and director Dave Harper died unexpectedly on 25 August 2021. The immense stress that comes with projects like this undoubtedly impacted his health, although we also know that he would have stopped at nothing. Everything that has been achieved is amazing, yet, at the same time, such achievements are never worth this. The impact within the project team was immeasurable and personal, and responding to his death was both urgent yet impossible. It meant that Dave's vision for the venue had to be taken over by others, who were also grieving, and who became more determined than ever to make things work in his legacy. It meant stepping back as researchers, and stepping up as friends, allowing the amazing community built around Pop Recs to come together and support each other.

A memorial gig at the Pop Recs venue was held in Dave's memory on 3 December 2021. The Dave Harper Music Award sessions, held with groups of 16–24-year-old SEN (special educational needs) students and run in conjunction with training provider Springboard, culminated in Pop Recs winning the award for Supporting Partner of the Year at the Springboard North East Annual Awards in late autumn 2022.

List of References

AHF (n.d.). *Architectural Heritage Fund.* https://ahfund.org.uk/projects/high-street-west/

Assemble (n.d.). *Granby four streets.* https://www.assemblestudio.co.uk/projects/granby-four-streets-2

Back on the Map (n.d.). *Our projects.* https://backonthemap.org/our-projects/

BBC (2021, 26 August). *Frankie and the Heartstrings heartbroken over drummer's death.* British Broadcasting Corporation. https://www.bbc.co.uk/news/uk-england-tyne-58341308

BBC (2022, 6 March). *The rebel women of Sunderland.* British Broadcasting Corporation. https://www.bbc.co.uk/programmes/p0brnf9c

Clark, K. (2022, 14 July). Here's how historic buildings in the heart of Sunderland could look as work begins on restoration scheme. *Sunderland Echo.* https://www.sunderlandecho.com/business/heres-how-historic-buildings-in-the-heart-of-sunderland-could-look-as-work-begins-on-restoration-scheme-3768310

Gillan, T. (2021, 13 June). The story of Sunderland's Binns family and their links to the anti-slavery movement. *Sunderland Echo.* https://www.sunderlandecho.com/heritage-and-retro/heritage/the-story-of-sunderlands-binns-family-and-the-legacy-behind-the-shop-3269954

Historic England (n.d. a). *Heritage at risk.* Historic England. https://historicengland.org.uk/advice/heritage-at-risk

Historic England (n.d. b). *Heritage action zones – Breathing new life into old places.* Historic England. https://historicengland.org.uk/services-skills/heritage-action-zones/breathe-new-life-into-old-places-through-heritage-action-zones/#Complete3

Historic England (n.d. c). *Celebrating the success of Sunderland's heritage action zone.* Historic England. https://historicengland.org.uk/whats-new/in-your-area/north-east/celebrating-sunderland-heritage-action-zone/

Historic England (n.d. d). *Living in a grade I, grade II* or grade II listed building.* Historic England. https://historicengland.org.uk/advice/your-home/owning-historic-property/listed-building/

HSW Site Stories (2021). *Local edible heritage stories.* HSW Site Stories. https://hswsitestories.wordpress.com

InvestSundUK. (2022, 19 July). 170–175 High Street West: A Partnership Approach. YouTube. https://www.youtube.com/watch?v=GttYMjv11w0

The Newsroom (2018, 12 December). Regeneration of 'forgotten' city centre buildings given cash boost. *Sunderland Echo.* https://www.sunderlandecho.com/news/regeneration-forgotten-city-centre-buildings-given-cash-boost-189444

North East Culture Awards (2022). *Finalists.* North East Culture Awards https://necultureawards.com/2022/en/page/finalists

OpenHeritage (2020). *A successful crowdfunding campaign.* OpenHeritage. https://openheritage.eu/timeline/a-successful-crowdfunding-campaign/

Seagull City (2022). *173 High Street West and female anti-slavery campaigners.* https://wp.sunderland.ac.uk/seagullcity/female-anti-slavery-campaigners/

Springboard (2022, 8 April). *Springboard and Pop Recs join together to launch the Dave Harper Music Award.* Springboard. https://springboard-ne.org.uk/springboard-and-pop-recs-join-together-to-launch-the-dave-harper-music-award/

Summer Streets Festival (2022). *A little bit about us.* Summer Streets Festival. https://www.summerstreetsfestival.com/aboutus

Sunderland City Council (n.d.). *Community Led Local Development.* Sunderland City Council. https://www.sunderland.gov.uk/article/14307/Community-Led-Local-Development

Sunderland Culture (n.d.). *Rebel women project.* Sunderland Culture. https://sunderlandculture.org.uk/rebelwomen/

TOWN (2023). *Sunniside Sunderland.* TOWN. https://sunnisidesunderland.com

TWBPT (2019a). *Open heritage.* Tyne and Wear Building Preservation Trust. https://www.youtube.com/watch?v=RmyFtVz4ZfQ

TWBPT (2019b). *#hswsunderland.* Tyne and Wear Building Preservation Trust. https://www.youtube.com/watch?v=Lpy4Rs0eVi8

Youngs, I. (2013, 9 October). *Frankie and the Heartstrings: Record shop boys.* British Broadcasting Corporation. https://www.bbc.co.uk/news/entertainment-arts-24437766

The OpenHeritage team has included: Martin Hulse of TWBPT; and Loes Veldpaus, John Pendlebury, Emma Ormerod, Miranda Iossifidis, and Ashley Mason of Newcastle University.

London Community Land Trust: A Model for Non-Speculative Property Development in London

By Levente Polyák and Giovanni Pagano

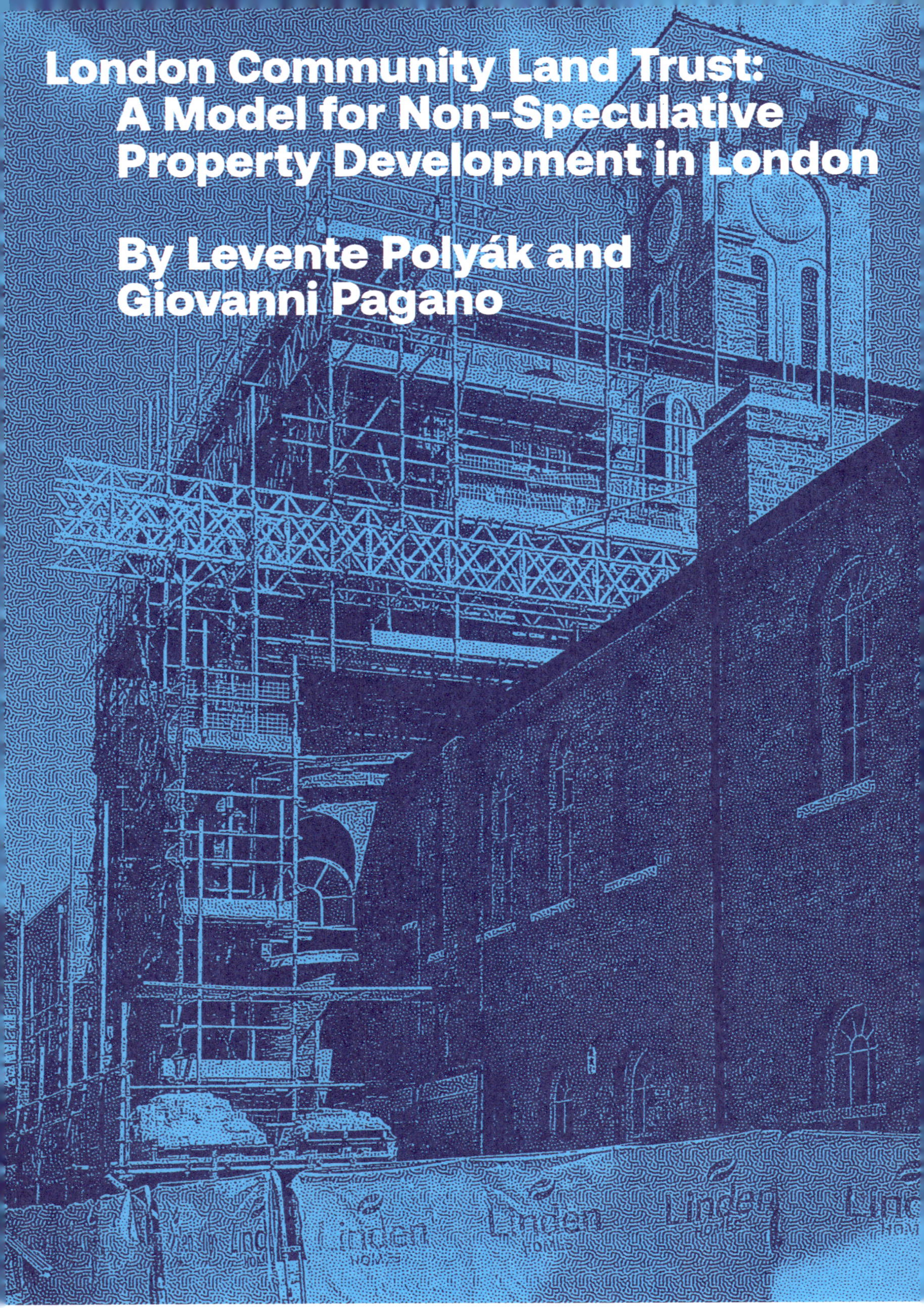

London CLT is London's first Community Land Trust, which was established in the former St Clements psychiatric hospital, in the Mile End area. The CLT provides affordable housing, allowing long-term residents who would otherwise be priced out to stay in the area, countering the tendencies of displacement and housing unaffordability (Fig. 1). Supported by the Greater London Authority to work with a private developer and a social housing association, the CLT was allocated 23 (out of 252) homes, distributed among privately owned and social housing units. Besides these homes, the CLT also promotes community engagement and is actively working on the creation of a community centre at the St Clements site. As one of the first urban community land trusts in the UK, London CLT has set a model of community-driven property development and adaptive heritage reuse, which has inspired a veritable movement in the UK and Continental Europe.

From hospital to housing

Located on an important road connecting the City of London with the county of East Anglia, St Clements was built in 1848 following the design of the architect Richard Tress and opened in 1849 as a workhouse – a place where poor people were sent who had no means of supporting themselves. In the 1860s, the workhouse's function shifted towards being an infirmary. In 1909, the workhouse closed, and was reopened in 1912 under the management of London County Council, caring for more than 600 chronically ill patients. Part of the site was destroyed during the Second World War, after which it became a fully-operational hospital. In 1959, the complex became a psychiatric hospital under the National Health Service (NHS). The hospital closed in 2005 and was then unoccupied for about ten years, falling into dereliction.

St Clements is situated in East London, five kilometres from the City of London, a very central location within the London agglomeration (Fig. 1). From being a relatively deprived area with working-class families, the neighbourhood became a centre of immigration in the 20th century. In recent decades, the financialisation of London real estate resulted in rising housing prices and the displacement of less affluent residents. East London's problems of gentrification and affordability were among the main motivations for developing a CLT in the area.

Fig. 1
CLT in London. Map

Timeline	1819—2020
1849	A workhouse opened at the St Clements site
1909	The workhouse closed
1912	The complex reopened as a hospital run by London County Council
1944	Part of the complex was destroyed during the Second World War
1948	The complex reopened as a hospital run by the National Health Service
1959	The complex became a psychiatric hospital
2005	The St Clements site was closed in a deteriorated state
2007	East London CLT (later London CLT) was established to bid for a site in Tower Hamlets borough
2009	The St Clements site became the focus of London CLT
2010	London CLT, as part of a consortium with Igloo Regeneration, bid for the site
2011	The bid for St Clements was won by Linden Homes, Galliford Try, and architects John Thompson and Partners (JTP)
2012	Community consultation events with JTP Architects (November)
2012	The Meanwhile Mixed-Use working group was formed within the CLT
2013	Shuffle Festivals took place at St Clements
2013	Planning applications for the site were submitted
2014	Shuffle Festival exhibition was hosted at St Clements (January), and the festival relocated to the adjacent Cemetery Park

2014	Planning applications for the site were approved and construction began
2015	Unsuccessful application to the National Lottery Fund, for renovation of the John Denham building
2016	Community share offer
2017	First CLT residents moved in
2020	Construction finished

St Clements occupies a long site, stretching from a major road (Mile End Road) to the Tower Hamlets Cemetery Park. Originally, the complex was built to face the street, while today it is better connected with the cemetery. The St Clements site includes 19 buildings and building parts, a combination of old and new.

"St Clements reveals a very symmetrical and orderly way to deal with the poor. It seems almost an industrial process as you enter off the main Bow Road into the reception wards and then move into the site with the chapel, the workshops, and then the fever wards, the mortuary, and the cemetery. Some people see it as a trajectory."
Nicola de Quincey

Community organisers at the charity Citizens UK identified St Clements as a potential site for a CLT, and established London CLT in 2007 in order to bid for the site. In 2010, the Mayor's Office opened the site to competitive bidding. London CLT presented a bid with Igloo Regeneration, an ethical real estate company, proposing a community-led design process – but was outbid by Linden Homes (a brand of a leading construction company) and Peabody (a social housing association). Nevertheless, political support resulted in London CLT joining the winning project in order to test the CLT model in an urban setting.

In 2014, planning applications for the site were approved, and demolition and construction began. The first residents moved into their CLT homes in 2017. Since 2015, London CLT has been working on raising funds to renovate the John Denham building and convert it into a community venue.

In the new urban design proposal by JTP Architects, heritage research played a significant role. This research, conducted by Nicola de Quincey, aimed to establish not only the evolution of the site, but also to understand the significance of each historical layer and addition to the complex (Fig. 2). The research findings informed decisions on which buildings to retain or demolish when opening up space for new volumes, as well as on where to place new structures to correspond to the original layout of the site.

2

4

Fig. 2
Construction site around the Clocktower

Fig. 3
Interior of the John Denham building

Fig. 4
Entrance to the Tower Hamlets Cemetery Park

"Besides the individual buildings, the historic pattern of the complex was respected when we tried to think of opportunities for new build between the old buildings."
Nicola de Quincey

The original St Clements site consisted of listed Victorian buildings and ancillary buildings of a more recent era. Research into the complex's temporal layers through demolitions and additions was conducted to inform decisions about which structures to prioritise, what to save, and where to open space for new constructions. Erecting new building volumes was also necessary to cover the renovation costs. The urban design scheme proposed by JTP aimed to restore the site's symmetry and to build on the precedents of previous buildings that had since been demolished.

3

The heritage protection structure of the St Clements site is complex. Three structures on the site (the Boundary Wall, the John Denham building, and the Administration building) are Grade 2 listed monuments. The whole site is curtilage listed, meaning that every single building on the site is protected. In addition, the site is located within the Tower Hamlets Cemetery Park conservation area, meaning that any demolition must be approved and special attention has to be given by the local authority. These layers of protection signify that every single structure on the site had to be treated carefully. The organisations Historic England (Historic Buildings and Monuments Commission for England) and English Heritage (English Heritage Trust) demonstrated a keen interest in the site and worked closely with the architects, developers, and the council's conservation officer.

The adaptive reuse of St Clements was designed by JTP Architects. The focus of the reuse process was to create a predominantly residential-led development: most buildings were turned into apartment complexes, except the John Denham building at the front. Besides historical research, the design decisions were also based on studies of the view of the Clocktower from different parts of the site. Moreover, there were a series of other regulations in play when designing the site's adaptive reuse. Some were of a logistical nature, such as ensuring access for fire service vehicles, and how to remove waste – significant challenges for a long, thin site with vehicular access only at the northern end. Despite efforts by Historic England to retain as many workshops as possible, some had to be sacrificed to ensure emergency access. Another key aspect of the urban design was to allow free access to the site via Mile End Road in the north and the Tower Hamlets Cemetery Park in the south. For the residential blocks, it was important that their design did not distinguish between CLT homes, privately owned apartments, or social housing units.

JTP's approach was to run a charrette or community planning process, inviting local stakeholders to 'come, co-design St Clements'. Preceded by a campaign inviting the press, local stakeholders, schools, and community groups, the charrette was organised in November 2012, including an exhibition with historical materials, dialogue workshops, hands-on planning workshops, and walkabouts. The ideas collected and the consensus developed during the workshops by more than 350 participants led the design team to create a vision for the area, feeding into a planning application that gained unanimous approval by the Tower Hamlets Planning Committee.

About a third of the site today consists of existing, retained buildings and two-thirds of new build, resulting in a variety of building styles, combined with open spaces, some of them semi-private gardens, others publicly accessible. The renewed St Clements site has 252 homes, 58 of which are social rent homes provided by the Peabody social housing association. In order to integrate the CLT within the community, its 23 homes are dispersed throughout the site.

Tools for affordable real estate

The St Clements site is governed through cooperation among a variety of actors. London CLT, one of the first urban CLTs in the UK, is a community benefit society, a not-for-profit limited company – a model widely used by community land trusts. People join CLTs as members, either because they are interested in buying a home in the long term, or because they like the project and choose to support it (Fig. 5). Others have an academic or professional interest in the project. The London CLT has about 3,000 members made up of residents who own CLT homes, the communities and campaigners from areas around CLT sites, and stakeholders who might invest their expertise in the CLT. These three membership categories are all represented in the board of trustees consisting of 15 people. Besides the board, the CLT also has subcommittees focusing on finance and risk; development; human resources; impact measurement; and allowing more in-depth discussion about these issues. Members have the right to vote and stand for elections. Membership requires the payment of a nominal sum of £1.

London's housing shortage has led to great demand for affordable housing, and so London CLT developed a well-designed selection procedure for its homes. CLT homes are allocated to local residents with a deep connection to the area (e.g., those who have worked in the area for at least five years); unstable housing situation (in risk of losing their homes); financial eligibility (not catered for by social housing programmes); local involvement (social connections in the area); and a supportive attitude towards the CLT's values and mission (potential future CLT advocates).

At the St Clements site, London CLT supported the establishment of a residents' association (including CLT, private, and social housing residents) that would participate in decision-making related to the site. This organisation has already been formed with a representative from each building, and is to be formally constituted as a resident management company to take over once the developers have left. Once the development is finished, the site will be handed over to a freeholder, the Ricardo Community Foundation (named

Community Land Trust

Community Land Trusts are a model of community-led development, where local organisations develop and manage homes and other assets important to their communities, such as community enterprises, food-growing, or workspaces. By owning land (or leasing it from public owners) and leasing apartments, entire buildings, or other types of properties to individuals, families, or community groups, CLTs can control the use and price of such properties. CLTs can therefore use this leverage to guarantee that spaces in their management remain affordable, based on local income levels. Each CLT has a different governance system but they all share some characteristics: they are controlled by local residents in a democratic fashion. CLTs are described in the Housing Regeneration Act of 2008: while any legal format that complies with that Act can be considered a CLT, most are established as community benefit societies, a legal format updated in 2014 that refers to membership organisations operating for the benefit of a community.

The CLT's communities manager works with residents through allocations and supports them in the process of accessing their new homes. He/she also develops specific training for residents and campaigners, about what being a CLT resident means. Once the new residents are in their homes, the communities manager works with them to look at ways to transform the neighbourhood, by building up community leaders, developing community spaces, or by other means.

Section 106 agreements

These agreements are planning obligations based on the 1990 Town & Country Planning Act. They are private agreements made between local authorities and developers and can be attached to a planning permission. The land itself, rather than the person or organisation that develops the land, is bound by a Section 106 Agreement, something that any future owners will need to take into account. Section 106 agreements are drafted when it is considered that a development will have significant impacts on the local area.

Funding Community Land Trusts (CLTs)

There are different ways to fund CLTs. In the most typical case, CLTs act like regular developers, but approach a charity or a socially minded bank that provides loans at low interest rates. In addition, CLTs receive government subsidies or grants to provide affordable housing. The CLT then constructs the homes and sells or rents them, using these revenues to refinance the mortgage. In other cases, more classical housing providers such as housing associations develop homes in partnership with CLTs: in these cases, the housing association finances and builds the homes and then transfers the freehold to the CLT and leases back the homes from the CLT. In some cases, public finance in the form of affordable housing subsidies can lower the costs of establishing a CLT.

after the economist David Ricardo, whose family lived in the area) made up of different stakeholders on the site, including Peabody, the CLT, the local council, the Greater London Authority, Linden Homes, Galliford Try, and the residents' management company.

St Clements is a site where real estate pressure as well as various public policies are in play, regarding the sale of public land, housing provision, heritage protection, as well as natural ecosystems. One of the key dimensions of public policy at St Clements relates to housing. The St Clements site is subject to a Section 106 agreement (a legal agreement between a developer and the local planning authority), which stipulates that new developments should provide 30% affordable housing. In such cases, the developer constructs all of the homes, then looks for a housing association or similar organisation to take on the future management of the affordable housing units. The CLT homes account for some of the affordable units, with the remainder of that 30% being covered by other models such as shared ownership schemes.

The main costs of the CLT are construction finance, usually through social investment from large donors or community shares. The London CLT's first revenues came in 2016 from a community share offer with Ethex, a not-for-profit Positive Investing organisation. The minimum investment was £100 each, with a return on investment of about 5%. About 130 investors (some from the surrounding communities, others being large donors) contributed £450,000, which covered architect fees and planning preparations for London CLT's Lewisham site, allowing the CLT to gain time and raise additional funds.

The most important source of revenue for London CLT was from the sales of the first homes at St Clements. Due to rising property prices, a surplus – between the purchase price paid to Linden Homes at a time of lower home values versus the price subsequently paid by the homeowners – allowed the CLT to generate some income. CLT home prices at the beginning of the process were about half the market price, but are now around one third. In the long term, however, such profit margins are unlikely to provide a source of income.

Mortgages are another important source of funding for CLTs on the buyers' side. London CLT managed to engage lenders who understand the specificity of a CLT: the Ecology Building Society and Triodos Bank were the first institutions to offer mortgages, before other mainstream lenders.

London CLT has a 250-year lease on its units in St Clements, and it can sell and underlease to the residents. The CLT sells properties at prices that are linked to the median income of the borough. When a resident wants to move on, they have to sell their property back to London CLT at a rate that is linked to median income in the borough.

"The idea behind this model is that wages are the best way to determine if something is affordable for the people living in the area. Our houses are affordable in perpetuity."
Hannah Emery-Wright

Besides funding the planning and construction process, setting up a CLT also has costs: in the case of London CLT, its parent organisation Citizens UK initially invested some staff time in the CLT's work. In addition, the National CLT Network gave the London CLT a £10,000 catalyst grant for capacity building.

Reconnecting with the neighbourhood

After years of vacancy and decay, one way to reconnect the site with the neighbouring communities was to open St Clements for various activities. This idea was implemented by the CLT's Meanwhile Mixed-Use working group established in 2012, aiming to bring events to the site before and during some phases of the construction. When the events and festivals organised at St Clements outgrew their original scale, the not-for-profit community enterprise Shuffle was established in 2013 to continue the activities. Shuffle's focus was on a mixture of high-calibre art, film, and community programming and curation, focusing on themes connected to mental health.

"St Clements is a lot of stories, and a lot of those weren't good stories. People grew up hearing 'If you don't eat your greens you will go to St Clements.' We wanted to change these narratives."
Lizzy Daish

Culture had an important role in building relationships and support for the St Clements redevelopment project. In order to explore the St Clements site, Shuffle organised cinema screenings in the former patients' social club and outside, and worked with gardeners to plant a flower garden from seeds donated from the Cemetery Park, and with edible plants to be used in the café opening on the site. Shuffle organised two large events at St Clements in 2013, a several-month summer festival and a ten-day winter festival in November.

Shuffle also conducted an oral history study among the local communities, concentrating on the last iteration of the complex as a psychiatric hospital, organising the testimonies of people who had been patients of the old institution into an exhibition in January 2014, using the gardens and the John Denham building (Fig. 5). Soon after the exhibition, demolition began at the site and Shuffle moved its festival to the Cemetery Park, where it organised four seasons.

Besides securing affordable homes, the CLT has also been leading a campaign to turn the John Denham building, a listed building at the front of the St Clements site, into a community space. With many constraints and large spaces that limited its potential use for residential units, the building was also listed as an 'Asset of Community Value', referring to its significance to the wider community, thereby giving the community

Asset of community value

An asset of community value (ACV) is land or property of importance to a local community. Under the Localism Act of 2011, ACVs are subject to additional protection from development. When the owner of an ACV wants to sell the property, they must inform the local authority; if a community group wishes to purchase the asset, they can trigger a moratorium for six months, allowing them to raise necessary funds. ACV status can be used by the local planning authority as a factor to refuse planning permission for full or partial change or demolition, or can force the local authority to buy the asset if it is under threat of long-term loss to the community. ACVs across the UK include more than 800 pubs, sport facilities, and stadiums as well as parks.

Fig. 5
The John Denham building

additional time to raise funds to purchase the building. Reusing the John Denham building as a community space would provide the area with a focal point, where neighbourhood residents with different ways of life could meet.

The impacts of the London CLT on St Clements, its neighbourhood, and on the city are manifold. Opening the site from Bow Road through to Tower Hamlets Cemetery Park turned St Clements into a public space accessible to the broader community. By offering affordable housing to people involved in the neighbourhood, CLT homes are contributing to easing the effects of London's housing crisis. With its temporary use events and participatory governance model, London CLT has engaged local communities to share their memories of the site on one hand, and shape its future on the other. The involvement of local residents in the CLT board and subcommittees, as well as their participation in local campaigns, contributes to improving their skills and capacities for mobilisation and self-determination.

"It's not enough just to build affordable homes: we want to have a lasting impact in the areas we work in, by empowering our residents as individuals or leaders of the community."
Hannah Emery-Wright

At the city level, London CLT has created a precedent that showcases how CLTs can work in an urban setting under strong real estate pressure. While previous CLTs had worked predominantly in rural areas where local communities came together to buy land, London CLT has opened the way for urban CLTs and shown how to apply political pressure in order to secure land. Reaching beyond the St Clements site, London CLT is involved in setting up other CLTs across London, and provides peer learning opportunities for other initiatives from across the country. However, gentrification trends in the neighbourhood can only be slowed if more sites become a CLT.

List of References

Department for Communities and Local Government (2011). *A plain English guide to the localism act*. Department for Communities and Local Government.

Department for Communities and Local Government (2011). *Assets of community value – policy statement*. Department for Communities and Local Government.

De Quincey, N. (2013). *Heritage statement and addendum. St Clements Hospital, listed building consent application*. JTP.

Engelsman, U., Rowe, M., & Southern, A. (2018). Community land trusts, affordable housing and community organising in low-income neighbourhoods. *European Journal of Housing Policy*, 18(1), 103–123.

FMDV (2018). *Mapping finance for community land trusts (synthesis document)*. Fonds Mondial pour le Développement des Villes (FMDV).

Harrington, C., & Seagrief, R. (2012). *The community land trust handbook*. National CLT Network.

Hill, D. (2015, 26 July). Ringing London's changes at St Clements in Mile End. *The Guardian*. (https://www.theguardian.com/uk-news/davehillblog/2015/jul/26/ringing-londons-changes-at-st-clements-in-mile-end)

Kip, M., & Oevermann, H. (2022). Neighbourhood revitalisation and heritage conservation through adaptive reuse: Assessing instruments for commoning. *The Historic Environment: Policy and Practice*, 13(2), 242–266.

Kruger, R., DeFilippis, J., Williams, O. R., Esfahani, A. H., Martin, D. G. & Pierce, J. (2020). The production of community in community land trusts. *City and Community*, 19(3), 638–655.

Lang, R., & Mullins, D. (2019). Field emergence in civil society: A theoretical framework and its application to community-led housing organisations in England. VOLUNTAS: *International Journal of Voluntary and Nonprofit Organizations*, 31, 184–200.

Patti, D., & Polyák, L. (2017). *Funding the cooperative city*. Community finance and the economy of civic spaces. Cooperative City Books.

This case study is based on interviews with: Charles Campion, architect at JTP; Tom Chance, president of the National CLT Network; Lizzy Daish, co-founder of Shuffle and former board member of London CLT; Hannah Emery-Wright, communities manager at London CLT; Nicola de Quincey, architect and heritage specialist at JTP; Rosy Smith, resident at St Clements, member of the residents' association, and former board member of London CLT.

B
Enabling Collaboration: Financing Projects

By Volodymyr Kulikov

Funding is a vital part of an adaptive heritage reuse (AHR) project. Covering the expenses is the only way to keep the mission alive. But it is also one of the most challenging tasks, due to increasing pressure on non-profit organisations to become financially self-sustaining, including those in the heritage domain (Proteau, 2018). Many heritage-related projects seek support from the limited sources of public finance; consequently, competition is strong and the methods of securing funding have become more sophisticated. The market drives high expectations of non-profit leaders and managers to acquire advanced financing, fundraising, and business-planning skills.

This overview summarises the observations gained during the OpenHeritage research project and incorporates analysis of the relevant secondary literature. For more detailed information about the financial management and business models explored during the OpenHeritage projects, see the deliverables published on Openheritage.eu (de Roo & Novy-Huy, 2020, 2022; Kulikov & Tönkő, 2021).

Inclusive business models and sustainable funding

The OpenHeritage project studied a variety of financial and business models and concluded that inclusive business models and sustainable funding suit the best adaptive heritage reuse projects aimed at maximising public good. Within OpenHeritage, inclusive business models refer to: 'ways in which the costs of adaptive heritage reuse relate to the benefits and the role of individuals and communities within that model'. The inclusive business model is then understood as the 'ways in which the costs of adaptive reuse relate to the (financial and societal) benefits and the extent to which all groups of civil society, particularly local communities, participate and benefit within that model' (de Roo & Novy-Huy, 2022, p. 6). Sustainable funding is a holistic approach to resource integration, aimed at long-term financial security without compromising the social and heritage values of a project or programme. It relies on a combination of external and internal financial and non-financial resources, and minimises negative impacts on society and nature. It is consistent with the project's social mission; it mobilises civic networks, facilitates self-financing, and maximises present and future values for stakeholders. Sustainable funding of adaptive heritage reuse projects mobilises necessary resources for investment and operation costs, serves the needs of the local community, strengthens connections between people and their surrounding environment, and creates benefits and additional value beyond the project site (Kulikov & Tönkő, 2021, p. 78).

Stará Tržnica

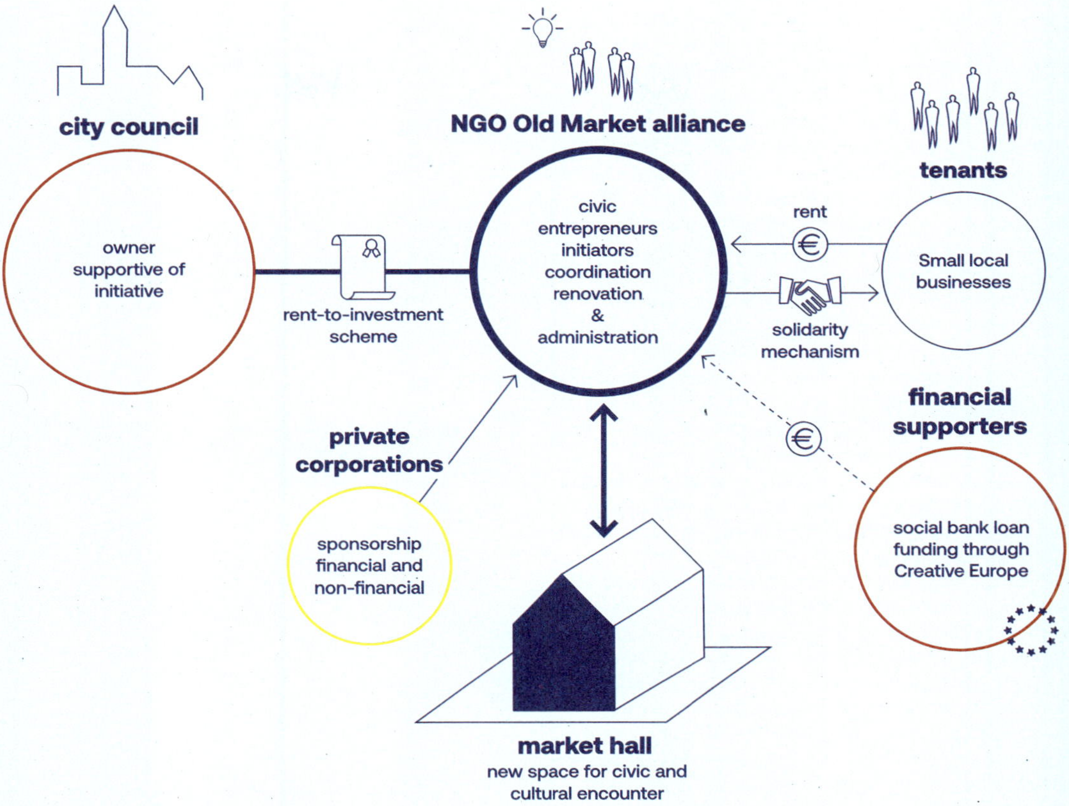

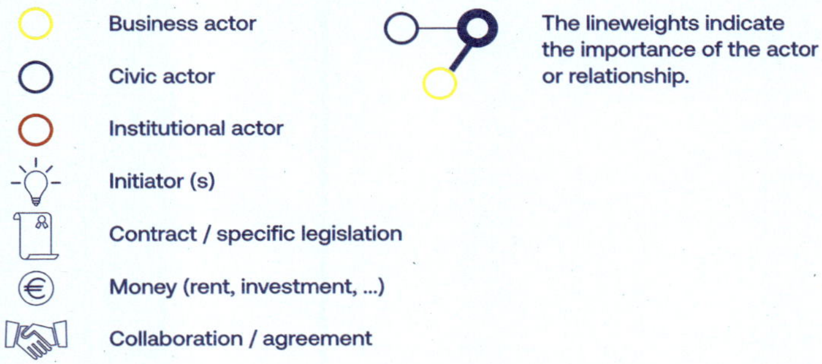

Fig. 1
Financing the Stará Tržnica project

Most adaptive heritage projects or programmes imply investment and operational costs. Investment costs are one-off expenses for accessing the site: purchase or transaction costs, construction, and renovation. Recurrent or operational costs include rent, interest payments, building maintenance, personal expenditures, etc. (Roo & Novy-Huy, 2020, p. 10). To cover investment and operating costs, projects and programmes need to generate revenues or secure external funding. Most organisations managing adaptive heritage reuse revitalisation projects observed by OpenHeritage have non-profit status. Non-profit does not mean 'no profit'. 'Non-profit' is a tax and legal status, ensuring that the revenues generated by an organisation are reinvested into its activities, and so generating income to cover operational (sometimes also investment) costs is vital for the organisation. The status of non-profit organisations varies in different countries, but in most cases revenue can be used to pay rents, salaries, and other transactions except for taking profit out of the company.

Funding instruments

A funding model combines different funding sources into a constellation unique to every adaptive heritage reuse project. Nevertheless, we can identify the main sources for European adaptive heritage reuse projects. They include internal funding (revenues generated by the organisations), external funding (bank loans, public money, private donations, etc.), and non-monetary resources such as volunteer work.

An internal revenue stream can contribute to a positive cash flow within the project. It can be generated by selling products or services, or asking for rent, membership dues, subscriptions, etc. Ideally, recurrent income covers recurrent costs or (at least) most of them (Roo & Novy-Huy, 2020, p. 10). The example of Stará Tržnica in Bratislava shows that stable income significantly contributes to funding diversity and is essential for a sustainable funding model (Fig. 1). It also allows organisations to remain independent from public and private donors. Social enterprises that generate income also look attractive in the eyes of the right investors (Bugg-Levine et al., 2012). Generating income often comes at the cost of complications of accounting, and may sometimes subjugate the project's mission. To mitigate this risk, project managers should try to identify an optimal level of commercialisation that does not undermine the fundamental values of the project. In other words, they should seek a model of 'commercialisation without over-commercialisation' (Bortolotto, 2020).

Donations from private persons, foundations, and businesses are an old tradition of supporting heritage organisations and projects. Ideally, donors become long-term project partners and help with resource integration tasks besides providing capital. For example, a family-owned enterprise, Lindéngruppen, is the main sponsor of the Färgfabriken project presented below. However, project managers should be aware of the increasing power of large donors within strategic decision-making, and create a govern-

Fig. 2
Brewery in Stará Tržnica

Fig. 3
Cooking school and community kitchen in Stará Tržnica

3

2

ance structure that ensures the independence of their projects. They should build an inclusive governance model based on checks and balances to empower all stakeholders (Lynch, 2011). In the case of Färgfabriken, creating a foundation and separating Färgfabriken's daily operations from the company helped ensure its curatorial independence. Additionally, by obtaining support from the Swedish Government, the Swedish Institute (public funds), and some international agencies, Färgfabriken diversified its funding and made the governance model more inclusive. Similarly, Jam Factory in Ukraine has relied on a sole benefactor when turning a Neo-Gothic former industrial building into an art centre focused on presentation, research, and development of contemporary art in Ukraine and East Central Europe. As the project is in a developmental stage, the governance model is not yet elaborated, providing more influence for the donor than in the case of the Swedish example.

Pooling funding includes several financial instruments, such as crowdfunding, cooperative community funds (peer-to-peer funding), and impactful investment. These financial instruments have been successfully applied in housing cooperatives and other community-led economic initiatives (Patti & Polyák, 2017). Many heritage-oriented projects, such as LaFábrika detodalavida in Spain or Promprylad.Renovation in Ukraine have successfully employed this funding tool. Pooling funding can be a powerful tool to mobilise communities and increase the diversity and inclusiveness of projects. On the downside, crowdfunding is usually a short-term solution; communities are often loose and cannot maintain adaptive reuse projects in their continuity. Crowdfunding is very demanding in promotional activities and thus might distract project managers from their primary goals. Studies show that crowdfunding can be used for small (and 'light') projects, together with traditional grant financing (Bonacchi et al., 2015, p. 194).

Public funds seem like the most natural source of external funding for adaptive heritage reuse projects aiming to generate public good. Governments (at various administrative levels) can provide direct financial support for heritage projects (grants and loans) or offer fiscal (tax) relief. Adaptive heritage reuse projects often receive public money as grants or subsidised loans. This instrument might be less flexible and prompt than money from the private sector, and public funding usually demands greater transparency and accountability. The Lisbon Lab of OpenHeritage, Marquês de Abrantes, is publicly financed, and shows the positive and negative aspects of such an investment structure.

Private or bank loans, mortgages, and guarantee loans can provide relatively quick access to funds to cover investment costs. However, if the project does not set profitability as a goal, bankers will likely see it as philanthropy, not an investment. Since most of the cases studied within the OpenHeritage project aimed to maximise social values rather than profits, traditional banks do not consider such initiatives 'normal' business cases. However, an emerging ecosystem of ethical and social financial institutions can support inclusive and sustainable adaptive heritage reuse projects with their resources.

International funding agencies, such as the European Commission or the EEA and Norway Grants scheme, support adaptive heritage reuse projects financially and often provide conceptual scaffolding and strongly encourage networking. However, competition for funds is usually strong, and small-scale projects may lack sufficient resources to prepare convincing applications. Also, projects of local relevance might have low priority for international organisations unless they are part of a larger consortium.

Finally, non-monetary contributions such as payment-in-kind, barter, volunteer work, DIY, and other in-kind donations are important resources. Volunteering hours help to reduce expenses on service work. But project managers should use volunteer work responsibly, distinguishing between volunteering and hidden employment (unpaid work). They can reduce the risks of perpetuating systematic inequality by setting up uniform and transparent principles of payment or accepting free work.

Diversity, social value, and well-matching

The cases below show that funding and governance models are closely related. A specific governance model can extend or restrict the pool of available resources, and strengthen or weaken the process of revenue integration. For instance, inclusive governance results in a shared mission and project benefits among many stakeholders. At the same time, it means shared responsibilities – possibly including financial risks. The importance of risk-sharing between various stakeholders is even more pronounced in times of economic crisis. A well-chosen funding model enforces cooperation with the communities and among the stakeholders. It has an impact on a larger territorial scale. It contributes to environmental, social, and economic sustainability.

Importantly, funding sources should be well-matched. As each funding type has its advantages and disadvantages, when designing the business model of a project, it is essential to consider how well the different funding sources complement each other. If funding sources are not well-matched, it can result in conflict between stakeholders and jeopardise the project's mission.

Additionally, social value cannot be neatly separated from financial tasks. Positive forms of co-responsibility and co-management contribute to a shift from maximising economic value to maximising social value. On the other hand, creating social value cannot rely only on 'claiming' resources from external actors (public authorities, donors, etc.) and contributing to raising and/or integrating resources. The ability to generate revenue to cover at least some operational expenses helps to keep the organisation fit and adaptable to public expectations.

Finally, funding diversity makes an adaptive heritage reuse project more resilient and resistant to economic disruption and business cycles. Diversification of funding resources reduces the risk of shocks from external factors. It also can be a tool for achieving a project's essential social goals, such as engaging stakeholders, sharing power, and building a stronger community around the project or programme. However, fundraising efforts consume time and energy that could be spent on a project's social missions; diversity therefore adds to the complexity and makes a project more challenging to manage.

List of References

Bonacchi, C., Pett, D., Bevan, A., & Keinan-Schoonbaert, A. (2015). Experiments in crowd-funding community archaeology. *Journal of Community Archaeology & Heritage*, 2(3), 184–198.

Bortolotto, C. (2020). Commercialisation without over-commercialisation: Normative conundrums across heritage rationalities. *International Journal of Heritage Studies*, *27*(9), 1–12. https://doi.org/10.1080/13527258.2020.1858441

Bugg-Levine, A., Kogut, B., & Kulatilaka, N. (2012). A new approach to funding social enterprises. *Harvard Business Review*, 90(1), 119–123.

de Roo, J., & Novy-Huy, R. (2020). *Financial guidelines: How to build a project-plan, project-structure and financial plan for community-led adaptive reuse projects* (OpenHeritage: task 4.1 and 5.4). OpenHeritage. https://eurodite.eu/wp/wp-content/uploads/2021/02/20201112_Financial-guidelines.pdf

de Roo, J., & Novy-Huy, R. (2022). *Inclusive business models. How to build an inclusive business model around your adaptive heritage reuse project*? (OpenHeritage deliverable 5.6). OpenHeritage. https://openheritage.eu/wp-content/uploads/2022/11/Inclusive-business-models-for-sustainable-heritage-reuse-processes.pdf

Kulikov, V., & Tönkő, A. et al. (2021). *Finalized report on European adaptive reuse management practices* (pp. 78-95). OpenHeritage. https://openheritage.eu/wp-content/uploads/2021/05/Finalized-Report-on-European-Adaptive-Reuse-Management-Practices.pdf

Lynch, B. (2011). *Whose cake is it anyway? A collaborative investigation into engagement and participation in 12 museums and galleries in the UK.* Paul Hamlyn Foundation.

Patti, D., & Polyák, L. (2017). *Funding the cooperative city: Community finance and the economy of civic spaces.* Cooperative City Books.

Proteau, J. (2018). Reducing risky relationships: Criteria for forming positive museum-corporate sponsorships. Museum Management and Curatorship, 33(3), 235–242.

(https://openheritage.eu/lviv-jam-factory/)

(https://openheritage.eu/la-fabrika-de-toda-la-vida/)

(https://promprylad.ua/en/)

(https://openheritage.eu/marques-de-abrantes-portugal/)

Färgfabriken, Sweden: An Art Space in Stockholm, Built on Private Sponsorship

By Levente Polyák and Sophie Bod

Färgfabriken ('paint factory' in English) is a platform and exhibition venue for contemporary cultural expressions, with an emphasis on art, architecture, and urban planning (Fig. 2). It is located in a former paint factory building in Lövholmen, an industrial zone in southwest Stockholm. Since its creation, Färgfabriken has not only become a key cultural institution in Stockholm, but has also pioneered a model of building inclusive, participatory processes through art and dialogue. Through a cultural agenda that combines architecture, arts, and urban planning with contemporary societal issues, Färgfabriken remains a significant actor in Stockholm, with a great impact on the development of the surrounding area and on the inclusion of a great variety of stakeholders in decision-making processes. With a private company as the building owner and main sponsor of its activities, Färgfabriken demonstrates how cultural institutions can rely on private assets and financing for their operations. The creation of a foundation and the separation of Färgfabriken's daily operations from the company ensures the curatorial independence of the art venue.

From factory to *Kunsthalle*

Färgfabriken's building was constructed by Helge Palmcrantz in 1889 in Lövholmen, an industrial zone in southwest Stockholm (Fig. 1). Originally called the Palmcrantz House, it was specifically designed to accommodate the reaping machine, mower, and machine gun production of the Palmcrantz company. In 1902, it became a paint factory for the Wilhelm Becker company. In 1974, Ulf G. Lindén became managing director of Beckers and in 1985 his company, Lindéngruppen, acquired Beckers, including the company's properties in Lövholmen.

Ulf G. Lindén and the Lindéngruppen were key protagonists in the creation of Färgfabriken. When paint production ceased, the art-lover Lindén began to make plans for a cultural venue. By 1994 the building was abandoned, practically a ruin, with its walls standing but without a roof and with trees growing inside the main hall.

"This was just a ruin. The wall was there, this iron construction in the main hall was intact, but there was no roof. Beckers said we could take over, use it for free, if we could find a sponsor for reconstruction. I thought this would be a suicide mission, but we understood that it is architecturally an amazing space."
Thomas Lundh

The creation of Färgfabriken resulted from a collaboration between the Association of Swedish Architects (Svenska Arkitekters Riksförbund), Alcro-Beckers, ColArt, and a group of

Fig. 1
Färgfabriken in Stockholm. Map

Timeline	1889—2020
1889	The factory was built by industrialist Helge Palmcrantz, to accommodate the company's production
1902	The paint firm Beckers moved into the building
1985	Beckers was bought by Lindéngruppen, owned by Ulf G. Lindén
1987	The Beckers Art Award was established
1994	The paint factory ceased production and Lindén began planning a new cultural venue
1995	The Färgfabriken Foundation was established, basic renovation started, and a first exhibition *Triangular* was held in May
1996	*Interpol* exhibition and first important events concerning architecture
1998	Stockholm's European Capital of Culture season, with a major contribution from Färgfabriken
2001	Lindéngruppen sold the Alcro-Beckers decorative paint business
2001	*Stockholm at Large* exhibition, introducing the Färgfabriken method
2008	Jenny Lindén Urnes, the daughter of Ulf G. Lindén, took over the company and the foundation's chair; Jan Åman resigned as director
2009	Industrial activity ceased at Lövholmen, with all factories relocated
2010	*Building Blocks* exhibition
2011	Second renovation of the building by architect Petra Gipp
2012–2013	*Stockholm on the Move* exhibition
2020	Färgfabriken's 25th anniversary

Lindéngruppen's role in facilitating the creation of Färgfabriken is due to the engagement of Ulf G. Lindén, its former owner. When paint production ended at the Lövholmen facility, Ulf G. Lindén, inspired by his love of art, decided to use the space as a cultural venue. While Lindéngruppen's sponsorship is a philanthropic gesture and a continuation of the company's engagement with arts through the Beckers Art Award, Färgfabriken as a cultural venue also helped the company explore new ideas for its own development. Meanwhile, the creation of a foundation and the separation of Färgfabriken's daily operations from the company also ensured the curatorial independence of the new cultural centre.

artists and architects. The Beckers paint company was interested in building a collaboration with architects, in order to open up a new market for its products. Coincidentally, a group of artists and architects including Jan Åman, Thomas Lundh, and Elizabeth Hatz had long discussed opening a space for art activities and reflection on architecture and contemporary art.

Beckers' longer-term plan was originally to demolish the building, but the group was offered free use if they could find a sponsor for its renovation. However, with pressure from the artists, the building received heritage protection from the municipality. Beckers was also persuaded by the artists' involvement and their capacity to raise funding. Consequently, in 1995, a foundation was created with the participation of Alcro-Beckers (still owner of the building), ColArt, and the Association of Swedish Architects, with Alcro-Beckers taking a more important role.

Färgfabriken opened in May 1995 with a series of international art exhibitions that gave the organisation visibility at the national level. In parallel with these exhibitions, Färgfabriken began to organise seminars on architecture and urban planning, and received additional municipal funding to run activities exploring the future of the Lövholmen area.

"Färgfabriken became famous as a free space: not managed by the city or the government, it was a non-religious, non-political and non-profit foundation."
Pernilla Lesse

Färgfabriken defined itself as a *Kunsthalle*, which encompasses different and broader activities than an art museum or gallery. Building its unique profile among art institutions, the organisation focused on emerging artists and creators rather than established stars, and created a communication platform. In contrast to art institutions owned by the state, city, or private banks, Färgfabriken was conceived as a free place where more open discussions and exhibitions can be held without external control. In 1998, Stockholm was designated the European Capital of Culture and Färgfabriken, as its main partner, gained international visibility. In 2001, Lindéngruppen sold Alcro-Beckers, the decorative paints business of Beckers, to the Finnish company Tikkurila but retained ownership of the Färgfabriken building.

"It was quite new for a cultural institution to have a very open, transparent collaboration with partners outside the cultural field. And for that we got lot of criticism, mostly from the traditional cultural scene, that we were not serious, that we were mixing money with culture."
Thomas Lundh

The 2001 exhibition *Stockholm at Large* can be identified as one of Färgfabriken's main turning points. The event brought together urban planners, project managers and students, to look at the city from a distance. For the first time in

“We need to aim towards the future and use our amassed knowledge and experience as a force to go forward. We have to be at the forefront of where a cultural institution can be, to challenge the status quo and get new ideas – being this platform where different worlds and interests come together as they have not done before.”

Joacim Björk

Fig. 2
Färgfabriken in Stockholm

Sweden, a diverse group of local stakeholders came together and discussed issues concerning the development of the city of Stockholm and various towns in the metropolitan agglomeration. Participants joined various thematic groups and were asked to look at different issues relevant to the analysis of the city and the vision for its development. Urban segregation soon emerged as a key issue and, for the first time, Stockholm was defined as a very segregated city, with little communication among different neighbourhoods. The results of this participatory workshop were so unexpected that it immediately resulted in both media attention and a strong public reaction. As a result, Färgfabriken became well known in Stockholm and gained the status of a 'national cultural brand'. Its model of bringing together different stakeholders was labelled the 'Färgfabriken method' and was adopted in various cities within the framework of the New Urban Topologies series.

"We need to aim towards the future and use our amassed knowledge and experience as a force to go forward. We have to be at the forefront of where a cultural institution can be, to challenge the status quo and get new ideas – being this platform where different worlds and interests come together as they have not done before."
Joacim Björk

Although participatory and multi-disciplinary focus groups are increasingly common practice in current urban planning and management, *Stockholm at Large* caught Stockholm public opinion by surprise at the time. The events triggered a broad interest in collaborative ways of addressing urban challenges and building interdisciplinary dialogue around urban challenges.

Transforming industrial buildings and areas

Lövholmen had been an industrial site for over one hundred years. Although factories began to close in the later decades of the 20th century, the area was overlooked during Stockholm's building boom of the 1990s. However, basic infrastructure and public services provided to Lövholmen, and new environmental regulations prompting the remaining factories to relocate further from the city, ignited new interest in regenerating the former industrial district.

As a practical arrangement, once industries had left Lövholmen, landowners began to offer buildings to artists and designers, protecting their properties from vandalism and attracting a critical mass of art and design activities to the area. Recognising this transformation, local authorities also started to support individual artists with studio grants, and Färgfabriken with funding for activities.

Although a large proportion of the area remains abandoned, the presence of Färgfabriken and of other small art studios that slowly settled in the surroundings suggests a particular vision for the future development of the neighbourhood. Plans for the area are dominated by residential complexes, threatening the survival of the cultural initiatives that have settled there.

"With the right actor, you can create a model that would provide some hipness for the commercial developer, and studio spaces for the artists. Otherwise, they would be just thrown out and the area would become a sanitised version of what you have now."
Jan Rydén

In the mid-1990s, Färgfabriken was basically locked in a guarded site, as the surrounding industries were still operational (Fig. 3). It was dangerous even to smoke a cigarette outside, due to chemicals in the air. Moreover, despite improvements in basic infrastructure and public services, the area was still very poorly connected with the city centre, and suffered from negative perceptions often linked to drug abuse and poverty. Nevertheless, the building had quite a charming character, and the team accepted the challenge of starting to work there after the first renovation in 1995.

When discussions began with the groups of artists, the building was in such bad condition that Beckers longer-term intention was to demolish it. The building lacked many basic amenities: it had a dirt floor, no toilets, ventilation system, heating, or hot water, and its roof was open. The artists neverthe-

The Färgfabriken method

This method is the realisation of the founders' vision for the cultural institution, with events and exhibitions helping to discuss important societal issues. Involving a variety of stakeholders, organising workshops to create exchange between different positions, mediating between different professional and lay languages, and supporting such discussions through exhibitions and artistic research have all become trademark formats of Färgfabriken's projects. The art context has proven to be fruitful for discussions, liberating ideas and enabling empathy instead of confrontation.

3

Fig. 3
Färgfabriken's industrial neighbourhood in Lövholmen

Fig. 4
The southern facade of Färgfabriken

less recognised the building's value, and contacted the municipality's heritage department seeking protection for it. The department acted quickly, assigning the building heritage protection.

Through their contacts at the Association of Swedish Architects, the initiators approached Skanska, the large construction company active in the area, and received 600,000 SEK (Swedish krona) that allowed basic renovation of the building: restoring the roof, opening the water system, levelling the floors, and installing heating in some of the spaces. The renovation was designed by architects Catharina Gabrielsson and Staffan Henriksson, specialists in industrial architecture. After the first renovation, although the building was suitable for work, it was still quite uncomfortable and unwelcoming, with many cold spaces.

4

Following a change in the foundation's leadership in 2009, Lindéngruppen stepped in, stabilised Färgfabriken's finances, and funded the renovation of the building to upgrade the organisation's facilities, turning the building into a state-of-the-art cultural venue. This second renovation was designed by Petra Gipp and was completed in 2011. As a result, the atmosphere of the building has been altered, becoming more polished and comfortable (Fig. 4). The ground floor gave space to a new restaurant, adding to Färgfabriken's financial stability.

"Our vision is to keep much of the historical value of the area. It has so much industrial and cultural history; these are things that should be part of the future of the area, and not be replaced by a sterile space."
Karin Englund

The ground floor, besides the building's main entrance, accommodates the Färgfabriken Kafé and an additional event space. The first floor hosts the large main hall, Färgfabriken's most important space, which is characterised by monumental pillars and a raw factory interior and is used as the institution's central exhibition space. Next to the main hall, two smaller project rooms provide space for smaller exhibitions and workshops. The same floor also hosts the staff office plus a shop selling books, catalogues, and artefacts related to the institution's cultural programme. On the top floor, events, talks, workshops, and occasionally private events take place in a spacious and bright loft space.

The Färgfabriken building enjoys legal protection. Local authorities were responsive to the need to protect industrial heritage, and immediately agreed to collaborate with the artists; this enabled the renovation to happen, which had a fundamental role in protecting the site from demolition.

A new vision for Lövholmen

Once Färgfabriken was launched and its building renovated, the biggest challenge for the organisation was to generate public interest in its activities and motivate them to visit an area they would not otherwise have gone to. The media coverage resulting from the success of Färgfabriken's events and exhibitions was definitely helpful in attracting a larger audience.

Among factories already abandoned or about to close, Färgfabriken has been a catalyst for attracting new initiatives to the area and building relationships with them. Continuously reaching out to other art spaces and studios in Lövholmen, Färgfabriken has created a variety of collaborations with different local initiatives. For instance, products from local designers and works by local artists are sold in Färgfabriken's shop under the label 'Created in Lövholmen!'

In the decades since its establishment, Färgfabriken has been directly engaged in the discussion about the future of Lövholmen. Following an exhibition about Lövholmen in 2007 that explored the possibilities of keeping existing buildings and the industrial character of the area, Färgfabriken has taken on the role of initiating, coordinating, and hosting a series of exhibitions, events and discussions about the area's transformation. Recently, the foundation received a grant from the municipality's cultural administration, to collect knowledge about the area, mapping local actors, building networks among them, and serving as a gathering point for their discussions. Färgfabriken has devoted a space to this discussion, where opinions, ideas, and feedback are collected. An online questionnaire complements this platform in the virtual space.

While Färgfabriken enjoys relative autonomy due to its organisational structure and the foundation's backing, it has also received significant support from public administrations keen on using culture as an instrument for urban renovation and the rehabilitation of industrial sites. However, the relationship with the Stockholm municipality lacks more concrete projects, a clearer vision, and more consistent funding for longer-term collaboration between them.

Despite the lack of municipal ownership in the area, municipal regulations can have a strong impact on the future of Lövholmen. Zoning regulations demand that new residential areas have active uses on ground floors. This gives an opportunity for more diversity in the future development of the area, and the chance for Färgfabriken to coordinate efforts to keep artistic production in the neighbourhood.

Since its creation, Färgfabriken has had a strong influence on the surrounding area's transformation. The mere presence of a cultural venue meant a lot for the regeneration of the area. During the first exhibitions, it was seen as irrational that such a centre was established in such a remote and disconnected area. Soon, however, the city developed an interest in improving Färgfabriken's surroundings with streetlighting, public transport and even a school. Moreover, when some of the neighbouring factories closed, various buildings became incubators for small companies and studios for artists. Many of the foundation's activities are in some way or another related to the surrounding neighbourhood, have impacted its recent development, and are still playing a crucial role in the design of future plans. In the past decade, Färgfabriken has essentially become a gathering point to discuss the future of the Lövholmen area, seeking to retain working spaces and cultural venues as part of its future development, aside from the inevitable residential complexes.

Besides its impact on its immediate surroundings, the foundation has influenced the ways in which urban planning dilemmas are discussed in Stockholm. Through its debates, Färgfabriken played an important role in raising awareness of the need for infrastructural development, and the Färgfabriken method brought many diverse actors around the same table to debate shared topics. Such a working dynamic is very interesting, since it facilitated collaborations and conversations between stakeholders that otherwise would have not met. Moreover, it made people aware of a diversity of working logics and environments.

Fig. 5
Event venue on the top floor of Färgfabriken

The Färgfabriken staff have been keen to share their experiences and contribute to the creation of similar venues. The organisation's model has also been reproduced in other contexts. Between 2008 and 2011, the organisation was engaged in creating Färgfabriken Norr (Färgfabriken North) in Östersund, north Sweden, helped by EU funding, but this experience was discontinued after Färgfabriken withdrew from running the venue and wished to hand over the operations to the municipality. Since 2012, through the New Urban Topologies project, another version of the institution has been operating in Mostar, Bosnia and Herzegovina, built up by Färgfabriken and its local sister organisation.

Autonomy through diversity

In the early years of Färgfabriken, its founders explored a variety of funding sources to help run its activities. The first exhibitions, for instance, were covered by Development Aid funds and by the Swedish Institute, both focusing on cultural exchange. Färgfabriken's economic model has been consolidated in the past decade, but a large part of the foundation's budget is linked to grants and sponsorship. The building used by Färgfabriken is owned by Lindéngruppen. As such, the foundation depends on a lease that is usually renewed every three/four years. Lindéngruppen remains Färgfabriken's main sponsor, contributing around 3 million SEK (€285,000) to the organisation each year.

At the time of Färgfabriken's opening, the organisation's members approached the Ministry of Culture for funding. Not being a museum or a private gallery, Färgfabriken was initially not eligible for funding, but subsequent changes to eligibility criteria gave the organisation access to 800,000 SEK (equivalent to €80,000) per year. Furthermore, yearly grants are provided by the government (one million SEK, or €93,000), and the region (450,000 SEK, or €42,000). Some activities are financed by EU funds through international collaboration networks.

Besides this combination of private engagement and public funding, the foundation has looked for ways to attract more support from third parties (Fig. 5). Because the projects exhibited at Färgfabriken are rarely 'standard' art projects, it is important that the foundation does not rely solely on the art world for sponsorship, but on other sectors too. This is the main reason why the initial focus on arts and architecture was eventually extended to include urban planning. In this sense, when the foundation decided to add urban planning as one of the main subjects tackled, there was a real need to draw interest from a broader range of actors and stakeholders. By opening up to urban planning, much more funding became available from a variety of European sources as well as in partnership with the Swedish Institute. The projects exhibited at Färgfabriken are as diverse as the stakeholders with which it builds partnerships.

Färgfabriken's governance follows the classical organisational structure of a foundation. The organisation's operations are overseen by a board of nine people, of which the director is Jenny Lindén Urnes, daughter of Ulf G. Lindén and owner of Lindéngruppen. The board members also include two architects, a former politician, an acclaimed artist, and a banker, reflecting the need for a multi-disciplinary approach and the making of the foundation as a complex network, bringing together a diversity of interests, occupations, and visions. The board meets four times per year and mainly controls the financial side of the organisation, rather than its agenda. The latter is left almost entirely to the Färgfabriken staff to define.

The building now hosts two organisations: Färgfabriken as the cultural organisation, overseen by the foundation; and Färgfabriken Events, which manages the restaurant and other commercial events. Färgfabriken's everyday tasks, together with the design and management of exhibitions at the *Kunsthalle*, are made possible by a team of five employees and three project managers. A collaborative leadership is very telling of the way in which the Färgfabriken team has decided to work, one that rejects any strongly hierarchical management structure.

As for many organisations, COVID-19 was not an easy period for Färgfabriken. The organisation had to postpone or cancel many events: for instance, one of Stockholm's largest design and craft markets, organised by Färgfabriken every March with over 100 artisans, had to be called off. Färgfabriken operated the space according to health guidelines and regulations, forcing the organisation to reduce the number of visitors and cancel opening events. However, compared with many art venues across Europe, Färgfabriken was still very fortunate, in that it could host many exhibitions during the pandemic, made possible by relatively flexible national regulations. The hope is that Färgfabriken has a long-term future and will not be displaced by higher economic interests.

List of References

Hårsman, B. (2006). Ethnic diversity and spatial segregation in the Stockholm region. *Urban Studies*, 43(8), 1341–1364. https://doi.org/10.1080/00420980600776434

Immler, N., & Sakkers, H. (2014). (Re) Programming Europe: European capitals of culture: Rethinking the role of culture. *Journal of European Studies*, 44(1), 3–29. https://doi.org/10.1177/0047244113515567

Schmitt, P. (2016, June). Experiments and innovations in 'soft' urban planning: Urban living labs. *Casual: Co-creating Attractive Sustainable Urban Areas and Lifestyles. Policy Brief #3: Urban Europe*. Nordregio. https://www.nordregio.org/wp-content/uploads/2018/03/CASUAL-PB-3_1.pdf

Schmitt, P., Smas, L., Perjo, L., & Tunström, M. (2016, 22–24 June). *Urban planning through exhibition and experimentation in Stockholm*. REAL CORP 2016. 21st International Conference on Urban Planning, Regional Development and Information Society. https://programm.corp.at/cdrom2016/papers2016/CORP2016_21.pdf

Smas, L. (2016, Iss. 4). Exploring new forms of urban governance. *Nordregio News*. http://www.diva-portal.se/smash/get/diva2:1128939/FULLTEXT01.pdf

The case study is based on interviews with: Joachim Granit, artistic director of Färgfabriken; Pernilla Lesse, managing director of Färgfabriken; Thomas Lundh and Elizabeth Hatz, co-founders of Färgfabriken; Jan Rydén, former curator at Färgfabriken; Karin Englund, curator at Färgfabriken; Joachim Björk, board member of Färgfabriken.

Stará Tržnica, Slovakia: The NGO-Led Regeneration of the Old Market Hall in Bratislava

By Levente Polyák and Lukács Hayes

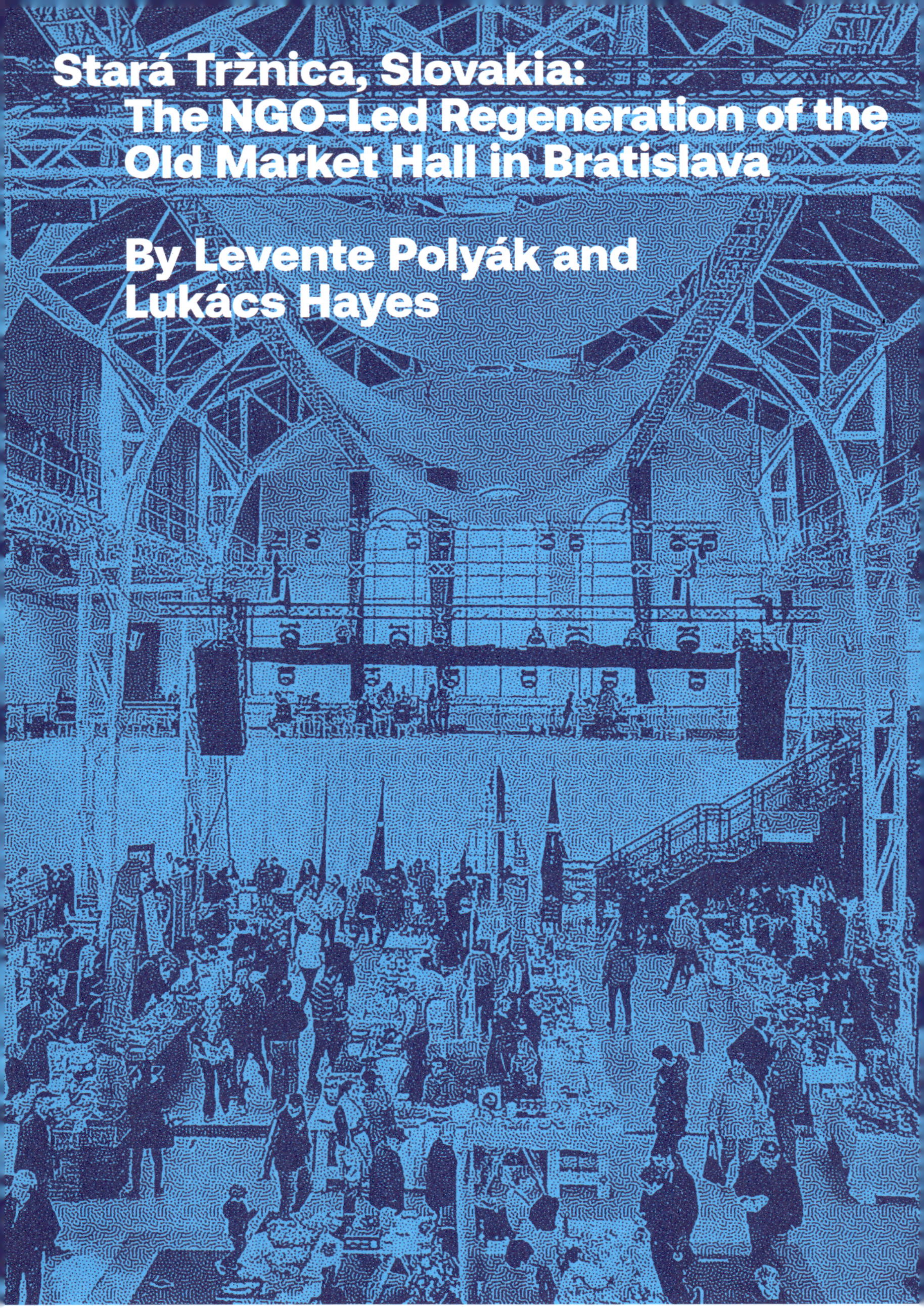

Stará Tržnica (Old Market Hall) is Bratislava's historic market building, located in the city centre. The market closed in 1960, following protracted but unsuccessful attempts by the municipality to maintain its viability. Years later, the hall reopened with a redevelopment plan proposed by the NGO Alianca Stará Tržnica (Old Market Hall Alliance), combining a Saturday food market with cultural events on other days, together with two cafés, a grocery shop, a cooking school, and a soda water manufacturer (Fig. 2). Rethinking the opportunities of the Old Market Hall allows the organisation to run the building in an economically sustainable way, while gradually renovating it and creating a new event venue and meeting space in the heart of the city. Since reopening, the investment and management model has been recognised as an innovative mechanism for more inclusive use of a public property while reinvesting revenues in its renovation and activities. The Stará Tržnica model has inspired a series of initiatives across Slovakia and Czechia.

From vacant building to a thriving venue

Bratislava's Old Market Hall, designed by architect Endre Makay and engineer Gyula Laubner, opened on 31 October, 1910. The building, situated at the edge of Bratislava's historical centre, was built with steel structures inspired by Gustave Eiffel, and was considered a daring novelty in the city (Fig. 1). The Old Market Hall operated as a municipal marketplace until 1960.

During the communist era, the market lost its appeal and was gradually depopulated. Between 1960 and 1989, the building hosted a television warehouse, studio, and a variety of cultural productions. Between 1989 and 1996, it stood empty until a renovation in 1996. However, the renewed market function was short-lived due to a lack of demand, with most vendors closing shop. The remaining vendors failed to compete with supermarkets, providing little revenue for the market hall, and the building incurred significant losses for the municipality of approximately €30,000 per year. In the years following its closure in 2008, the market hall was occasionally used as a stage set for TV shows and gala events. The building hosted around 15–20 private events annually, but was otherwise unused for around 350 days each year.

The building's original spaces were modified at various times. In the 1990s, the municipality renovated the hall and constructed small shops along its edges. In 2013, when the Old Market Hall Alliance gained access to the building, the market hall was fragmented into smaller spaces divided by walls, rem-

Fig. 1
Stará Tržnica in Bratislava. Map

Timeline	1910—2018
1910	Construction of the market building, designed by Gyula Laubner
1960	The building ceases to function as a market and is turned into a TV warehouse and studio
1989	The building becomes vacant
1996	The municipality launches the building's renovation
1998	The municipality rents out the renovated building for use as a market
2004	The market is in decline and underused
2008	Following a long dispute, the municipality cancels the rental contract and the building again becomes vacant
2011	Discussions begin about a new programme for the building
2012	Establishment of the Old Market Hall Alliance
2012	Proposal by the Old Market Hall Alliance to run the building
2013	The City Council votes to approve the Old Market Hall Alliance plan
2013	The Old Market Hall Alliance begins to operate the building
2016	The Old Market Hall Alliance begins its Living Square programme to revitalise public spaces around the market
2017	The Old Market Hall Alliance's investment breaks even
2018	Matúš Vallo, a founder of the Alliance, becomes mayor of Bratislava. The Living Square programme becomes a key objective of the municipality

iniscent of a poorly functioning shopping mall. Besides damaged floors and other surfaces, the building's infrastructure was also dilapidated, with defective heating, cooling, air-circulation, and electrical systems.

The Old Market Hall Alliance, an NGO established to elaborate a special programme for the building, was created by a team of 11 professionals from different disciplines. Among the founders, one had run concerts for 20 years; another had organised food markets for years, and was ready to bring that experience to the market hall. When the 11 founders met, they all nurtured the same ambition – of finding a way to revive the market hall. The original idea was not to take over the management of the building, but to create a project that explored its history and the reasons for its failure. By 2012, those ambitions had gradually changed: they increasingly saw their role not only as authors of a study, but as developers of the project itself.

In 2012, the Alliance submitted a proposal to the municipality for running the market hall, including a detailed economic model and supported by many expressions of interest from various organisations. The proposal was to organise a weekly market every Saturday, combined with other events on weekdays, and permanent leasing of smaller shops within the building to different services related to the market. The Alliance built up broad public backing for the proposal. Support from various communities in the city helped the association convince the municipality of the public interest in the proposal. Due to its detailed planning and considerable public support, the building was handed over to the Alliance through a concession procedure, voted on by the city council, rather than a public procurement process.

The Old Market Hall Alliance received the keys to the building in September 2013. The first event, a food market, was organised on 22 September, and was followed by regular market days, first once a month and then twice a month after the first year. In 2014, the building's various spaces piloted 'pop-up' uses, which informed the renovation of these spaces in subsequent years. Following a trial period and temporary closure for renovations, the market hall reopened in March 2015. Since September 2015, the weekly Saturday market has operated continuously (except during the first COVID-19 lockdown, when it closed for 2½ months), with other events gradually developed to complement it.

"What works is the blend of programmes, multi-functionality, the combination of activities that don't generate revenue with those that do: this way, we can subsidise the former. This is a really strong message – that the most precious day is given to the public."
Ján Mazúr

The Old Market Hall Alliance created an agenda centred around the food market. During the week, the building is used as a concert venue, a ballroom for companies, a conference hall, and workshop space. The food market was never

2

3

4

5

Fig. 2
Saturday market in the Old Market Hall

Fig. 3
A revitalised public space in front of the Old Market Hall

Fig. 4
Cafeteria in Stará Tržnica spilling into the street

Fig. 5
Between events in the Old Market Hall

intended to generate revenue for the Market Hall; its objective is to attract visitors and make the market hall work. The Saturday market is conceived as an inclusive and sustainable event: children's theatre sessions are organised every week, and there are dedicated spaces for children and seniors, with no obligation to purchase anything (Fig. 2). Local minority communities are regularly invited to present their cuisine and music at the hall. The building also has a composter and a collection facility for used oil. Most transport to and from the building is organised by cargo bikes.

The food market hosts approximately 20–30 vendors during summer and 100 in winter. One of the largest events is the Christmas market, which attracts more than 20,000 visitors annually, and includes a street market, thereby uniting the indoor and outdoor spaces.

The food market has also cultivated various synergies among other tenants and venues within the market hall: the café has an open door towards the market and plays music on Saturday mornings; restaurants and the cooking school buy unsold vegetables, to ensure that the vendors have no unsold produce. The bike-sharing shop offers a home-delivery service for grocery purchases.

The outward-facing spaces that look onto the neighbouring square and streets are rented out to permanent tenants. These businesses all contribute to the market hall's operation in their own ways, through specific activities or resources, or by adapting their opening hours and services to the needs of more vulnerable groups.

Besides the Saturday market and other events in the main hall, the building hosts a variety of other activities (Fig. 4). Lab is a cafeteria and fabrication lab on the ground floor, including a basement workshop with woodcutters, laser cutters, a 3D printer, and other tools for digital fabrication. It works on a prepaid membership basis and contributes to an emerging community around the Lab. Next door is a bike-sharing shop that offers a delivery service for marketgoers. Another tenant is Foodstock, a restaurant that composts all its organic waste, thus inspiring a planned waste system for the entire market and the neighbourhood. Foodstock also helps with the community kitchen, organised on Saturdays, where various minorities present their cuisine and products. There is also a grocery store, which provides food and other items that are produced as locally as possible. On the other side of the market is a wine bar that opens throughout the day, offering local wines at affordable prices. Inside the market hall, there are other businesses: a soda manufacturer, in which the Old Market Hall Alliance is a major shareholder; and a brewery that is also responsible for maintaining the square in front of the market hall.

In March 2020, the COVID-19 pandemic forced Stará Tržnica to shut completely. While the Old Market Hall suspended many social and cultural activities for more than a year and a half, the building served as storage for the city of Bratislava, storing materials, providing a space to make basic packages for homeless or older people, and producing protective equipment and face shields that were distributed to hospitals around the area. During this period, the Old Market Hall lost considerable revenue, and survived on savings generated by previous events and through contributions from partners.

Throughout the pandemic lockdown, Stará Tržnica supported its food vendors by delivering food packages until the market reopened in May 2020. During the second lockdown, the Old Market Hall was kept open by following stringent health and safety regulations stipulated by health authorities. The venue continued supporting its community by hosting the Christmas market, which provided an opportunity for many designers and artists, who lost their stores or market stalls during the pandemic, to sell their products.

Renovation in stages

When rethinking the building, the main concept was to create a space as multi-functional and flexible as possible; a large, open space that could host various activities, ranging from markets and conferences to concerts. In order to make the space adaptable to different events, specific, versatile, and easily arranged tables were acquired to support all these events.

One of the biggest challenges in the process was to coordinate the different phases of the renovation with activities that constantly had to adapt to new circumstances. A month after the Alliance took charge of the building, a fire inspection revealed 54 security issues. Complying with safety regulations was a costly process: simply repainting some surfaces with fireproof paint cost €50,000, while revising the fire safety system, installing a new lightning rod, new doors, fire extinguishers, fire alarms, and a regulated heating system cost around €100,000–150,000.

After making the spaces secure, the following phase included renovating the shops and other street-front spaces, fixing their water and electricity systems so that they could be rented to tenants. This was followed by renovation of the toilets, floors, and lights – important details that enable the individual operations. In some cases, future tenants agreed to fund the renovations, with their costs subsequently subtracted from rental fees.

"Our goal was to open the space physically and mentally.
We benefited from heritage protection:
we wanted to make use of the advantages of the building
as it was built in 1910."
Gábor Bindics

Bratislava's Old Market Hall is a nationally protected cultural heritage building. The protection concerns the hall's columns and windows, and the outer appearance of the building. Consequently, no modifications are allowed to the building, especially those that that would impact its external appearance. For minor interventions, ranging from changing the external colours of the building to insulating windows, the Alliance required permission from the regional heritage office. In order to better insulate the building, for instance, an expensive solution was implemented: a second, thicker glass layer was built inside the market hall, in order to retain the original appearance of the building but adapt it to events that require heating during winter (Fig. 5).

On a regular basis, the Alliance must obtain municipal approval for all phases of the renovation. The Alliance is required to inform the municipality of all investments in the building as these, including newly purchased equipment, will belong to the building owned by the city. Before each expenditure, the association must provide an investment plan to be reviewed by a specific committee – consisting of three municipal officers and two or three representatives of the Alliance. The committee scrutinises each item of the plan before submitting it to a municipal vote. Besides this committee, there is also another contractual body created between the Alliance and the municipality, consisting of four people from the Municipal Assembly, that reviews and supervises the association's activities.

Rent-to-investment scheme

The Alliance conceived the new market hall's model to be economically sustainable and financially separated from the municipality, with no public subsidies involved. Under the 15-year (ten years + five years extension) contract the Alliance pays the municipality a symbolic rent of €1 per year and must invest €10,000 per month in renovating the market hall for the entire duration of the contract (amounting to €120,000 euros per year and almost €2 million overall). The monthly investment cannot include in-kind work, but does account for investments by the tenants. Each item of investment is overseen by a supervisory board that includes municipal officers and members of the association.

Reinvesting in the building

Before engaging in the contract with the municipality, the Alliance consulted various experts to estimate the renovation costs. Even without utilising any high-tech equipment during the estimation process, simply renovating the floors, windows, and complying with all fire safety requirements was estimated to cost between €700,000 and €1 million, with at least €400,000–500,000 required to make the building operational. After five years, slightly more than €1 million had been spent on the building, making the market hall fully operational in the technical sense. By the second year, the Market Hall started generating revenues, and by the third year the economic model began to work. In March 2019, the initial bank loan was repaid and the Market Hall broke even. After the basic renovation items, the Alliance then began investing in more value-related equipment such as a composter and other extras.

The renovations began with a loan from Erste Bank. At the time, the bank opened a social banking division with about €10 million to support projects that would be considered too risky by traditional loan schemes. The Market Hall Alliance received a loan of about €200,000 at an interest rate of 4%. As the association did not own the market hall, it could not use the building to secure the loan; therefore, members of the association offered their own personal properties as collateral.

The market hall generates a variety of revenues. Marketing collaborations provide about one-third of the total revenue. Volkswagen and Orange contribute approximately €50,000–60,000 annually, in cash or services. Orange, for instance, provides minimal financial support but contributes high-value services amounting to around €100,000 in recent years. Orange provided machinery (worth €70,000) for the Lab, and installed internet throughout the building (worth €20,000).

Orange also provided 'big data' to the association, about people passing by the market hall, in order to better understand their needs. Volkswagen contributes in a similar way, partly funding the renovation of the square in front of the building. Rental fees contribute another third of the revenues. Besides the market hall's large open space, the building contains a variety of smaller venues, accessible from the neighbouring streets, that are rented out to tenants on a regular basis. Market hall tenants are selected based on open calls, thematic connections, potential cooperation with other tenants, as well as the social value created. The last third of the revenues is provided by large events. A considerable proportion of the market hall's revenue comes from about 16 solely private events per year. The fee for hosting a private event can amount to several thousand euros (up to €6,000 per day) – for which the association provides many services, including setting up the space. The great success of the Old Market Hall has generated higher revenues than originally anticipated, enabling the Alliance to already invest six or seven years upfront in the building's renovation.

Since its creation in 2012, the Old Market Hall Alliance has been expanded to include both active and advisory members. The Alliance is the main tenant of the market hall and holds the 10+5-year contract with the municipality; in turn, it rents out the building's various spaces to businesses and events. The Alliance has also invested in some of the activities in the building: for instance, it holds 50% of the shares in the soda manufacturing business located on-site.

Voluntary work played an important role in building up the new market hall. Highlighting their own initiative, members of the Old Market Hall Alliance offered weeks of unpaid work, also supported by various forms of community involvement and institutional support. A wide range of cultural institutions and national embassies also pledged their support to the Alliance, which proved to be an important symbolic resource in securing municipal approval.

Although there is no formalised structure for bringing together the tenants besides one-to-one contracts, the Old Market Hall Alliance organises regular tenant meetings to focus on opportunities for mutually beneficial cooperation. Some tenants began to cooperate spontaneously: for example, the soda manufacturer and brewery supply all the bars and restaurants, the events communicate with the venues, and the grocery store sources from the market vendors.

Generating public space

In its original role, Bratislava's Old Market Hall had always been a public space, connected to a large public square outside the building. After the 1960s, with the building converted into TV production studios, the square gradually lost its public function and was increasingly occupied by car parking. For the Old Market Hall Alliance, opening the square and reconnecting it to the market hall creates public value and also contributes to the building's economic model.

The Old Market Hall Alliance has also been engaged in the revitalisation of neighbouring public spaces. Investment in these public spaces has had an important impact: with small interventions (e.g., €5,000 invested in tables and chairs), the square in front of the market hall has been filled with life, especially during summer and autumn months, attracting hundreds of people.

Bringing new activities into the market hall had a strong impact on its surroundings: more people are using the area, small businesses have flourished in the neighbouring streets, and the bars that used to serve only older men have also become popular with young people. On a daily basis, the market hall accommodates about 90–100 workers: that means a lot of workplaces, many of them new jobs that were created with the reopening of the building. In some cases, the market hall works as an incubator; for example, a baker who rented a stall in the market later opened a bakery across the street. In other cases, the market, especially with its street food events, competes with other restaurants in the city centre and takes some of their clientele.

The Alliance, reassured about the positive effects of its interventions, subsequently submitted proposals to the municipality about how to develop, programme, manage, and administer the neighbouring areas and public spaces. Meanwhile, it helped revitalise premises in the neighbouring streets, bringing in new tenants (including shops for design, bicycles, and books) in the ground floor of a badly neglected building adjacent to the market hall.

The contract developed between the Old Market Hall Alliance and the municipality has created a precedent for other initiatives. The model was first reused in the vicinity of the Market Hall: the previous owner of a long-vacant neighbouring building invited the Alliance to implement the same model used in the market building, namely to secure tenants that – although not necessarily paying commercial rents – can act as catalysts for the building and wider area.

On a broader scale, the Stará Tržnica model has inspired a variety of other initiatives across Slovakia. The Alliance advised the team regenerating the Rožno Monastery; the initiators of Nová Cvernovka in Bratislava; was involved in establishing events on the rooftop terraces of Prague's Lucerna Palace; and in the regeneration of the Cloister in Brno. These places have also established a network based on the exchange of experiences.

Politically, the Old Market Hall model has proved that the civic-led management of publicly owned properties can be beneficial both to the municipality and the city's communities: It has been instrumental in convincing politicians and property owners to open up their buildings for civic uses. This model has hence paved the way for several initiatives, from Nová Cvernovka in Bratislava to Kino Úsmev in Košice.

Social impact

Besides underlining the many environmental and educational initiatives of the new market hall, the Alliance also developed a method to measure social impact in a monetary way. If the Old Market Hall was run in a fully commercial way, renting out all the building's spaces at a market rate, it could generate €16,000–20,000 more. This sum corresponds to the overall rent subsidies the Alliance offers to activities with a strong social, environmental, or educational dimension.

List of References

Garriga, S., & Garcia-Fuentes, J. M. (2015). The idealization of a Barcelona model for market halls renovation. In Cinà, G. & Dansero, E. (Eds.), *Localizing urban food strategies. Farming cities and performing rurality*. Politecnico di Torino.

Gejdošová, K. (2017). *The new old market hall in Bratislava*. URBACT blog. https://www.blog.urbact.eu/2017/08/the-new-old-market-hall-in-bratislava/

Morales, A. (2009). Public markets as community development tools. *Journal of Planning Education and Research, 28*(4), 426–440.

Patti, D., & Polyák, L. (2017). *Funding the cooperative city. Community finance and the economy of civic spaces.* Cooperative City Books.

Patti, D., Polyák, L., & Torresan, M. (2019). *Il rilancio dei mercati. Spazio pubblico, servizi comunitari ed economia circolare*. Cooperative City Books.

Polyák, L. (2019). *From privatisation to community use*. Magazyn Miasta. http://magazynmiasta.pl/2019/10/02/from-privatisation-to-community-use/

SozialMarie. (2016). *Dobre & Dobré: Project fulfilment evaluation and external reviews*. https://sozialmarie.org/files/5077/pdf_en.pdf

Bartha, G. (2010). Rethinking the marketplace: A story of resistance and proactivity. In Steierhoffer, E. & Polyák, L. (Eds.), *Anatomy of a street.* Art Netwörk Agency.

Sík, E., & Wallace, C. (1999). *The development of open-air markets in east-central Europe.* International Journal of Urban and Regional Research, 23(4), 697–714.

The case study is based on interviews with: Gábor Bindics, co-founder of the Old Market Hall Alliance; Ján Mazúr legal expert of the Old Market Hall Alliance; Illah van Oljen, co-founder of the Old Market Hall Alliance, formerly responsible for the food market; and Veronika Hliničanová, responsible for the Old Market Hall Alliance's public spaces programme.

Jam Factory, Ukraine: An Adaptive Heritage Reuse Model in Lviv?

By Iryna Sklokina

Jam Factory is an interdisciplinary centre for contemporary arts, located in the revitalised space of a former jam factory in Lviv, Ukraine (Fig. 2). Through educational activities, exhibitions, and research, the centre reflects current processes in Ukrainian and international art and culture, and provides opportunities for public dialogue. The impressive Neo-Gothic building, together with several adjacent buildings from later periods, is located in Pidzamche, a historical industrial district of Lviv. From 1872, it was the site of an alcohol factory owned by Kronik and Son. The building subsequently underwent several changes of function, and stood vacant from 2008, when the vegetable-processing unit producing jam was closed. Several grass-roots artistic and cultural initiatives temporarily used the building in the following years, including Contemporary Art Week which set in motion to performance art in Lviv.

In 2015, the Jam Factory site was purchased and its revitalisation initiated through Harald Binder Cultural Enterprises (HBCE). This was the first step in a further two-year process of consolidating six adjacent plots containing other factory buildings owned by different legal entities. The project team worked on institution-building, including grant programmes, an educational lecture series, exhibitions, and art fellowship residences. Implementation of the revitalisation project commenced in October 2019. It includes restoration and adaptation of the two buildings listed as monuments of local significance, as well as construction of new, additional premises. Jam Factory is seen as a mixed model, receiving support both from the owner and external grants, and generating income through the building itself. Completion of the renovation works and construction of the complex is scheduled for September 2023.

Fig. 1
Jam Factory in Lviv. Map

Timeline	1826—2023
1826	Moses Kronik opens a tavern in Zniesienie village, producing and selling alcoholic beverages
1875	Josef Kronik, grandson of Moses, receives permission to produce alcoholic beverages alongside his father Leib, who also trades in wines at the same address
1909	Josef Kronik receives the prestigious title of a 'Purveyor to the Court' (Hoflieferant) in Vienna
1921	The firm Józef Kronik i Syn is relaunched after the First World War and mostly run by the local Jewish businessman Schulim Wallach
1939	Lviv is annexed to the Soviet Union. The Kronik factory is nationalised, its director, Schulim Wallach, is arrested and his fate is unknown
1941–1942	Nazi Germany occupies Lviv. Moritz Kronik is shot while attempting to escape the Janowska concentration camp. The synagogue adjacent to the factory is burnt down
1945	Return of the Soviets. The building hosts wine base (from 1946, Lviv Wine Plant) under 'Ukrholovvyno' company
1958	Vegetable and fruit processing unit is located in the building.
2008	Production ends. The building is purchased by Oleksiy Kurylyshyn, who allows temporary cultural uses. First 'Days of Contemporary Art' take place
2015	The building is purchased by the Harald Binder Cultural Enterprises and revitalisation as an art venue starts. Activities and programmes launched
2020	Restoration and construction process starts after collection of all the permissions
2023	Opening of Jam Factory

The initiative by a cultural entrepreneur

In 2015, the Jam Factory site was purchased by Dr Harald Binder, a historian and cultural entrepreneur based in Vienna, with the idea of developing a revitalisation project for the future art centre. Harald Binder was already a well-known public figure in Lviv and Ukraine, as a founder of the Center for Urban History of East Central Europe in Lviv in 2004. The Center acts as a research and public history institution that engages different audiences in dialogue on unknown and challenging aspects of the past, and serves as a space for discussions on urban and cultural policies. It is also a successful case of adaptive reuse of a historical residential building (located at Bohomoltsia Street) as an office, exhibition space, accommodation for research fellows, conference hall, and café. With this background, Binder aimed to develop a new project serving the critical reassessment of contemporary Ukrainian and international art, and combining research, art production, and educational programmes. He therefore involved Bozhena Pelenska (formerly Zakaliuzhna), a cultural manager and independent art activist who was previously engaged in the temporary usage of the Jam Factory site (Fig. 1).

The decision to purchase the Jam Factory area and undertake the revitalisation project was motivated by several factors. Firstly, due to the temporary uses during 2008–2014, the site had become firmly associated with the idea of an art centre. The very name 'Jam Factory' was invented by temporary users and became common among Lviv residents. The building was also mentioned in the media as a place of cultural life, and a 'second life' of the former factory. Pelenska promoted the idea of an art centre in the building as well, notably by organising the international workshop 'Regeneration of Industrial Buildings in Ukraine' in 2014 (Regeneration 2014), where invited experts shared their experience and drafted some ideas for reuse of Jam Factory. Secondly, Binder considered it reasonable to begin another project in Lviv, because there was no other institution of contemporary art in the city, and few in Ukraine at that time. Under such circumstances, its possible impact could be much greater than, for example, another art centre in Vienna. What made this project especially ambitious was the location of the building in a historically rich district, which was perceived as post-industrial and depressive (Fig. 3). The initiative differed significantly from the very common strategy of investors redeveloping historical properties in downtown Lviv. The idea of Jam Factory as a trigger for revitalising Pidzamche was already present in discourses, but no practical steps had been taken to implement it. Importantly, the level of investment required to realise such a project in Lviv is still significantly lower than in other locations such as Vienna. Thirdly, the Neo-Gothic style of the main building was itself inspiring and hence highly appropriate for an arts centre.

Cultural activities and solidarity in wartime

Starting the development of the renovation project without a definite programme was part of a longer process of

2

3

4

Fig. 2
Jam Factory prior to renovation

Fig. 3
View of Żółkewska St. (now Bohdana Khmelnytskoho St.) with Kronik factory, 1930s

Fig. 4
Workshop of the MagiC Carpets art residency, involving teenagers from Pidzamche district

searching for an identity for the future arts centre. Importantly, this allowed a period of creative improvisation about the future, and enabled brainstorming with different specialists who were invited to give advice. The Stephan Rindler bureau initially proposed a contemporary art museum, but in the process of discussions the concept of the institution evolved into the current 'Center', which focuses more on public programmes than on displaying collections. This process of establishing an identity also contributed to the delays in the project timeline.

Testing potential new uses prior to the renovation work became a beneficial tool for the Jam Factory team. Initially envisioned as an art cluster with several resident organisations and independent artists, the team invited other actors to stage events in the temporary building, in many cases at no cost. In the process, the team concluded that, to implement its aim of promotion and stronger public outreach of contemporary art, a single institution with a strong educational agenda was more relevant to the local context than a cluster of independent actors with their own agendas. Jam Factory sees itself as an institution combining research, education, and production of contemporary art, in international cooperation but with focus on local contexts and the needs of local publics.

In 2017–2019, the Jam Factory team focused on research, communication with local residents and broader audiences, work with the neighbourhood, and building partnerships in Ukraine and internationally. As such, many activities commenced even prior to the renovations. Historical research was conducted in the archives and libraries of Lviv, Kyiv, Warsaw, and Vienna. An oral history and mapping project, 'Tell Your Story', was launched to learn more about the Soviet and post-Soviet periods and to engage local residents and former employees of Jam Factory. In November 2021, the art centre opened an exhibition and launched an audio walking-guide called 'Tracing the Memories of Pidzamche', based on interviews with local residents and in cooperation with Lviv craft producers who created special scents connected to the iconic objects of the district, including smells of industrial enterprises. Several partner projects were organised with contemporary artists, including those for children living in the neighbourhood. Each year, artists supported by SWAP (a British-Ukrainian exchange programme) pursue visiting fellowships at Jam Factory to develop their projects, also in cooperation with locals. Building partnerships in Ukraine and internationally was very helpful in gradually developing the institutional design and becoming more self-aware. Infopoint (a temporary building for educational activities and presentations) was renovated in 2017. Cultural events started there, and the building was also made available (in many cases at no cost) to other cultural initiatives. The main aim of these activities was a gradual change in the neighbourhood cultural scene, and more sensitive and organic development. In 2018 several applications were submitted for international partnerships and joint projects, such as the Harald Binder Cultural Enterprises annual grant programme, with the Jam Factory team as an operator. Non-governmental organisations from Ukraine were encouraged to propose artistic and educational projects. Jam Factory also became a member of Trans Europe Halles (a network of cultural centres initiated by citizens and artists, with members in 40 countries). Furthermore, educational events and the black box educational theatre programme started in 2018. In October and November 2019, the first exhibitions were hosted in another temporary exhibition and event space on neighbouring Mekhanichna Street. In 2020–2022, Jam Factory focused on renovation of the protected buildings and new construction of additional premises.

The COVID-19 pandemic did not affect the construction process, but hindered the international supply of construction materials. Several international cooperation projects switched to online models. In summer 2020, when the pandemic restrictions were eased, Jam Factory hosted international art residences of the 'MagiC Carpets' critical and social art platform (Fig. 4).

With the start of Russia's full-scale invasion of Ukraine in February 2022, Lviv became a backbone city oriented towards supply of the army and support for displaced people from other regions of Ukraine. Jam Factory started to provide stipends for artists at risk, and converted its premises to a refugee shelter. To provide stipends, Jam Factory collected international donations and organised charity events. After a short break due to the shock of Russia's major escalation of the war, the restoration and construction works continued – as a sign of hope for better, and a positive signal to the international community about the resilience of Ukraine and its culture. Jam Factory cooperates with artists who have relocated to Lviv due to the war, providing financial support, stimulating their return to creative work and integration into the local society, resulting in two collective exhibitions *Navigation* in 2022 and 2023. Other public activities during the war have included theatre performances, reading plays on the theme of war, exhibitions, and art residencies for diverse art collectives. The project '*How We Are Together*' specifically engaged parents and children, whose wartime traumas were addressed in art classes led by the artists and a psychologist. The Jam Factory team plans to complete the revitalisation process and fully launch the centre in September 2023 (Fig. 5).

The multi-layered heritage of Lviv and Jam Factory

The Jam Factory complex consists of several buildings from different epochs. The oldest part, dating from the mid-19th century, was supplemented by Neo-Gothic elements in the early 20th century and is listed as a monument of local significance. Other parts of the building complex also date from the pre-1914 period but are not listed, and some are from the Soviet epoch. Due to their close proximity to the listed monument, the new buildings are height-restricted (to 23.6 m) and a special 'historical and urban planning feasibility study' had to be approved.

Fig. 5
Ongoing restoration and construction

In many adaptive reuse and industrial-zone revitalisation projects in Ukraine, the major challenge is the legal status of the land plots. In official records, adjacent plots may have differing or inconsistent borders and unclear ownership; furthermore, many plots are also subject to legal investigation as a consequence of 'shadow' privatisation practices during the post-Soviet period. The State Land Registry is incomplete and not integrated with the planning, construction, and heritage databases, and was previously subject to corrupt manipulation. Consequently, the legal resolution of such matters is complex and protracted.

Bureaucratic inefficiency and the absence of established adaptive reuse schemes present major challenges for the project. More traditional restoration projects (e.g., adapting historical buildings into hotels and restaurants) are common in Lviv, but not the revitalisation of a complex of buildings, and plots with additional new buildings adjacent to historical monuments. Furthermore, officials employ a highly personalised approach, with decisions taken on the basis of personal relations, tastes, and some undisclosed personal agendas. The solution employed by the Jam Factory team was to strictly follow all official rules and to promote understanding of the importance of the project for the city. No informal connections (very common in the local context) were used. The good reputation of Harald Binder and his previous projects in Lviv, plus media coverage, acknowledgement of the Jam Factory project among urban activists in Ukraine, as well as the municipality's positive attitude, were all helpful in navigating the bureaucratic procedures. Nevertheless, adaptation of the project to local conditions and obtaining necessary approvals took much longer than initially anticipated.

Harald Binder (as a professional historian) and several other researchers developed a multi-layered understanding of the heritage values of the complex. First, the architectural heritage values are defined by the Neo-Gothic style applied to the industrial building, which is unique in Lviv. Second, the building is a witness to the industrial boom and rapid population growth in the second half of the 19th century, when the district performed production and transportation functions and served as a link to agricultural areas, with its numerous distilleries processing grain into various alcoholic beverages. Third, the enterprise represents the multi-national history of Lviv, and the history of the owner's Jewish family is part of the broader history of Jewish businesses thriving within the Habsburg Empire and during the interwar period, with extensive connections to other geographical localities. The disruption of the family history in the Holocaust is also part of Europe's dark 20th-century heritage, together with the silencing and non-remembering, during the Soviet period, of the factory's past and its Jewish ownership. Fourth, the living memories of those who worked in the factory during the Soviet period are also part of an intangible heritage, revived in the oral history and mental mapping project 'Tell Your Story'. Fifth, the temporary usage of the factory after the end of production and prior to its purchase in

2015 is another heritage layer because it is connected to the development of independent art initiatives in Lviv, such as Contemporary Art Week which catalysed many further fruitful initiatives.

With so many heritage layers, it was not easy to decide how to harmoniously develop the complex. One challenge is that the exact uses of some plots and buildings are unknown, because too few documents have survived. The Second World War was especially disruptive, with tremendous population changes associated with both the Holocaust and also post-war population exchanges (including resettlement of ethnic Poles to within Poland's newly revised borders, and influx of Ukrainians from Lviv's rural hinterland and other regions of Ukraine).

Another challenge of adapting the former industrial building to an art centre was the need to maximise its adaptability to diverse uses, such as exhibition space, theatre and performance, workshops, offices, and event halls. The project aims to preserve the structure of the whole complex, which is arranged around a comfortable courtyard, with the interior utilising temporary partition-walls and a movable stage to make the space more flexible. In terms of formal heritage preservation, only two buildings have protection status, and changes to the others are not regulated. However, the Jam Factory team decided to preserve the entire structure of the territory because the complex is perceived by locals as a single entity.

While the plots were consolidated in 2015–2017, the architectural project was gradually developed. First, there was a closed competition among five bureaus selected by a jury consisting of Ukrainian artists and scholars. All the architectural proposals had merit, but none completely fitted the concept and place. The proposal by Atelier Stephan Rindler (Vienna) was then partnered with the local AVR Development bureau due to their better understanding of Ukrainian building regulations. Adaptive reuse is always a compromise between preservation and change. Personally, for Binder, it was important to develop an understanding of heritage that includes the opinions of local residents and those who can be called a 'heritage community' (those with previous connections to the site, including former factory workers, artists, and activists). For the Jam Factory project, it is important that the listed and non-listed buildings facing the main street are perceived as a single complex. Therefore, most historic buildings have been left intact, contrary to some architects' proposals. In the process of adaptation, a new building, 'Black Box', was constructed. During the planning phase, it provoked discussions at the municipality level as being too radical a statement for a historical setting, which remains quite unusual for Lviv.

Harald Binder also owns the plot located behind the complex, where the synagogue was previously located (this served the entire district's Jewish community, and was destroyed during the Nazi occupation). This plot remains empty, with the future intention of memorialising the synagogue and the long-term silencing of the city's Jewish memory. The aim is for the Art Center to commission an artwork for this site. In one of the first temporary artistic events, in October 2018 the artist Taras Pastushchuk quoted passages from the Bible and used salt to demarcate the original floorplan of the absent synagogue (Fig. 6).

Facing financial challenges

Jam Factory employs a mixed economic model, combining: private non-profit investment, without expectation of return; various forms of income generated through the complex itself; and external funds from other institutions. It currently has full support from the donor, but a future priority is to become self-sufficient. The project includes a restaurant and a small bar that should generate profit, in addition to income from ticket and book sales and from leasing space. The current aim is for this income to cover the costs of building maintenance. Securing grants and cooperative projects is also important, but Binder considers this as an addition to the basic stable funding, which helps make the institution more resilient but cannot remain as the main source of income (and a source of precarity and frustration for the team). As Ukraine is not an EU member, Jam Factory is ineligible for many EU programmes, but it can apply in partnership with other institutions based in EU member states. From January 2020 Jam Factory participated in the EU-funded project (by the European Commission) 'Face to Faith'.

The Harald Binder Cultural Enterprises (limited liability company) and the non-governmental organization 'Jam Factory Art Center' exist side-by-side. HBCE owns the buildings and the biggest part of the territory and invests in the restauration. As for the operational costs, the Jam Factory team applies to a separate Harald Binder's foundation which also has a role in developing, scrutinising, examining the costs, and approving the team's proposals for the longer-term development. The NGO aims to become more financially independent over time through grant support from other sources. With Russia's full-scale invasion of Ukraine in 2022, the prospects for commercial functions at the site are difficult to access, but the team still aims to open the restaurant and other planned functions:

> "(...) renting the spaces, generating from the shop or parking, we cannot expect a lot of income, but we hope for the grants, because Ukraine moved into focus of attention, and culture is important especially during the war. But we realise we should be realistic."
> Harald Binder, 2023

Maintaining the buildings is costly, as is rent paid to the municipality, because HBCE does not own all the land and some plots are municipal. Despite its status as a cultural institution, Jam Factory does not benefit from reduced rent, and such proposals are difficult to broach under current wartime

Fig. 5
Performance by Taras Pastushchuk

conditions. Ukrainian legislation allows for special treatment of cultural and artistic NGOs (which can rent municipal property or land without tender procedures), but this does not guarantee that the rent will be affordable.

Common decision-making

Initially, Jam Factory developed as a private initiative. Binder and Pelenska are the core team responsible for drafting the idea and the strategic roadmap, both for the institutional development and adaptive reuse of the site. Until 2017, most tasks were outsourced to specialists on an ad hoc basis, including: accounting, land issues, detailed planning, legal expertise, land survey documentation, and architectural project design.

In 2017, Jam Factory started to move from the stage of contracting out all these processes, towards employing a regular in-house team. Two project managers were hired in 2017, and the team expanded considerably in 2019 (adding specialists in finance, communication, grant fundraising, planning and construction, office management, and project and construction management). In order to develop more efficient planning and management processes, the team requested long-term consultancy (coaching) from Olivearte Cultural Agency, which has relevant expertise in adaptive heritage reuse. In 2021, a new position of financial director was created in order to facilitate construction processes.

After the complex is fully launched, the team will expand further to include some additional, formal decision-making structures such as a General Assembly, management board, directors, and advisers (these changes are expected to be fixed in the new charter in spring 2023). At present, decisions are taken at the regular and irregular team meetings, meetings with coaches, and one-to-one meetings. As the project initiator, Harald Binder remains very active and will remain so until the point where the institution matures and builds capacity for sustaining its own development.

> "Harald always has the last word [as for the architectural project] but he also has this trust and always listens to different parties. And there's Herbert Pasterk [architect and designer] who is looking at that from the technical point of view ... So, we have corresponding discussions ... Actually, Harald worships history and has his own visions. All of us have a chance to express our own opinion but the final decision belongs to Harald. He always listens to everyone."
> Bozhena Pelenska, 2019

Some activities (especially larger events) utilise volunteers, but only in limited numbers at present. There is also a new proposal to engage work/study interns, who may subsequently become part of the team.

“Ukraine became a focus of interest more after 2014 [the Maidan Revolution]. We stopped being some kind of blank space for many organizations because we started talking about ourselves in a different way. This self-awareness, this change, this feeling that we as people living in this country have to change and stop waiting that someone from the top will change it for us. This awareness … of democratic transformations won’t be made down from the top, only bottom-up … And this understanding that we can change something, it affects people from other countries, and it gets interesting … A lot of people understand that they will reinforce and make their influence felt with the help of that cooperation.”

Bozhena Pelenska, 2018

A model for Ukraine?

The impact of Jam Factory is evident on several levels. The discussions on the architectural project had considerable impact on thinking around contemporary architecture in the historical context of Lviv. Discussions at Lviv City Council and gatherings of the municipal Commission on Architecture, Urban Planning, and Protection of the Historical Environment were heated and focused on possible ways of combining old and new. The project thereby became ground-breaking for Lviv, and contributed to changing opinions.

The Jam Factory team shares their experience in Ukraine at forums and meetings related to revitalisation in Ukraine and internationally. Although the first successful initiatives of adaptive reuse in Ukraine were almost exclusively commercially oriented and included only mass cultural events and festivals (such institutions as Art-Zavod Platforma in Kyiv and Art Factory Mekhanika in Kharkiv), there are now several initiatives with a special focus on socially critical art and contemporary art, such as the Dnipro Center for Contemporary Culture. Jam Factory was one of the first initiatives (along with the Izolyatsia platform for cultural initiatives, opened in Donetsk in eastern Ukraine in 2012) with special focus on socially critical art, and references to Jam Factory are now present in the narratives of other similar initiatives.

The previous uses of the Jam Factory complex as a space for informal art initiatives, and especially for Contemporary Art Week and Lviv Fashion Week, promoted the idea of Pidzamche district as a future 'creative hub' of Lviv, which became a discursive cliché. It also had some impact on the municipality's decision to select Pidzamche for a pilot regeneration project conducted in cooperation with the Krakow Urban Development Institute and Lviv City Institute, which aimed to improve urban management through local residents' participation and increasing the district's attractiveness to tourists. Ambitious public outreach by Jam Factory attracted new investment into Pidzamche district, including real estate developers who demonstrate differing levels of respect for heritage. However, there is also a risk that such changes may promote gentrification of the district.

The project emphasises financial self-sufficiency and community engagement, but is also part of the gradual shift away from dependence on the state and wealthier classes as supporters of culture and the social sphere. Jam Factory is instead supported by a private donor, who does not expect a financial return on investment but is instead motivated by the possibility of fostering social and cultural change.

Following regulations

Most importantly, Jam Factory represents a case of the gradual development of an adaptive reuse project, of establishing relations with the municipality and the Department for Protection of the Historical Environment, and with engagement of local communities and a number of experts. The project rigorously complies with all relevant rules and regulations, and strictly avoids involvement in any informal deals with officials or services (which, elsewhere, is quite common in the Ukrainian context). Implementation of the project has taken much longer than initially anticipated, but this has also enabled the team to gradually change the setting and work to build the project's reputation. This also helped to establish good relations with the local community and to react in a sensitive way to the challenges of the ongoing war, with relevant programmes targeting displaced persons, artists at risk, and parents with children.

List of References

Ackermann, F. (2018, 12 October). Stadtgeschichte als Gegenwart [City history as the present]. *Frankfurter Allgemeine Zeitung*. https://edition.faz.net/faz-edition/feuilleton/2018-10-12/de19b6ccf6a870d9abd4216bad7e-2be8/?popup=user.lf&fbclid=IwAR2Yi-wai5bfcVD1oEKws2GIAqxOs-7RVEA-7mon2TnaMv_J--K4RHWMUwUdY

Amar, T. C. (2015). The paradox of Ukrainian Lviv. A borderland city between Stalinists, Nazis, and nationalists. Cornell University Press.

Дрималовський, О. (2016, 20 February). Гаральд і його фабрика [Harald and his factory]. Zaxid.net.https://1n1383289

GIZ (2016). Муніципальний розвиток та оновлення старої частини міста Львова [Municipal development and renewal of the old part of the city of Lviv]. Deutsche Gesellschaft für Internationale Zusammenarbeit GmbH. https://www.giz.de/en/worldwide/32570.html

Jam Factory Art Center (2019, 10 October). Jam Factory Art Center у фокусі проекту OpenHeritage [Jam Factory Art Center in the focus of the OpenHeritage project] [video]. YouTube. https://www.youtube.com/watch?v=vS_351T8_T8

Janas, K., & Jarczewski, W. (Eds.). (2014). Urban regeneration. Polish-Ukrainian experience and inspiration. Krakow–Lviv. Institute of Urban Development, Kraków.

Jarczewski, W., & Maciej, H. (Eds.). (2011). Програма ревіталізації «Львів-Підзамче» 2012–2025 [Programme of Lviv-Pidzamche Revitalization in 2012–2025]. Krakow-Lviv: Instytut Rozwoju Miast w Krakowie; Instytut mista Lvova; Lvivska miska rada.

Могитич, Р. (2016). Фабрика горілки та підсолоджених трунків «Йозеф Кронік і син»: історична довідка. [Factory of vodka and sweetened drinks 'Yosef Kronik and son'. Historical reference]. Lviv.

Nielsen, J., Kharbedia, E., Hirzberger, J., & Yutchenko, A. (n.d.). Mind the gap. Revitalisation of old industrial spaces in Lviv. Jam Factory case. Jamfactory.tilda. http://jamfactory.tilda.ws/

Prokopenko, M. (2015, 9 November). New life of a Jam Factory. The Day. https://day.kyiv.ua/en/article/society/new-life-jam-factory

Родак, К. (2018, 19 March). Мистецтво з присмаком повидла і бюрократії [Art with a taste of jam and bureaucracy]. Portal.lviv.ua https://portal.lviv.ua/news/2018/03/19/mistetstvo-z-prismakom-povidla-i-byurokratiyi

Zakaliuzhna, B., & Mysak, N. (Eds.). (n.d.). Regeneration of industrial buildings in Ukraine. Outcomes of the workshop, held on 24–27 September 2014 in Lviv. Cultural Industries Association. http://culture.in.ua/media/7516/bro_2_preview.pdf

This chapter is informed by interviews with: Dr Harald Binder, founder of Harald Binder Cultural Enterprises (March 2019, January 2023); Yulian Chaplynskyi, chief architect of Lviv, 2015–2019 (February 2019); Bohdan Hrytsiuk, project manager at Jam Factory (December 2018); Kateryna Kovalchuk, AVR Development architectural bureau (January 2019); Yaryna Melnyk, associate of the Lviv City Institute, 2011–2015 (October 2019); Viktoriia Olishevska, associate of Lviv City Council, 2016–2018 (October 2019); Lilia Onyshchenko, head of the Department for Protection of the Historical Environment at Lviv City Council (December 2018); and Bozhena Pelenska (formerly Zakaliuzhna), director of Jam Factory (several interviews, conducted in November 2018–June 2019 and January 2023).

C

Enabling Collaboration: Supporting Regional Integration

By Hanna Szemző, Andrea Tönkő, Federica Fava, Katarzyna Sadowy

Regional integration is one of the three pillars of OpenHeritage's approach to heritage management. While initially quite open, the term was refined during the project, gaining meaning in relation to the other two pillars – stakeholder and resource integration. It describes the process by which adaptive heritage reuse (AHR) is incorporated into a larger territorial framework, and assumes that AHR is inseparable from working with the broader social, environmental, administrative, and economic context of heritage buildings/sites. Thus, the process includes diverse mechanisms that encourage the integration of adaptive reuse practices into urban and regional governance (e.g., commons-oriented governance, alternative concepts of ownership, circular economy via bottom-up adaptive reuse, etc.) while allowing heritage transformations to unfold.

What is regional integration?

The concept of regional integration put forward by OpenHeritage differs from traditional approaches in which it is associated with the idea of nested scales. That idea is aligned with the traditional focus of spatial planning on geographically confined plans, often organised in a vertical hierarchy, whereas our approach adopts a horizontal or 'flat' approach that deals with such spatial features and themes in a much more adaptive and relational way, operating across various scales and times (Leitner et al., 2007; Paasi, 2004). This type of neo-regionalist approach conceives regions as territories defined through social practices and discourses, where the scale might vary greatly by cross-cutting macro, micro, or trans-border dimensions (De Lombaerde et al., 2010, p. 23). Thus, regional integration becomes a cooperative strategy that engages with multi-actor collaborations to orient territorial imaginaries, steering divergent interests toward goals of spatial and local development. Building on heritage values and materiality, this entails engaging with a continuously adaptive process that operationalises heritage values to overcome territorial disparities. Regional integration in this sense describes a way to create conditions of inclusiveness, expanding the quality and quantity of opportunities for people to act.

In practice, realising regional integration is difficult, and stakeholders often face various challenges. The most widespread of these include regulatory overlaps, competency disputes, lack of time, and inadequate resources, as well as the difficulties of involving heritage communities and locals as partners in the process. The cases from both Warsaw (Praga

Largo Residências

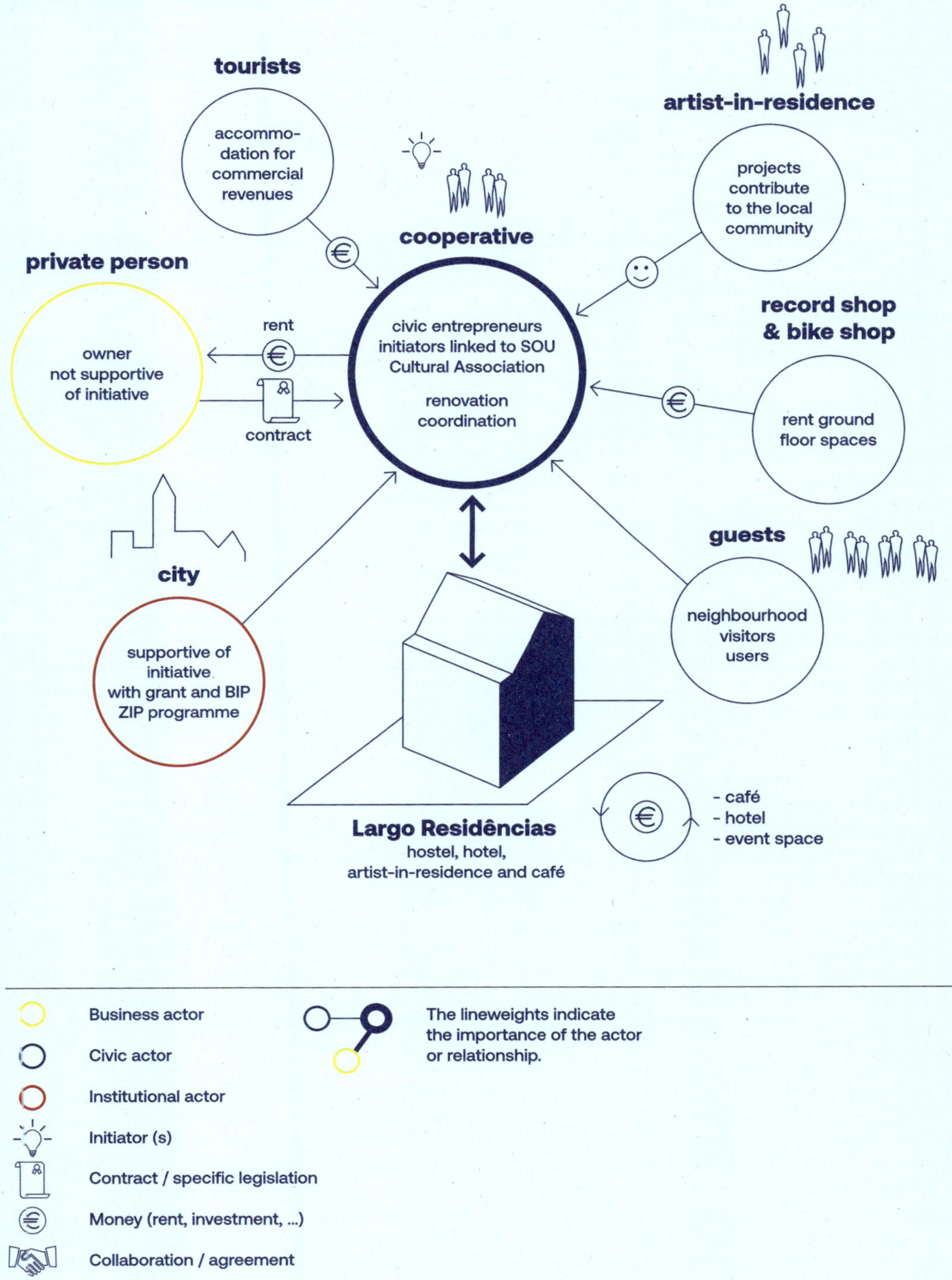

Fig. 1
Supporting regional integration at Largo Residências

neighbourhood) and Lisbon (Largo Residências) show that to achieve success – even temporarily – a wide spectrum of actors/stakeholders need to be involved, and territorial-level thinking is inevitable (Fig. 1). The Lisbon case also demonstrates how urban renewal is an essential component of success for regional integration. Importantly, whereas regional cooperation is already a widespread practice in numerous policy areas, heritage conservation and adaptive reuse work differently. Here, the regional scale is often missing, and in most cases the need to cooperate with other actors (local governments, NGOs, and other bodies) is less pressing. The Broei case (Ghent) describes an interesting local governance setup, in which the various levels and actors cooperate in a well-orchestrated manner.

Models of regional integration

There is no fool-proof recipe for pursuing regional integration; however, a few models can be discerned that outline the roles that various actors can/should play to yield the desired results. The status of the project initiator (public or civic organisation) as well as the extent of cooperation/pursuit of common interests among the stakeholders are two crucial factors that determine how these models work. Based on these, we introduce four models that serve different purposes: the *'common-interest-driven public model'* (Model 1) is devised for municipalities and public entities that wish to work in close cooperation with various local groups but hope to have the main say in the process. The *'common-interest-driven civic model'* (Model 2) describes the process for situations where a broad coalition of civic initiatives take the lead and are in charge of the main development. Model 3, the *'individual-interest-driven public model'* outlines a scenario that most resembles the classic, top-down-driven cooperation between actors and territories, which is adaptable for large-scale restructuring but characterised by democratic deficit. And finally, the *'individual-interest-driven civic model'* (Model 4) delineates a scenario where the main driver of activities is a bottom-up initiative or a small and medium-sized enterprise (SME) and where, despite existing networks, there is no supporting ecosystem and the various stakeholders do not necessarily strive in the same direction (Tönkő et al., 2022).

Model 1 – Common-interest-driven public model:

In this model the project initiators are public authorities (usually municipalities). Although the main project objectives are set by the municipalities, they always reflect the strong common interests between the different stakeholders, representing a guided, organic transformation beneficial to all parties involved. A major advantage of this model is that the municipality establishes bridges and dialogues with community groups, expert groups, and civic organisations, which are all intensively involved in almost all phases of the project. Both formal and informal relationships between these actors are very strong. The policy instruments developed by the municipalities include not just policies and territorial development plans but also formal cooperation agreements, contracts, and protocols that institutionalise their relationship with the main stakeholders. The dominant financial instruments include public (national and international) grants, funds, and loans. However, depending on the type of project, private actors may also contribute to the operating costs, typically in the form of rents. This is an ideal setup for large-scale interventions.

Model 2 – Common-interest-driven civic model:

The initiator of the project is a civic actor that develops strong cooperation with other stakeholders affected by the project. The project's success or failure depends largely on these formal and informal relationships, determined by strong and well-defined common interests. These interests can vary greatly depending on the nature of a project. In most cases, such projects are characterised by a mix of functions, and so a broad range of stakeholders (private sector, civic organisations, community groups, financial institutions, public authorities) contribute to its financial sustainability. An additional feature of the model is that, although the political instruments are determined by the local government, civic actors play a significant role. Building formal and informal networks with public authorities is very important; however, all actors must ensure that their cooperation remains transparent. The OpenHeritage cases studies mostly belonged to this category, showcasing that in an appropriate environment – provided first and foremost by local and regional authorities – civic initiatives can thrive, influencing city and regional development in very positive ways (Fig. 2). The Broei and Largo Residências cases both introduce such models (Fig. 3).

Model 3 – Individual-interest-driven public model:

The individual-interest-driven public model is very different in that it lacks both the broad coalition and the strong democratic element that are so important in Model 2. Although various stakeholders are present, there are no well-defined common interests; actors instead follow their individual goals, and their participation is often not a core activity for them. A top-down approach to planning and participation is apparent in the process, and even if the local authorities plan (and also implement) initiatives for citizen involvement (inviting public contributions to the planning process, conducting sociological surveys, organising public consultations, etc.), the potential of civic initiatives is under-utilised. Very often, these are large-scale adaptive reuse projects that aim to stimulate the region's socio-economic development through renewing the landscape and strengthening its tourism potential.

Model 4 – Individual-interest-driven civic model:

This fourth model introduces the possibilities and limitations of what a mission-oriented NGO (or an SME with an ethical, environmental, social, and/or artistic agenda) can contribute to regional integration

2

3

Fig. 2
Temporary use at Broei

Fig. 3
Neighbourhood festival in Intendente/
Largo Residências

through an adaptive reuse project. This situation is evident in the case from Warsaw, where neither the regulatory environment nor the public authorities are particularly cooperative. To survive, the initiator organisations are typically well-embedded within an expert network and can engage with the local community. They also have informal relations with local authorities, but are rarely perceived as long-term partners by them. The projects are usually small-scale, and financially dependent on their own funds, additional work (for SMEs, aside from their core business), volunteer work, and donations. Financial institutions do not play a significant role in their financing. At best, the regulatory environment does not hinder the implementation of these projects. Despite their difficulties and significant constraints, outcomes include strengthening local communities and preparing the ground for larger interventions.

Facing the barriers between authorities and communities

The models outlined above show that the success of regional integration depends significantly on the behaviours of local and regional authorities. They have the capacity to connect and cooperate with NGOs and the local population; accommodate the participatory approaches necessary for broadening the scope of actors involved; and to provide initiatives of various sizes the opportunity to develop. A concluding question is: what does cooperation on a regional level, and involving various actors, give to local politicians and decision-makers? How can municipal heritage protection/maintenance and reuse initiatives profit from engaging on a regional level? Local politicians (interviewed in early 2022) stated that cooperation actually provides many benefits, but that most are not specific to AHR projects.*

Most importantly, the long-term trend shows an increasing proportion of successful projects and fewer failures. Involving people with different organisational and social backgrounds – and often divergent interests – brings new ideas and strengthens the general vision of a project. This is essential, since AHR processes have a wide variety of possible applications, with varying outcomes and effects for local populations. However, once a compromise is agreed, this increases the local embeddedness of the project and contributes to its acceptance by a wider audience. Additionally, the common vision ensures an easier realisation phase, effectively lowering barriers. It was also mentioned that cooperation brings new ideas, innovation, and dynamics to projects; and creates a new perspective for the future, giving the various actors a say in how their neighbourhoods will develop.

Although in theory there are few downsides to cooperation among different tiers of government, in practice much depends on the attitudes of municipal leaders. The typical municipal bureaucratic structure does not support broad cooperation: most municipalities function within a silo structure, with each department focusing on a specific topic and knowing little about the others. Much depends on the specific municipal structures that are in place: more interdisciplinary teams, for example, encompassing regeneration rather than solely planning, appear better equipped to host heritage conservation officers and those responsible for overseeing adaptive reuse.

List of References

De Lombaerde, P., Söderbaum, F., & Van Langenhove, L. (2010). Problems and divides in comparative regionalism. In F. Laursen (Ed.), *Comparative regional integration: Europe and beyond* (pp. 21–39). Routledge.

Leitner, H., Sheppard, E. S., Sziarto, K., & Maringanti A. (2007). Contesting urban futures: Decentering neoliberalism. In H. Leitner, J. Peck, & E. S. Sheppard (Eds.), *Contesting neoliberalism: Urban frontiers* (pp. 1–25). The Guilford Press.

Paasi, A. (2004). Place and region: Looking through the prism of scale. *Progress in Human Geography*, 28(4), 536–546. https://doi.org/10.1191/0309132504ph502pr

Tönkő, A., Szemző, H., Fava, F., & van Gils, H. (2022). *Roadmap to enhance regional cooperation* (OpenHeritage Deliverable D5.7). https://openheritage.eu/wp-content/uploads/2023/03/Roadmap-to-enhance-regional-cooperation.pdf

* Interviewees included: Emma Tytgadt (Ghent); Csilla Siklódi (Pomáz); Mark Taylor (Sunderland); Martin Linne (Duisburg); and Jacek Grunt-Mejer (Warsaw).

Largo Residências, Portugal: Inclusion through Job Creation and Advocacy in Lisbon

By Levente Polyák and Jorge Mosquera

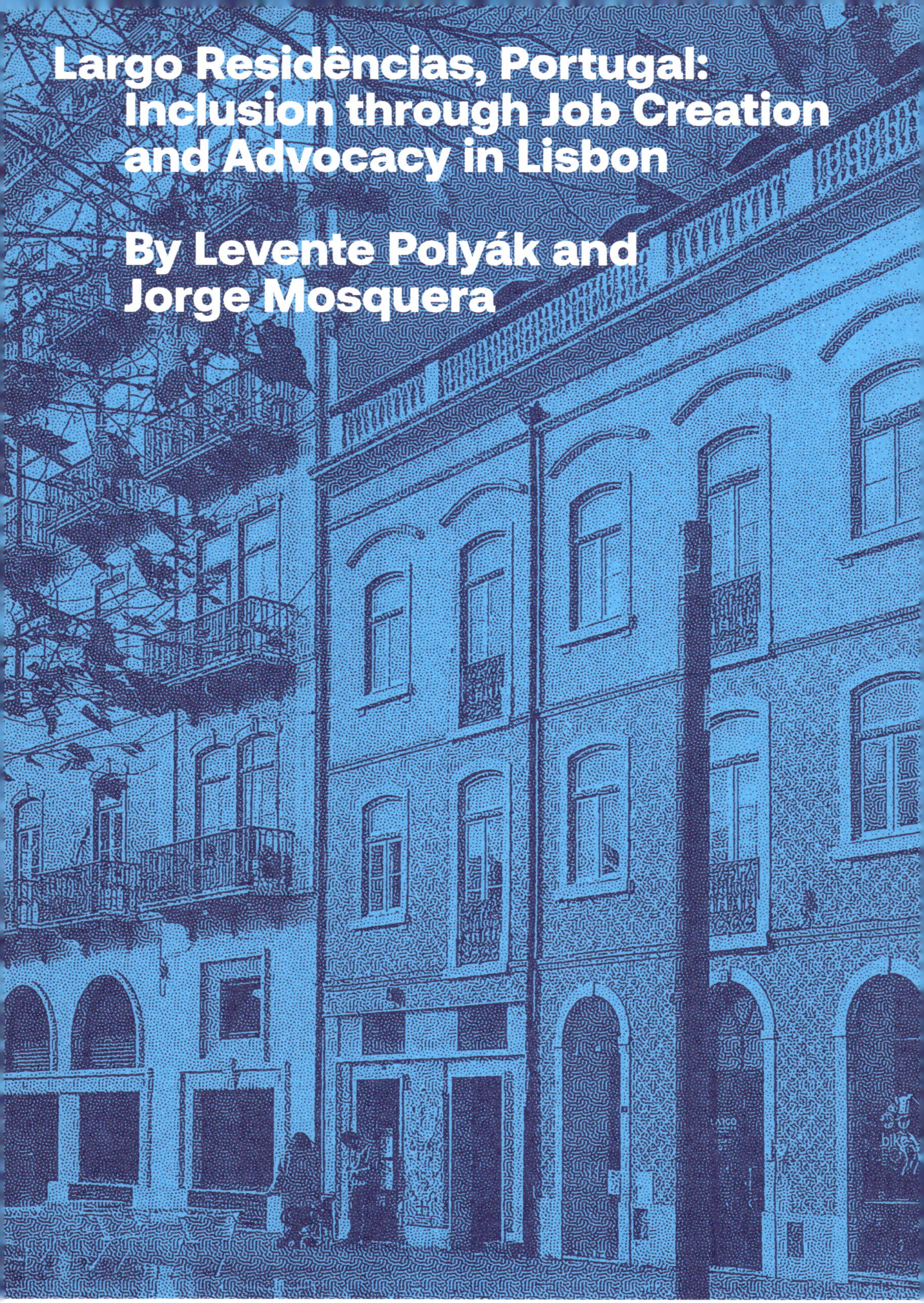

Largo Residências is a hostel, hotel, artist residence, and café in Lisbon's fast-changing Intendente neighbourhood (Fig. 2). The initiative is managed by a cooperative, and uses revenues from tourism and events to develop projects that support the cultural and social inclusion of the most vulnerable groups. In recent years, it has provided a social safety net for many of the area's residents as well as a community hub, spearheading the discussion about Lisbon's touristification and gentrification. Through its inclusive job policy, cultural events, and advocacy work, Largo Residências exemplifies the introduction of social inclusion to the cultural sector and has mobilised the local community for a more resilient neighbourhood, resistant to gentrification.

Largo Residências was previously based in a four-storey building dating from the late 19th century, located at Largo Intendente, the central square of the Intendente neighbourhood in the northeast of the historic centre of Lisbon. Originally built as a ceramic factory, in past decades it had operated illegally as a brothel, leading to judicial confiscation of the property. The new owner began renovation but soon passed it over to the initiators of Largo Residências who inherited the construction site. In 2011, a ten-year rental contract was signed by this initiative that completed the renovation and included an additional floor, adapting the building for commercial and artistic purposes, creating a hostel, hotel, artist residency space, and a café hosting community gatherings.

Under pressure from tourism-driven real estate development transforming the city's historical areas, in 2021 Largo vacated the building on Largo Intendente. The cooperative moved its operations to a state-owned former military complex in the adjacent neighbourhood, contributing to the transformation of the barracks into social housing and community facilities.

Fig. 1
Largo Residências in Lisbon. Map

Timeline	1850 — 2022
1850s	Construction of the ceramic factory by the Viúva Lamego family
2011	Largo Residências rents the building on Largo Intendente
2011	Renovation of Largo begins
2012	The first residências begin
2013	The rental contract is revised
2013	The café opens
2013	Renovation of Largo is completed
2017	Conflicts begin with the landowner, who seeks to sell the building
2018	Largo breaks even and pays back the cooperative members' loans
2019	Municipal regulation to limit new tourism facilities in historical areas
2020	COVID-19 crisis: Largo acts as a quarantine facility
2021	Largo's rental contract is discontinued
2021 — 2022	Largo launches temporary events at a new location, supporting the development of future social housing and community facilities

From ceramic factory to cultural venue

Largo Residências was initiated by members of SOU Cultural Association (SOU Associação Cultural), an association set up by the dancer and cultural producer Marta Silva. SOU previously had a venue in Lisbon's Mouraria neighbourhood, organising performing arts classes and cultural programmes. Looking for a suitable space for an art venue in Intendente, SOU members found the building at Largo Intendente that was in relatively good condition, making renovation more feasible (Fig. 1). The many rooms of the building suggested establishing an artist residency, at a time when tourism was non-existent in the area (Fig. 2).

As all SOU members were inexperienced in tourism, commerce, and property management, they all took on new professional tasks and had to rely on external advice to perform well. Legal and economic advice helped to develop Largo Residências as a social cooperative, and called for the participation of new members. The architectural firm Ateliermob, which originally conducted the renovation process, soon became a member of the cooperative.

The concept of a studio/artist residency space sustained by a tourist accommodation facility was developed in a gradual process with inputs and ideas from the community surrounding SOU. Largo launched its cultural and social programming while renovating the building with other members of the cooperative, under the guidance of Ateliermob. The hostel opened gradually, accepting guests in its completed rooms while renovations were still under way, in order to balance the renovation expenses with the hostel's revenue. The first two years were financially difficult, as the hostel was only partially operational and at that time remained closed during winter due to considerable heat loss in some rooms. The café studio opened in 2013, and soon became a beloved cultural and nightlife venue. Within three years, Largo was ready and fully operational.

From 2011 to 2021 Largo Residências operated as a multi-purpose space combining social, cultural, and commercial functions. The resident artists' apartments were situated on the top floor. Besides offering them accommodation for a period of two to six months, Largo Residências supported artists, architects, cultural producers, and researchers in fields as diverse as plastic and visual arts, dance, theatre, literature, and performance. Largo required residents' projects to contribute to the local community and its territory. Besides the residents' spaces, the top floor also hosted Largo's production office. The first and second floors (each about 200 m²) were dedicated to short-term rentals, hosting tourists but also Largo's collaborators. The first floor had eight private rooms with en suite bathrooms, while the second floor housed a hostel of nine rooms, with shared bathrooms, kitchen, and living rooms.

2

3

Fig. 2
Largo Residências in Lisbon

Fig. 3
A room in Largo Residências

Fig. 4
Cafeteria on the ground floor of Largo Residências

Fig. 5
Community event in Intendente

4

5

"Visiting the building – and knowing that hairdressers and cafés are the most important meeting points – we thought we should have a café, as it would be the meeting point for not only our workers but also our neighbours and local people."
Marta Silva

On the ground floor, Largo had a cafeteria, a studio and a shop occupying around 150 m^2 (Fig. 4). The café contributed to the economic viability of the entire socio-cultural project and created a meeting point for the community. The studio was one of the workspaces for artists-in-residence and a venue for showcasing their work. Besides its own venues, Largo's ground floor also hosted the bike.POP shop and the Largo Loja vinyl record store, both of which contributed to the organisation's financial sustainability.

Largo Residências was part of the historical tissue of Intendente. The building has a typical facade with ceramic tiles that refer to its original function as a ceramic factory run by the Viúva Lamego family, making it one of the most spectacular landmarks on the square.

The building enjoys heritage protection because it is located within the protection zone around two classified buildings, making any change in the facades of these buildings complicated and time-consuming due to the need for approval by the Ministry of Culture. When the rental agreement was signed, the building's structural condition was not entirely clear. Incongruities are common in Lisbon buildings constructed in the 19th century, because liberalisation of construction procedures during the 20th century allowed structural and non-structural walls to be modified without following a plan. Consequently, many buildings that were modified during the past decades reveal unanticipated problems during subsequent renovation. In the case of Largo, there were many construction and technical issues to solve, such as the absence of structural walls, and an electricity system non-compliant with current legal standards, which forced the architects to constantly re-adapt their design according to the emerging needs of the building.

Largo Residências had been working on embracing both the tangible and intangible heritage of the building and surrounding neighbourhood. For example, in order to highlight the building's past as a ceramic factory, Largo developed a variety of urban walks and visits to explore the ceramic tiles once produced in the building and used across the neighbourhood and wider city.

Under the pressure of tourism

Intendente is a historical neighbourhood in Lisbon, located approximately 1.5 km northeast of the city's central square, Praça do Comércio. Despite its central location, in the last decades of the 20th century the area was largely neglected by city councils and developers. Over time, Intendente therefore became one of the most affordable yet also cosmopolitan

Touristification

This concept describes the process of adapting the urban realm to the needs of tourism. It commonly implies the redistribution of resources from local to touristic uses, and often triggers real estate speculation that results in a gap in rental availability and greatly increases housing prices for residents.

and multi-cultural areas of the city. In the 1970s, with the demolition of some of the most deprived neighbourhoods of Lisbon, many families from these areas moved to Intendente, bringing with them drug and sex businesses. As a result, the Intendente neighbourhood became isolated and had a negative reputation throughout the city.

Around 2010, the city council commenced a process to revitalise Mouraria and Intendente, the two neighbourhoods connected by Largo Intendente. The mayor at the time, António Costa, moved his office to Largo Intendente for three years, to bring attention to the area's regeneration. Following the physical renovation of Largo Intendente, the area has been radically transformed, becoming a conflict zone between citizen-led initiatives trying to improve local residents' living conditions versus investors buying up buildings and converting them into hotels and short-term rental apartment complexes. This evolution coincided with tourism assuming a greater role in Lisbon's city economy, with many sectors specialising in tourism, as well as a boom in short-term rentals in central areas of the city.

Intendente's recent transformation is the result of a combination of local and global processes. One important aspect is the recent liberalisation of the housing market in the 2000s. As a vestige of the fascist regime in Portugal (which ended in 1974), rental prices had been frozen since the 1940s, which strongly affected Portuguese cities with significant rental markets. As a result, the lack of funds for landlords to maintain their properties led to the structural deterioration of buildings across entire neighbourhoods. Since 2004, new governmental and municipal policies have opened the housing market to private investors. With the economic crisis of 2008–2009, and under pressure from the IMF, European Commission, and European Central Bank, Portugal privatised many public buildings, revised rental laws, and lifted the rent freeze, leading to massive transformation in Portuguese real estate as well as mass evictions.

Troubled by the economic crisis of 2008, Portugal has not only embraced the liberalisation of its housing stock but also the creation of fiscal programmes that attract foreign investment. International funds have been injected into the housing sector to promote tourism facilities and luxury apartments. Besides a few public spaces and social housing in peripheral areas of the city, there has been little public investment in refurbishing the existing building stock. Cuts in government funding forced municipalities to sell many buildings, including in Intendente, and contributed to increasing the value of private properties, thereby exacerbating the effects of gentrification and touristification.

When opening its doors in 2011, as the square was a construction site, Largo Residências only had a few neighbours: old bars, sports pubs, and an 82-year-old saloon. Largo's most direct engagement took place at the street level, with members of the cooperative talking to passers-by, getting to know residents in local bars, gaining their trust and inviting them to visit Largo Residências. This work included mapping the area's social memory, collecting local stories countering the (largely negative) mainstream narratives of the neighbourhood, instead presenting an image of a place with strong community ties and solidarity networks, via festivals, exhibitions, and radio programmes. Slowly but steadily, Largo Residências gained the features of a community centre around which people from the neighbourhood started gathering.

"We were keen on not acting as gentrifiers but to strengthen the networks of local commerce, local shops, and help the residents who suffered the most from the crisis and austerity first, and from tourism and real estate speculation afterwards. In a certain way we were trying to reorganise community in the neighbourhood."
Tiago Mota Saraiva

Aware of the risks of gentrification and touristification, Largo became a key actor in mediating between public institutions and the local community, and in organising juridical support to enable local associations and shopkeepers to resist pressure from real estate developers. Besides its daily activities, Largo Residências also runs a wide range of initiatives aimed at strengthening the local community: theatre projects, dance workshops, exhibitions featuring the artists-in-residence, and street festivals. Largo Residências is also at the source of many cultural events and programmes focusing on the life and personal stories of local residents (Fig. 5). These include Companhia Limitada, a theatre piece based on local stories of solitude and diseases, and Escuta, a radio programme interviewing a variety of local actors.

"The projects developed in Largo Residências use art to empower people and to bring a reflexive way of thinking about what is happening in their personal lives as well as in the urban surrounding."
Hélène Veiga Gomes

A cooperative model for a fragile area

New municipal policies supporting social and cultural initiatives coincided with Largo's ambition to run a space that can secure its economic sustainability. As renovations began in the area, Intendente and Mouraria were identified by the city council as candidates for BIP/ZIP, a seed-funding programme to support organisations and initiatives operating in priority neighbourhoods of Lisbon.

In order to facilitate the best use of this funding, the municipality established local coordination offices (GABIPs) in some of the priority areas, acting as governance institutions involving borough municipalities, local stakeholders, and community organisations. Largo Residências assumed an important role in the local GABIP process and developed a relationship of trust both with local communities and municipal offices. Aware of their work in the neighbourhood, municipal offices

The BIP/ZIP programme

This programme was launched by the Lisbon municipality's Department of Housing and Local Development in 2010 to promote strategic partnerships in the city's priority neighbourhoods. The programme pinpointed 67 priority areas that were considered as 'social territorial fractures', and were distributed heterogeneously throughout the city's centre and periphery. The priority areas include social housing areas, informal settlements as well as historical neighbourhoods with high unemployment rate, insecurity, poor accessibility and urban hygiene, and lack of services. The BIP/ZIP programme offers seed funding of up to €50,000 to initiatives, selected through an open call, allowing local organisations to carry out small projects that can act as catalysts for change. The total annual budget is approximately €1.5–2 million.

GABIP

GABIP offices are present in BIP/ZIP neighbourhoods, and consist of a coordinator from the municipality, and an executive committee including local key stakeholders in the urban regeneration process. These committees usually involve local associations, elected officials, and representatives of the Department of Housing and Local Development, but elected officials from other departments may also take part. The GABIPs allow the municipality to move decision-making to the local scale and share it with local actors.

Cooperatives

Cooperatives are 'autonomous associations of persons united voluntarily to meet their common economic, social, and cultural needs and aspirations through a jointly owned and democratically controlled enterprise' (International Cooperative Alliance). In cooperatives, economic benefits are distributed proportionally to each member's level of participation. Democratic decision-making in cooperatives implies that each member has an equal vote, no matter how large their financial contribution.

increasingly reached out to Largo Residências to evaluate urban development, and Largo assumed a role of mediating between citizens and the local authorities.

In the first phase of conceiving Largo Residências, the initiators did not have tourism in mind, but were instead focused on cultural institutions and events as potential clients to bring performers and artists to Largo. Within a few years, this focus was extended as more and more tourists began to visit Intendente. Besides opening to tourists in general, Largo has maintained its residency profile: more than 20 cultural institutions regularly book rooms in the hotel.

In order to renovate the building, set up the organisation, and pay the rent for the first months, Largo needed significant upfront investment of approximately €200,000 (€150,000 was needed to create the cafeteria and other ground floor spaces, and another €50,000 was spent on renovating the first floor). The Largo Residências cooperative raised money from various sources: €50,000 was invested by cooperative members and another €50,000 came from municipal funding. The remaining €100,000 was generated through Largo's economic activities. As an additional aid to the organisation's cash flow, the construction contractor deferred their fee of €50,000 until after the hostel's opening, an arrangement that enabled Largo to quickly complete the renovation. Moreover, Ateliermob offered its architectural services pro bono, in exchange for rooms to host the practice's interns.

The renovation was organised incrementally, so that when a floor was ready it opened and began to generate revenue; this allowed the renovation to continue on the other floors. Finally, a grant of €50,000 from the BIP/ZIP programme helped launch Largo's activities but could not be spent on infrastructure or renovation.

By 2017–2018, Largo's revenues allowed the organisation to repay the original cooperative members' investment. Largo Residências's business plan was based on using commercial revenues (hotel and hostel) to support the cultural and artistic projects, cover workers' salaries, and improve their working conditions. While the hotel and hostel are responsible for most of Largo's profit, the cafeteria, despite its initial ambitions, does not generate revenue for cultural activities. Nevertheless, its community function and the six jobs that it provides makes it an integral part of the project. Largo's main expense is the commercial rent paid to the building's owner. While the rent was originally set at €8,000 per month, this was lowered to €6,000 following protracted negotiation, due to the significant structural problems encountered in the building and the necessary renovations.

Largo Residências has the organisational form of a cooperative, a model considered by initiators as suitable to represent an entity combining commercial, cultural, and social activities, and including the organisation's workers in decision-making and ownership. The cooperative was founded by three members, and was later joined by ten members. All members had different backgrounds and professions but shared

"We were keen on not acting as gentrifiers but to strengthen the networks of local commerce, local shops, and help the residents who suffered the most from the crisis and austerity first, and from tourism and real estate speculation afterwards. In a certain way we were trying to reorganise community in the neighbourhood."

Tiago Mota Saraiva

the desire to develop a social programme in the Intendente neighbourhood. The members did not make equal financial investments but have equal decision-making power. The cooperative has three sectors – one taking care of cultural activities, another responsible for accommodation, and the third for the cafeteria, with each sector having a coordinator.

A social safety net for vulnerable people

Largo Residências has had multiple impacts on the Intendente neighbourhood. While it arguably contributed to the area's gentrification through its nightlife venue and tourism facilities, the organisation also created a variety of services in the neighbourhood that benefit local residents. Relying on its local network with residents and other associations created in the past years, Largo has effectively constituted a welfare net that takes care of vulnerable residents facing eviction or other destabilising life situations. For many local residents, joining activities organised by Largo was conceived as an empowerment process, with increasing personal security, as well as new networking and job opportunities.

Largo's employment policies have also contributed to social integration. The organisation has created a variety of employment opportunities for people living in Intendente, mostly in the cafeteria and the hotel. Until 2021, Largo employed 15 workers, with 80–90% living in the neighbourhood and 30% having a highly vulnerable social background. Of the 15 employees, 6.5 positions were created in the cafeteria, 5.5 in accommodation, and 3 in the cultural department. Additional projects and festivals allow Largo to occasionally employ more people. By providing training and jobs, Largo Residências has also helped several vulnerable people change their lives and formalise their residence or citizenship status, welcoming them within a community that values equality and personal empowerment.

Besides conducting its own activities, Largo Residências has been engaged in advocating social inclusion policies. Through the local GABIP structure, Largo has advanced proposals for a law to empower the elderly, a section of society who may be isolated and often victims of exploitation and fraud. At both the local and national levels, Largo has been advocating housing-related legislation. Largo members are working on a new institution of cooperative housing to design processes of cooperativism in the city centre.

> "Largo is an important connector that can boost and organise people and civil society and can interact with important social movements. They try to put housing rights into the mainstream political and social agenda."
> Luis Mendes

Largo Residências also had an impact on municipal policies related to tourism. In October 2019, a new regulation prohibited new tourism facilities in Lisbon's historical areas. However, tourism facilities that reuse a formerly vacant building and accommodate social and cultural projects for local development and housing, are exempt from this ban. Clearly, the regulation has been inspired by Largo Residências, aiming at limiting extractive real estate speculation and promoting a new, more sustainable and responsible logic of tourism.

During the first months of the COVID-19 pandemic, Largo suspended all of its activities to offer rooms to the Central Hospitals of Lisbon to host people in need. This situation led to financial difficulties for Largo, exacerbated by pressure from the building's owners who sought to sell the building to be converted into another high-end hotel in central Lisbon. The original rental contract on Largo Intendente concluded in 2021 and was not renewed.

The end of the rental contract signalled the fact that all this advocacy work was not enough to protect Largo Residências against the real estate pressures faced by most initiatives and residents in central Lisbon. The cooperative's vulnerability as a tenant of a private landlord offered a cautionary tale, and the future of Largo Residências is envisioned in public or community-owned properties.

By the time the cooperative had to leave Largo Intendente, members of Largo Residências, aware of pressure from the changing real estate market, had been negotiating a new location for several years. Largo temporarily opened its new venue in a state-owned former military barracks, about 500 m from Intendente, with the neighbourhood festival Bairro em Festa.

In order to sustain its programmes during this transitional period, Largo partnered with other organisations to carry out cultural and social activities at the site. They worked on improving the artistic residence programme while developing a programme for refugees with the idea of integrating diverse groups of artists, creators, refugees, homeless people, and neighbours. While the military barracks is planned to become a social housing facility, Largo Residências, together with other local organisations, will use the complex until the start of the construction works and envisions inclusion in the future project.

List of References

Branco, R., & Alves, S. (2020). Urban rehabilitation, governance and housing affordability: Lessons from Portugal. *Urban Research and Practice, 13*(2), 157–179. https://doi.org/10.1080/17535069.2018.1510540

Carmo, A., & Estevens, A. (2017). Urban citizenship(s) in Lisbon: Examining the case of Mouraria. *Citizenship Studies, 21*(4), 409–424. https://doi.org/10.1080/13621025.2017.1307602

European Agenda for Culture. (2014). *Policy handbook on promotion of creative partnerships*. https://ec.europa.eu/assets/eac/culture/library/reports/creative-partnerships_en.pdf

Galhardo, J. (2014). Le mythe du ghetto de la Mouraria à Lisbonne: La mise en récit d'un territoire plastique [The myth of the Mouraria ghetto in Lisbon: A plastic memory]. *Articulo – Journal of Urban Research* (Special issue 5). https://doi.org/10.4000/articulo.2430

Gomes, P. (2020). The birth of public space privatisation: How entrepreneurialism, convivial urbanism and stakeholder interactions made the Martim Moniz square, in Lisbon, privatisation-ready. *European Urban and Regional Studies, 27*(1), 86–100. https://journals.sagepub.com/doi/full/10.1177/0969776418823052

Nofre, J., Martins, J. C., Vaz, D., Fina, R., Sequera, J., & Vale, P. (2019). The 'Pink Street' in Cais do Sodré: Urban change and liminal governance in a nightlife district of Lisbon. *Urban Research and Practice*, 12(4), 322–340. https://doi.org/10.1080/17535069.2018.1449010

Patti, D., & Polyák, L. (2017). *Funding the cooperative city: Community finance and the economy of civic spaces.* Cooperative City Books.

Pincha, J. P. (2019, 30 October). *Alojamento local em Lisboa: Graça e Bairro das Colónias passam a ser zonas de contenção.* Publico. https://www.publico.pt/2019/10/30/local/noticia/novos-alojamentos-locais-proibidos-parte-centro-lisboa-1891975

Sánchez-Fuarros, I. (2017). Mapping out the sounds of urban transformation: The renewal of Lisbon's Mouraria quarter. In C. Guillebaud (Ed.), *Towards an anthropology of ambient sound*. Routledge.

Tulumello, S. (2016). Reconsidering neoliberal urban planning in times of crisis: Urban regeneration policy in a 'dense' space in Lisbon. *Urban Geography*, 37(1), 117–140. https://www.tandfonline.com/doi/abs/10.1080/02723638.2015.1056605

The case study is based on interviews with: Marta Silva, founder of Largo Residências; Tiago Mota Saraiva, architect, Ateliermob; Hélène Veiga Gomes, anthropologist, Escuta; Roberto Falanga, adviser to the BIP/ZIP programme, Universidade do Lisboa; Ana Jara, activist, politician, elected municipal councillor; Luis Mendes, journalist, Universidade do Lisboa.

Praga Lab, Poland: The Heritage of Warsaw's Other Side

By Katarzyna Sadowy, Dominika P. Brodowicz

Praga is part of Warsaw, Poland, but has such a distinctive character that it is often perceived as being a separate area. Such a distinction has strong path-dependence, which even today impacts both the image of Praga and its actual urban form. The name 'Praga' is usually used to describe the entire part of the city located on 'the other side' of the Vistula River, which cuts Warsaw in two not only physically but also in economic, social, and cultural terms. The habit of calling this area Praga persisted even as the area grew, and today it encompasses seven (out of 18) districts, with only two of them officially named so. The Praga Cooperative Heritage Lab and the area for its interventions lie within the Praga North district, encompassing the traditional and historical part of Praga (Fig. 1).

In 2020, Praga North's population was 63,442. The district experienced population decline over the preceding decade, from 71,009 people in 2010 and 66,495 in 2015. The Praga North and South districts have Warsaw's highest rates of unemployment among working age inhabitants.

This dynamic yet troubled environment results from the profound transformation initiated in 1989, which was most effectively carried out in other parts of Warsaw but is still in progress in Praga North. Trade and industry were previously large employers, but the area lost its economic base as a result of radical structural shifts in the local labour market. During the 1990s and early 2000s, it remained less attractive for investments than the west part of the city. During the last decade, two factors pushed Praga towards a new reality. On one hand, there was public investment: revitalisation programmes and construction of the metro line connecting it to the city centre. Private investment followed, encompassing transformation of former industrial sites, mostly for residential uses and high-end retail and leisure. Praga's long-neglected heritage became many things, including: an object of attraction for a consumerist city, a barrier to development, and an element of a neglected past.

Fig. 1
Praga Lab in Warsaw. Map

Timeline	1902—2022
1902	Construction of a bakery
After 1945	Centrally planned economy and nationalisation of production sector
After 1989	Transition towards free market economy, reinstatement of local governance
2010	Bakery ends production
2012	Failed venture to reuse the Bakery as a club/restaurant
2015	Opening of Museum of Praga
2016	Opening of Creativity Centre
2019	New tenant plans to adapt the Bakery as a restaurant/workshop space
2020	Bakery listed as a monument; COVID-19 halts the tenant's plan; end of the contract with the municipality
2021	Community Hub (Dom Kultury) finds new location in adapted Konopacki Palace
2022	*Praca Praga* exhibition; Praga Lab's circular workshops

Praga North as an ambiguous place of industrial heritage

Warsaw has been the capital of Poland since the 16th century, but the historic Praga (a small part of which is called Praga today) was incorporated into the city in the late 18th century. Even as a part of the capital city, it remained underdeveloped, with built environment of poorer quality and with inhabitants of lower skills and income. Praga experienced radical transformation in the late 19th century, under Russian occupation. The construction of a railway connecting Warsaw to Russian markets, and the lifting of custom duties, opened new economic possibilities. Industrialisation was the strongest economic growth factor that Praga ever experienced, and remained so during subsequent intensive stages of industrialisation: between the two world wars, in an independent country; and after 1945, during the centrally planned economy. Before the Second World War, Praga developed mainly due to the private sector and entrepreneurs: from such captains of industry as Wedel (owner of the famous chocolate factory), to those who owned several plots of land and developed them for various manufacturing ventures, to craftspeople, pedlars, and vendors at the famous Różycki Bazaar. The grey economy constituted a significant element of this thriving but chaotic environment.

Trade and manufacturing allowed economic development in Praga, but the remaining tangible elements of these two activities differ. Traditionally, Praga lacked places visited by the upper class and wealthier customers. Even while factory owners relocated production halls to Praga during the 1920s and 1930s, flagship stores and offices remained on the other side of the river (Fig. 2).

Therefore, trade consisted of wholesale operations on one hand, and very modest stores, markets, and street vendors on the other. Różycki Bazaar was famous – especially during the post-war period of the centrally planned economy, when the network of contacts and tradition of the shadow economy provided unusually abundant opportunities. Nevertheless, the area lacked affluent department stores, elegant restaurants, or cafés that could become appreciated as heritage assets. Apart from 'Różyc' there is no specific built heritage, in architectural or artistic terms, related to the area's trading tradition.

Industrial sites and buildings were the most characteristic tangible elements of the area. Work, in factories or in trade, is in fact Praga's heritage, manifested not only in large (post-)industrial sites, but intertwined in all manners with the urban fabric of the district. Significant investment and large-scale production resulted in several spill overs, including craft and repairs. There were many small workshops and repair services along the streets; the inner courtyards of the tenement houses were often sites for small workshops or warehouses; and people were sewing, mending, and repairing things in their own crowded flats.

The durability of the local heritage varied in the 20th century and during the transition period initiated in 1989. Large industrial sites maintained their role relatively late, despite many drawbacks caused by destruction and looting during the two world wars. After 1945, some industrial buildings were adapted for other uses (e.g., offices), but many were modernised and equipped for new phases of manufacturing. The most famous among them were the Wedel chocolate factory (for some time called 22nd July as a state-owned company) and the Koneser Vodka Factory. Pollena Uroda produced cosmetics that were known in all Polish households during the 1970s and 1980s, while Avia was a manufacturer of advanced aircraft engines. All of them operated as production sites in Praga from the early 20th century and until the 1990s or early 2000s. Also, mid-size production sites, such as the 3rd Mechanised Bakery (experiment case for Praga Lab) operated for over a century. The history of small workshops and individual craftspeople is more difficult to follow, but several places (especially those offering repairs) had been known in Praga for decades.

Fig. 2
Abandoned Michel Mill in Praga

Praga displays three elements of continuity:

- Conservation of built heritage and continuity of use of a specific site;
- Existing built heritage (factories, workshops) adapted for new uses;
- The presence of specific types of industry, craft, and repair sectors in the area (but not necessarily contemporaneously).

Numerous large factories were adapted for new uses, with some level of preservation of the built heritage but entirely new societal linkages and meaning. Some sites (including those that were municipally owned) remained vacant and fell into disrepair. Paradoxically, the most durable element of Praga's heritage turned out to be an intangible one: skills, and traditions of work and craft.

Now, after 30 years of transition, it is probably too late to look for a strong community connected by the experience of work in Praga's former factories, even if some memories and emotional relations are still present. Yet, the community of art and craft found its new form, better adapted to modern expectations. This group is struggling for several reasons, facing both threats and new opportunities.

Transformations

In Praga as elsewhere, the transformation of former industrial sites encompasses market-oriented investments of international and local developers. The Koneser Centre is marketed as a supra-local hub of commerce, elegant restaurants, hotel, conference centre, and Museum of Vodka as a tourist attraction. The large site of the former Pollena Uroda factory has been adapted and developed as housing, with services and stores for white-collar clients of above-average income. Property developers have become strong players in Warsaw, benefiting from the market-oriented strategies and policies of the City of Warsaw.

Praga North was included in both of the City of Warsaw's revitalisation programmes, spanning 2005–2013 and 2015–2022. The municipality also owns and manages numerous sites and buildings throughout the district. Municipal investment, including construction of a second metro line, is currently one of the strongest factors for change in Praga. Even though Praga North still generally lacks large public institutions, there are two whose work is connected to Praga heritage and which are very active in creating links between the past and the future: the Museum of Praga (a branch of the Museum of Warsaw) and Dom Kultury Praga (DK Praga, local Community Hub). It is worth mentioning that both organisations are based in heritage buildings. The Museum of Praga occupies a historic tenement house from the 19th century, a listed monument in a listed area, with modern extension (elements of Jewish ritual buildings were also discovered), while DK Praga is located in a historic mansion of the well-known Praga entrepreneur, Ksawery Konopacki. Both institutions support workers' heritage, but their locations and buildings are not related to places of production.

Praga still retains a strong presence of artists, the creative sector, and micro-entrepreneurs. At Targowa Street, the municipality established the Creativity Centre (Centrum Kreatywności Targowa 56) to support the creative sector. Since 2020, the centre has been privately operated by the Chamber of Commerce. Several curators of the Museum of Praga, entrepreneurs, and activists also live in the district. Physical proximity facilitates easier informal contacts but, during the Praga Lab activities, bottlenecks were observed regarding cooperation between actors, including a lack of time, common space, occasion to meet, and several gaps in information flow.

Experimenting with activating tools

The heritage community was involved in testing various tools alongside Praga Lab. These were structured via three groups of activities: the Bakery, Made in Praga, and the Living Memory Exhibition (LME). The goal was to create a basis for new solutions, embedding the local economy and society in the heritage of work, and to support heritage-driven uses of the existing sites. Heritage sites included both listed and unlisted locations. The goal was common, but the three paths differed in terms of their starting points. Praga Bakery was a *place*, chosen as a case study. Made in Praga focused on *people*, and the contemporary heritage community of art and craft. LME presented the *potential* for reinterpreting heritage, and the often unknown and underestimated potential of places and people.

The Bakery (in Polish, Piekarnia) located at 2/4 Stolarska Street, became an object of a series of Praga Lab workshops held in 2020, which focused on adaptive reuse, including both tangible and intangible heritage of the place. The site was included in the register of monuments in 2020 and remains nearly unchanged since its construction in the early 1900s.

However, in order to prepare the Bakery for business and social activities, it requires substantial renovation estimated at costing more than 4 million PLN (around €920,000). For over a century, Piekarnia served its original function, as a small complex with workplace and residential functions in one location. It is currently a municipally owned property administrated by the district's Property Management Office (ZGN). The site is precious and attractive, yet is currently unused and its future remains uncertain. To develop proposals and recommendations for the future use(s) of the Piekarnia site, a workshop was organised based on the well-established practice of the Warsaw branch of the Association of Polish Architects (OW SARP). The teams that participated in the workshop were chosen via an open call. In addition to reflecting heritage values, both the proposal and final recommendations were required to be community-oriented and to encompass the principles of a circular economy.

The first one chosen, mamArchitekci, focused on a non-profit solution. The second, Zaczyn, developed a not-only-for-profit idea for bringing life back to the Bakery. Both teams proposed that the Bakery should be a combination of workplace and residential complex, which reflects its original functions (Fig. 3).

The concept by mamArchitekci included organising an open tender for investors with documented experience in community-focused projects and the ability to ensure capital. The solution was based on a 20-year or longer horizon; necessity of waivers or discounts on operational costs from the public owner granted to the operator; starting activities in stages, to generate income early and use it for subsequent phases of adaptation; and flexibility of functions (the possibility of modifying these to match the changing needs of users/customers).

In the concept based on the not-only-for-profit approach, the Zaczyn team proposed two separate entities located in the Bakery, working in the form of a consortium. Each should have separate goals and scopes of activity. One would focus on a social programme and community- and place-making. The other, called the operator, would be dedicated to property administration and management, together with monitoring the investment process. The proposal would also necessitate a lease period of at least 20 years from the City of Warsaw (currently, leases on public properties are for three to five years, with possible extension but without any formal guarantee). Zaczyn also advised exemption from rental costs and even reimbursement of utility costs. It was suggested that tenants should have the option of subletting the space on a commercial basis, which under current legal conditions is not possible with public properties.

The published recommendations detailed the financial analysis, institutional solutions, and sustainable approach to the technology applied to the architectural design.

The aim of the workshops was to search for solutions for the Bakery, but the conclusions could be applicable to sim-

Long-term cooperation

Two concepts for socially responsible reuse were proposed for the Bakery. Financial and managerial analysis showed that the basis of the feasibility would be a long-term contract between the city (the site's owner) and new tenant. A near-term perspective of just a few years (which is typical of municipal contracts) would be much too short – either to ensure a return on investment or to create a long-term plan of cooperation with various stakeholders who might gradually become involved with the place: a 20-year lease period would be appropriate.

3

Fig. 3
Visualisation of Piekarnia from before it has been Stolarska Street

Fig. 4
Art workshop, sculpture TU

4

ilar historical workplaces not only in Praga district or Warsaw, but also in other Polish cities, which are filled with similar post-industrial gems.

Openness, cooperation, respect for heritage, and a will to bring together a wide range of stakeholders were also reflected in the Made in Praga project, which was similarly announced via an open call in 2019. Its aim was to support better connections between the local economy and artistic activity through Praga's tangible and intangible heritage, by empowering business entities through various financial and non-financial tools.

Initially, Praga Lab planned to support only one applicant. However, the quality of submissions was high, and so strongly connected with the heritage of work, that three candidates were chosen. The first was Natural Born, whose creator, the artist Anna Szuflicka, combines art with responsible manufacturing. Her work focuses on the design and production of small items of interior decor such as lamps, clocks, and candlesticks. The brand aims to produce simple and functional objects in small series. All products are made locally in Praga district, in cooperation with local artisans. Second, Look Inside is a vintage store created by Marek Rykiel and Janek Rygiel, who are also co-organisers of the Cuda Wianki festival and creators of the Museum of Polish Clocks. By selling used items, they offer them a second life. They repair some items prior to sale, which is not only a manifestation of circular economy practices but also authentic to the spirit of Praga district. Third, Pedet.shop, created by Katarzyna Osińska, consists of three brands, one of which, Praga Warszawa (Warsaw souvenirs), became a focus of cooperation with an artist. Her projects stemmed from her own local patriotism and wish to create a positive image of Praga districts among inhabitant of left-bank Warsaw as well as tourists and newcomers.

Between 2020 and 2022, despite the coronavirus pandemic and numerous lockdowns in Poland, Praga Lab carried out all planned activities with the winners of the Made in Praga competition, including mentoring and advisory sessions, incorporating the development of a business model. Praga Lab decided to become a partner in the fourth Cuda Wianki festival, which is organised cyclically and promotes a vintage culture and waste-reduction paradigm, but also creates a positive image of the area and popularises Nowa Praga among Warsaw residents and tourists. The festival's fourth edition took place in 2020 and was a great success, not only for the number of artists and entrepreneurs taking part but also the number of people encouraged to visit Nowa Praga.

The results of cooperation among local entrepreneurs and artists, through Made in Praga, were satisfactory, yet the impact of COVID-19 and economic difficulties resulting from the energy crisis in 2022 are yet to be revealed for the long term. Nevertheless, the role of craft turned out to be so significant that the Praga Lab decided to run Co.Creative workshops in February 2022. The aim was to mark once again that the district's heritage comprises not only monuments and conservation practices but a heritage of work, repair, and production. The workshops also enabled the direct involvement of a broader heritage community. Free public events were offered in the form of training for people who were not necessarily involved in the fields covered by the daily workshops, but who were eager to learn about those fields through their own activity and through interaction with others.

Three further workshops were organised in cooperation with DK Praga, Praga Museum of Warsaw, which were held at the Pałacyk Konopackiego (Konopacki Palace). The first was a production workshop, based on the idea that small-scale and local production of items builds the identity of places and creates relationships with customers, contractors, and the local community. In this context, the workshop was focused on reusing clothes and materials. The workshop was titled Circular Sewing and run by Paulina Leszczyk, representing the Kompromis brand. During the workshop, new items were created using second-hand clothes that the participants purchased in the neighbourhood. The design for a 'zero waste' backpack was shared online by Paulina Leszczyk.

The second, an art workshop, was hosted by Józef Gałązka, a Warsaw-based visual artist and sculptor. It involved constructing an 'unusual monument' as an artistic confrontation of the phenomenon of monument-mania. The result was a collaborative work between the artist and workshop participants, who began with a dialogue about Praga's identity from their personal perspectives (Fig. 4). The monument was dedicated to the district, and took the form of two letters forming the word 'TU' ('here' in Polish) This, according to the participants 'reminds Praga residents that the centre of the world is right here, not there or anywhere else. The materialised 'TU' is a guardian of what is close to our hearts, what is our own'. The sculpture consisted of elements that became part of a 'wandering exhibition', to appear on balconies across Praga as a flowerpot, candlestick, decoration, etc., thereby bringing art to everyday life.

The third event, Craft Café, is an example of how the work, art, and heritage of Praga blend with each other. The idea for this workshop was inspired by the work of Edward Manitius (primarily a designer and owner of a toy factory), which was presented at the same time at the Museum of Praga. Confectioners from Tadam! ran a workshop inspired by Manitius' project (a wooden box of sweets that serves as a toy, designed almost a century ago) and created Praga Bunny. During the meeting, participants were invited to create edible reproductions of an animal, based on the project and under guidance of confectioner Maks Szostak. The project itself proved to be a great success, and was awarded the Laurel of the Marshal of the Mazovian Voivodeship at the 15th edition of the competition.

All of the Co-Creative workshops were summed up during the last, common discussion and presentation of the results, accompanied by a seminar on circular economy principles, presented by the od.coop Foundation.

Fig. 5
The historic bakery building in its contemporary context

Szwedzka

Living Memory Exhibition *Praca Praga*

Praga long had a reputation as the most dangerous neighbourhood in Warsaw. Grey economy and crime-related activities were linked to the area's former image as a dirty and poor district of factories and workers. Such economic activities were replaced by conspicuous consumption in newly adapted post-industrial sites. Heritage connected to manufacturing, manual and craft work started to disappear from the narrative or else gained false aesthetic attraction.

The Living Memory Exhibition (LME) was organised as a tool to present an alternative image of Praga heritage to the broader public. The exhibition was entitled *Praca Praga* (*praca* means work in Polish), and work was the leading theme. The exhibition took place in February 2022, and five proposals were chosen:

Viola Głowacka, a young but already successful artist, fulfilled her dream of experimenting with an unusual space for artistic exhibition. Having already exhibited at locations including the Museum of Modern Art in Warsaw, she decided, literally, to set up shop in a pavilion of a modest bazaar. The artist presented her works inspired by the life of Praga, accompanied by ready-mades, objects bought at the same bazaar and from street vendors. She spent most of the day during the exhibition as any other seller at the bazaar, presenting her 'products' to the public, talking to visitors and other vendors.

Maria Kiesner opened her own studio, which is shared with several other artists, to the public. For visitors, it was an occasion to enter a post-industrial space that is usually inaccessible. The artist focused on representations of both lost and surviving symbolic buildings in Praga. Visitors could view the artist's paintings and the research materials that led to their creation. The goal was to present the studio as a working space, and to increase public awareness of the often-difficult conditions in which artistic work is undertaken.

Aga Szreder is an artist well known for her work in the specific medium of shadow sculpture. For LME, she presented the 'Worker' (in Polish, professions are gendered, so it was clear that this was a male worker). The sculpture was composed of ready-made objects related to the physical work: bricks, saws, and trowels. After dark, and with the use of artificial light, their shadows appeared as a grotesque military tank. This ambiguous eulogy of male, industrial work was confronted with images (on a looped video) of the hard, physical work of sculpting undertaken by the artist herself, with the 'Worker' presented in the window of the artistic studio.

Kasia Rysiak and Paulina Mirowska organised an exhibition around a chess set. The project resulted from a collaboration between several craftspeople and specialists, to create a durable and highly aesthetic product. The entire process of design, prototyping, and manufacture was presented during the exhibition through drawings, experimental pieces, tools, and artistic photographs. These were presented in the workspace, Pracownia Wschodnia, where both artists are part of an

Added value of local businesses

Made in Praga process, Co.Creative workshops, and the *Praca Praga* exhibition encompassed the presence of small businesses that offer several values important for the further sustainable development of Praga. They create strong ties to the place and are interested in its heritage; in their practices they are very respectful to various groups present in Praga, including those who suffer from social and economic inequalities; they are often strict about environmentally responsible means of production, repair, and consumption.

informal group. Visitors could learn not only about the heritage-driven process of manufacturing chess pieces, but also the principles and methods used by the group to adapt the space.

Following Warsaw's well-established tradition of craft confectionery, three siblings, Maks, Sonia, and Ania Szostak, founded Tadam! as a high-quality confectioner, which brings a bit of luxury and pleasure to Praga. For the exhibition, they proposed a comment on (over)consumption, mass production, and luxury: an edible golden egg presented in the window of their workshop. This plays upon the concept of the most luxurious Fabergé eggs, affordable for very few; and that of a 'surprise egg', which is affordable but of low quality. They proposed a product located in-between, contrasting the elegant arrangement of the window with the dilapidated facade of the heritage building.

Impacts through valuing local heritage

Praga preserved much of its original architecture, character, and identity, even as the industrial sites gradually lost their functions (Fig. 5). Today, the area provides a good case study for the reuse of a former industrial district, alternatives to market-driven commercial centres and housing, as well as to the dominance of top-down municipal investment. Praga is a unique example, not only in Warsaw, of empowering a local economy, and especially of micro-entrepreneurs, who often are not focused solely on economic gain, but are heritage- and culture-driven in their tangible and intangible spectrums. It became clear that such entrepreneurship needs to be based on networking (which resulted from Praga Lab's activities) and support from the public sector (whose long-term engagement remains to be seen) and must convey the role of work in both the district's heritage and its future. It is important to emphasise that for all actors involved in Praga, its character and community were important on various levels – ranging from inspiration, to history, and access to business opportunities, and certainly including architecture and the built environment. The keys to establishing cooperation were twofold: (1) strong relations to Praga and its heritage, either tangible or intangible; and (2) those actors who could be the gatekeepers of change, either as decision-makers or as pioneers of new solutions for heritage-driven initiatives.

Praga Lab was initiated in the context of the European Union's Horizon 2020 project OpenHeritage, and encompassed the core team: Katarzyna Sadowy (architect, economist), Maciej Czeredys (architect, heritage specialist), Dominika P. Brodowicz (economist, futurist), and Natalia Daca (dissemination and public relations specialist). It was supported by an advisory board, comprising: a historian/heritage specialist; cultural manager/local activist; circular economy specialist; and a specialist in public administration. Cooperation was established at both city and local levels, including: the City of Warsaw, Creativity Centre, New Craft Nów Association, the Museum of Warsaw, and Museum of Praga. Various actors were involved during the project, including the director of the Conservation Office, local entrepreneurs (art and craft), architects, sociologists, heritage specialists, and art curators.

List of References

Głowacka, K. (2016). *Echa dawnej Warszawy*. Skarpa Warszawska.

Kompromis. (n.d.). *Ubrania z materiałów z odzysku*. Retrieved 4 November 2022, from https://www.kompromis.store

Koneser Centre. (n.d.). *Centrum Praskie Koneser*. Retrieved 4 November 2022, from https://koneser.eu/en/

Leyk, A., & Wawrzyniak, J. (2020). *Cięcie. Mówiona historia transformacji*. Wydawnictwo Krytyki Politycznej.

Look Inside. (n.d.). *Look Inside – sklep vintage*. Retrieved 4 November 2022, from https://lookinside.pl

Miller, M. (2018). *Co dzień świeży pieniądz: Czyli dzieje bazaru Różyckiego. T. 1, Za cara, za sanacji i za Niemca*. Fundacja Laboratorium Reportażu: Narodowe Centrum Kultury.

Pedet.shop. (n.d.). *Pedet*. Retrieved 4 November 2022, from pedet.shop.pl

Pollena Uroda. (n.d.). *Bohema – Strefa Praga*. Retrieved 4 November 2022, from https://www.bohemapraga.pl/en

Praga Lab. (2021a). *Bakery*. Retrieved 4 November 2022, from https://ohpraga.pl/en/warsztaty/

Praga Lab. (2021b). Made in Praga. Retrieved 4 November 2022, from https://ohpraga.pl/en/made-in-praga/

Praga Lab. (2022a). *Praca Praga exhibition*. Retrieved 4 November 2022, from https://ohpraga.pl/en/wystawa/

Praga Lab. (2022b). *Co.Creative workshops*. Retrieved 4 November 2022, from https://ohpraga.pl/en/warsztaty-wy-tworcze/

Sadowy, K., Brodowicz, D. P., & Czeredys, M. (Eds.). (2021). *Piekarnia. In search of adaptive reuse models for architectural heritage*. OW SARP.

Sadowy, K., Czeredys, M., & Daca, N. (2022). *Notes Praski* [Praga Notebook].

Sadowy, K., & Lisiecki, A. (2019). Post-industrial, post-socialist or new productive city? Case study of the spatial and functional change of the chosen Warsaw industrial sites after 1989. *City, Territory and Architecture, 6*(1), 1–14.

Urząd Statystyczny w Warszawie. (2010). *Panorama dzielnic Warszawy*, 2010 [Warsaw Statistical Office. Overview of Warsaw districts, 2010].

Urząd Statystyczny w Warszawie. (2015). *Panorama dzielnic Warszawy*, 2015 [Warsaw Statistical Office. Overview of Warsaw districts, 2015].

Urząd Statystyczny w Warszawie. (2020). *Panorama dzielnic Warszawy*, 2020 [Warsaw Statistical Office. Overview of Warsaw districts, 2020].

Warsaw City Hall. (n.d.). *Warsaw revitalisation programme*. Retrieved 4 August 2022, from https://architektura.um.warszawa.pl/rewitalizacja

Broei, Belgium: The Legacy of Pleasure. The Adaptive Reuse of Devil Castle in Ghent

By Federica Fava

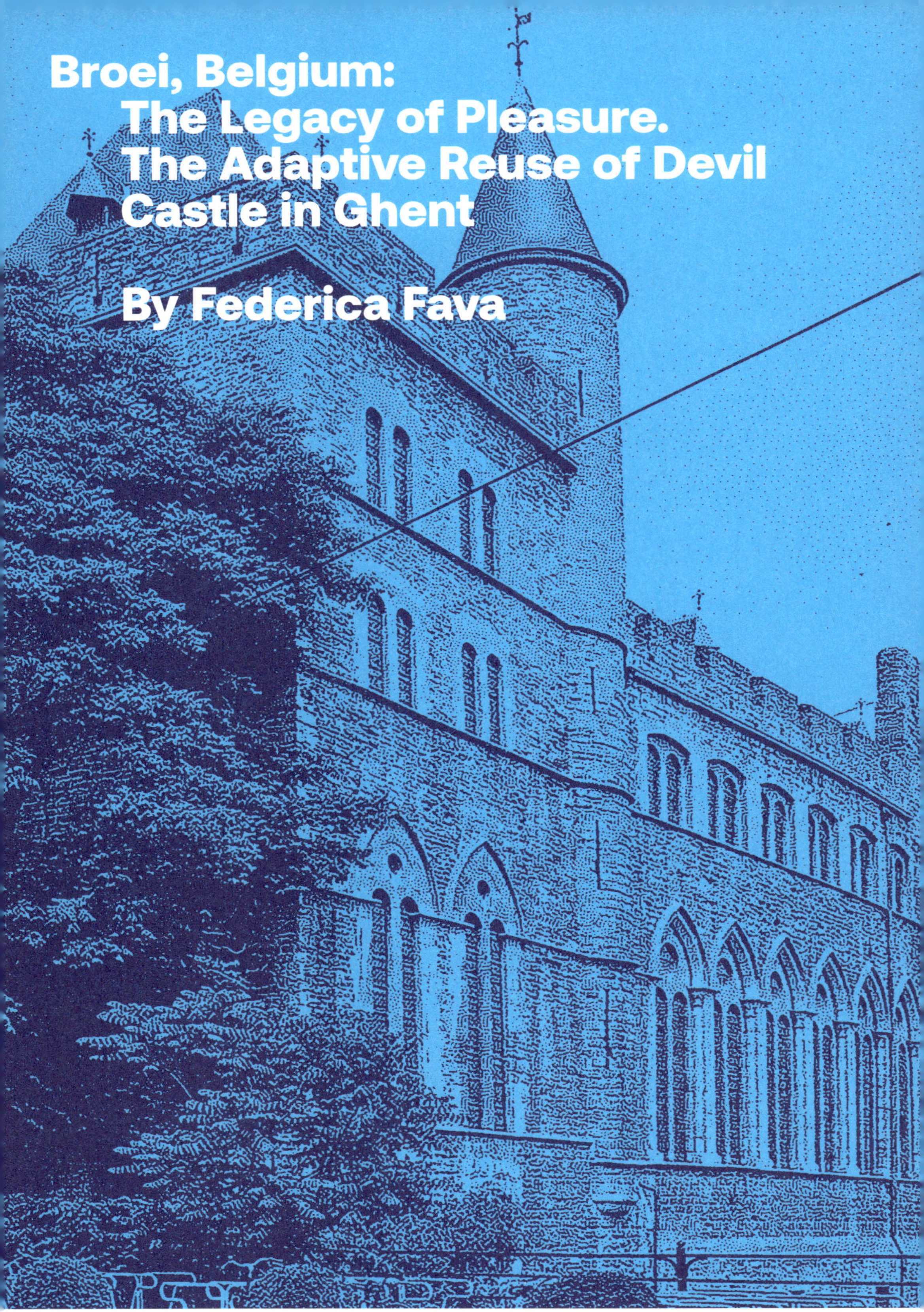

Broei is a non-profit organisation founded in Ghent in 2019, that functions as facilitator among parties, building a network grounded on mutual support and trust. Within the temporary approach to city development, Broei is a pioneer case, since it has evolved within a listed building (Fig. 2). Although Ghent has a long tradition of temporary uses, their application to cultural heritage is a novelty in the city scenario, presenting future challenges in terms of policy and sectorial integration in public administration. However, it is worth noting that Ghent is internationally known in matters of community-centre urbanism. Since 2014, the municipality has provided a Temporary Use Fund (annual budget €300,000) to support 'soft' adaptations of vacant assets, which goes hand in hand with the proliferation of new urban energies and skills. Emerging initiatives are subsidised at various levels (from €6,000 to €35,000) to be used to make buildings operational through standards of safety and habitability.

The motivation for introducing such policy instruments in Ghent is twofold. Firstly, they reflect the public recognition of a growing civic and active fabric of the city, reclaiming space in order to host activities that (potentially) have a large impact on the cityscape. On the other hand, they respond to development needs, providing participative planning tools adopted by the municipality to test possible renewal solutions. Beyond buildings, the main legacy of such experience is the creation of a social network that endures long after the conclusion of the initiatives themselves, thereby reshaping the relational structure of the city, or its urban brain.

"Reflecting on the legacy of temporary use in Ghent is not an easy task. We posed this question during the REFILL project (URBACT), a European project of knowledge exchange with nine other cities, where we want to focus on what happens after temporary uses. What we learned was that the biggest thing that consolidates after such uses is the network. During the projects there occurs a huge mobilisation of people. When a project stops, therefore, you need to be aware that a new collaboration exists and lot of people move from one place to another. This is what happened in Ghent. Moreover, funding temporary use also means to advance learning processes of those city departments that are closer to funded initiatives. And that's the most interesting evidence, namely you understand that the main legacy is not about buildings, but rather about people's evolution – as they become catalysts of the city."
Emma Tytgadt

The large body of experience regarding temporary uses in Ghent was crucial for advancing Broei. The collaboration with other initiatives such as NEST largely facilitated the setting up and launching of the project, providing appropriate contacts and knowledge to address complex urban operations. As mentioned, Broei is a temporary initiative, developed in the Castle Geeraard de Dueivelsteen, a 13th-century cultural asset located in Ghent city centre (Fig. 3), known as Devil Castle. The castle's name derives from its former owner, knight Geeraard Vilain, whose dark, somatic features inspired the naming of the old castle. Initiated in 2018, Broei was launched in 2020 as an open house, running from approximately May to October. Its primary mission is to give new functions to the old castle, discovering meaningful trajectories of development for the city of Ghent.

The project thus provides space, time, and resources to youth organisations that are willing to participate in collectively rewriting the castle's story while experimenting and testing their own ideas in matters of cultural, social, and entrepreneurial validity.

Groups or associations can apply to the yearly calls launched by Broei, choosing among three main topics: technology and sustainability; entrepreneurship and learning; expression and creativity. More generally, the project provides the opportunity for experimenting with new ways of making and living together, and offers a variety of cultural programmes (e.g., performance, exhibitions, lectures, etc.), thus making a positive contribution to improving living conditions in Ghent.

Overall, the openness of this space is mainly conceived in terms of 'safety', which implies the definition of an environment where everyone feels free to engage and experiment. On the other hand, safety is expressed with regard to relationships.

Fig. 1
The Castle, Ghent. Map

Timeline	1200—2024
1200	Construction of Devil Castle
1700	The former castle undergoes several adaptation and transformation projects
1800	Devil Castle used as orphanage for boys, an asylum, and then as fire station before being acquired by the Belgian Government and used as the National Archive from the late 19th century
2010	Closure of the National Archive; Devil Castle remains unused
2015	Devil Castle partially used for residential purposes; acquisition by Koiba
2016	Koiba asked Architecture Workroom Brussels to identify possible functions for the Castle
2018	Devil Castle hosts temporary cultural activities
2019	Broei non-profit organisation founded
2020	Test phase of reusing the castle by Broei
2022	End of reuse test phase
2023	Renovation work started
2024	Broei temporarily located in a new building supporting the European Youth Capital in Ghent

Fig. 2
Castle Geeraard de Dueivelsteen

Fig. 3
Community space in the castle

Fig. 4
The podium on the ground floor of the castle

2

3

4

Adapting a castle for the youth

In autumn 2015, having been for sale for five years, Devil Castle passed from the ownership of the Belgian state to Koiba, a Ghent holding that acquired the complex for €2.205 million. The final price barely exceeded the minimum auction price, originally set at €2.2 million, once again confirming that for urban assets to be open, some form of control over these 'new lands' is a prerequisite for commons-oriented forms of development. Unsurprisingly, the not-for-profit intention of the company has played a fundamental role in the promotion of a slower process of transformation, opting for prioritising research and participation, together with the socially oriented adaptive heritage reuse of the castle (Fig. 3).

In 2010 the National Archive, located in the castle since the late 19th century, was closed, leaving it empty for about five years (see timelines). To tackle uncertainties about the future function of the castle, the new owner embraced a more 'relaxed' relationship with time, by opening its premises up to experimental uses. To this end, the non-profit organisation Architecture Workroom Brussels conducted a study to understand appropriate (needed) uses that would return this space back to the city of Ghent. The findings highlighted an increasing need to respond to youth seeking employment opportunities, underlying the urgency of providing them with a continuously open-ended place. The large size of the castle, on one hand, and on the other its changing but constant historical social function that has unfolded throughout the centuries, have encouraged a process of rethinking the asset as a never-ending project in the process of scaling up the city transition towards more collaborative forms of development. Inheriting this ambition, Broei's goal has been to create a place where young people aged 16 to 30 can take the initiative, by exploring their interests and passions in a free and safe environment, grounded on principles of diversity and collaboration.

> "When choosing the name Broei it is because our idea was to create a place where things can brew, or grow. However, growing implicates a more regular process, a 'one way' growth that means to a certain extent you already know where you are going, what are your trajectories. Brewing instead entails a mounting and unpredictable energy, the forms or outcomes of which you do not know will be produced over time."
> Marie Vanderghote

In accordance with the mutational nature of the castle, it should be highlighted that, at the time of its acquisition by Koiba, it was already undergoing low-profile reuse, made possible through a specific legal instrument, the *Bruikleenoveeernkomst*. Adopted by the Municipality of Ghent as part of the city's anti-squatting strategy, the *Bruikleenoveeernkomst* is a temporary loan agreement, used to rent empty assets under a special regime of habitability. Covering the interim period between the old and new uses, the contract entails less stringent and more flexible building standards, allowing their occupation despite only partially complying with urban and building regulations.

Through this contract, in early 2015, part of Devil Castle was temporarily allocated to a group of young citizens for residential purposes.

Thanks to their involvement, the socio-cultural rehabilitation of the castle was initiated by opening its garden to the city for art exhibitions, after which the informal network of surrounding initiatives kept expanding. Marie Vanderghote, current Broei coordinator and former resident of the castle, states that it is from these activities that the seeds of Broei were planted.

Nowadays (February 2023), a growing constellation of actors revolves around the castle, 'condensing' new socio-cultural paths. To provide an overview: Koiba is the Ghent holding company. It purchased the castle in 2015 and opened it to Broei experimentation for free of charge use. The Municipality of Ghent funds temporary initiatives through the Office of Equal Opportunities, Welfare, Participation, Community Work and Public Green Spaces (*Gelijke Kansen, Welzijn, Participatie, Buurtwerk en Openbaar Groen*). The Interim Vastgoedbeheer is the company offering innovative solutions for managing vacancy, which managed the castle prior to its acquisition by Koiba. Broei is a non-profit, facilitating management of the castle and collaboration among organisations. ConstructLab is the construction partner involved in the re-functionalisation of the castle through a self-construction process. Timelab supports Broei and was mainly active in the initial phase of the project. Twenty-four youth organisations and community groups were using the castle in 2022.

Making fun, building togetherness

Prior to its occupation by the Broei community, the castle was completely empty. The introduction of basic services (e.g., bathroom, kitchen, etc.), together with spatial usages and construction, were determined through a process of co-creation with selected organisations in cooperation with the Construct Lab. This latter is a Berlin-based cooperative construction practice operating in different European countries, including Belgium, which specialises in participative design and construction.

Despite the diversity of uses over time and the connectedness of the entire space, in the last edition of Broei (2022) the functional organisation of the castle has reflected the following general scheme: the basement, adapted with minimum work, functioned as an events venue; the ground floor hosted a podium for cultural activities, from rehearsal to art performance and talks. This level also includes a bar and a community kitchen next to open workshop spaces. The main workshop spaces (e.g., wood, silkscreen printing, etc.), a darkroom, music and photography studio, are located on the first floor, along with staff offices and a silent room (the only room that can be closed) used for dance rehearsal and also psychological support services.

Participative approach

Since the 1990s, the City of Ghent has developed a participative approach to urban development, progressively grounding a time-based approach to the city's regeneration. The institutional innovation, which among others led to an annual budget for temporary uses, started with the establishment of neighbourhood managers (NMs), civil servants responsible for local networking activities. Depending on their needs, NMs connect citizens – and respective ideas – among them, as well as to the policy makers and/or vacant spaces. Currently, the City is organised into several neighbourhoods, each with its own NM. NMs are part of a municipal unit called Policy Participation, today formed of about 30 persons.

The open organisation of the castle responded to the need to create a place without pre-imposed learning paths and performance pressure, but instead prioritising collective enjoyment and fun. In this context, the heritage asset works as durable anchor for personal and community identity, while the transformability of the space is assured through the implementation of the open programme driving the project itself. Risks associated with the unpredictability of the process, and related anxieties, are thus faced through a shared approach to adaptive reuse, in both construction and management. In so doing, uncertainty becomes the basis for rebuilding the collective mindscape, using heritage for imaginative spatial and societal experimentation.

Transforming the construction site in a place of adventure, the realisation of the podium and of different structures to equip the ground floor (Fig. 4), shows a way to creatively tackle uncertainty, not only from the commonly known perspectives of defining future needs, who is involved, and what are the lasting resources, but also from a spatio-mental perspective. The ConstructLab methodology is based on participative design and construction phases, determined together with the final users in a short but full-time endeavour. In summary: a pre-design project is discussed with participants in order to collectively conceive a narrative for the place and then test it at the construction site. To involve non-expert actors, ConstructLab revisits in a social way the Fordist metaphor. In other words, it organises the process along a chain composed of small stations, where everyone can learn and be appreciated as a master of a constructive task while embedded in the wider project. In Bert Villa's words, the architectural process thus works as scaffolding for both buildings and communities, based on *stories of togetherness*:

> "In the adaptation process of the castle, there is a kind of crossing line between people's daily life and the castle functioning as public space which we create. I guess the new created patterns or habits, and the emotional attachment to such spaces, are the results of yearly work into the site. So, I do believe the steps you set out in the preparation of or first act in a building are very important and radical because they might influence a day-to-day behaviour of a space that otherwise might be more conventional than you would imagine at the beginning."
>
> Bert Villa

Although the COVID-19 pandemic significantly altered the ConstructLab methodology, during the last phase – when it was again possible to work collectively in the castle – the structures were assembled by a small team composed of ConstructLab members and the future users of the castle. The production of a manual was thus a way to overcome obstacles to collective-building during the pandemic, thereby providing users with instructions for modifying their own the space over time.

Fig. 5
Temporary exhibition about Broei and the castle

To perpetuate cross-pollination and peer-learning, the final setting of spaces includes a certain level of informality and disorganisation, as seen in the treatment of the entrance area, which was ultimately conceived as an urban space.

In terms of spatial and economic management, Broei benefits from different connection mechanisms (Fig. 5). As mentioned, it firstly relies on the free use of the castle without payment, and on municipal subsidies for temporary uses. For the project to advance, however, the combination of resources is crucial and includes: revenue from Bar Broei; rent revenues provided by the selected associations, with payments according to their development (starters, €50/month; pro, €125/month; and pro+, €250/month); and coming from occasional activities such as cultural events or parties; partnerships with different companies that provided material (in kind contributions) or economic support; and applying for subsidies to run associations' activities.

The overall management of the castle is the responsibility of the Broei team, which coordinates and supports the internal organisation of the castle in cooperation with selected organisations that are asked to become active partners in the project. Sub-organisations, for instance Broei Nest, have also been launched to provide psychological support to young people. Externally, the Broei team mediates with major actors such as the owner and the Municipality of Ghent, and by connecting with other initiatives within and beyond Ghent. In particular, informal relationships have been crucial to achieving understanding with public servants in matters of heritage protection or fire safety; while heritage-related constraints were mainly overcome through architectural temporary systems. The podium and all the new structures designed for the castle are not affixed to its walls. Moreover, the design of a metal mechanism was proposed to solve manifold issues: (1) to leave the castle untouched; (2) to make the wood structures totally reusable; and (3) to allow participants to (re)assemble the space in different ways, introducing an additional participative dimension to the construction process (which, in practice, was significantly constrained by COVID-19 restrictions). In terms of safety and security, continuous negotiation was fundamental to keeping the transformation process open to spatio-human experimentation. As Bert Villa recall, indeed, safety and fire regulations require specific indications about volumes and spatial occupation of any architectural intervention, which contrasts with the undetermined and participatory approach proposed by the group. A non-stop and direct exchange with local actors was thus instrumental to overcome tensions emerging from conflicting needs.

Growing by enjoying adaptive heritage reuse

In 2022, Broei concluded the last edition of the project. In the two preceding years, it initiated the reuse of the old castle, working through spatial and human structures (mentally) prone to and (physically) designed to change. Broei's success led the castle's owners to opt for its permanent transformation into a youth hub. During the renovation work, Broei will continue to develop within a new space proposed by the municipality for carrying out activities related to the European Youth Capital, taking place in Ghent in 2024.

The relational platform proposed by Broei shows that heritage-making can contribute to the welfare system of the city, providing non-prestructured – learning and playful – environments that are deemed crucial to orient the transition towards a healthy city. Although the connection with emotional-related aspects deserves further study, connection mechanisms that bridge people (needs) and (vacant) spaces are prerequisites in order to reckon and work with urban affectivities. In cities like Ghent, increasingly characterised by a physical-mental shortage of spaces for free leisure and experimentation, processual adaptive reuse becomes a mean not only to test new socio-spatial configurations but also to repair relational fractures with the ecological and institutional environment.

Nowadays, many European cities have adopted temporary tools to advance urban development, but which all too often contribute to urban speculation. However, Broei showcases a way to transform such approaches via a durable planning strategy, impacting on the social layer of the city and therefore on urban policy sectors beyond heritage. It is self-evident that partnerships with private actors – large as well as small entrepreneurs – are fundamental to collaborative urbanities in the long run. However, it is also essential to highlight the leading role of the public sector in nurturing the 'Ghent mindset' of temporary uses as the new normal – including more participative urban development, thereby opening up the city to joyful forms of growth.

List of References

Anzani, A. (2020). Mind and places. A multidisciplinary approach to the design of contemporary city. Springer.

AWB, MAAT, noA. (2018). Het Duivelsteen. Internal report commissioned by Koiba.

The City of Ghent. (2018). A journey through temporary use. Refill Network. https://refillthecity.files.wordpress.com/2018/03/refill-final-publication.pdf

Fava, F., Cannella, F., & Caudo, G. (2020). Interim report on the regional and territorial integration evaluation. https://openheritage.eu/wp-content/uploads/2022/12/Interim-Report-on-the-regional-and-territorial-integration-evaluation.pdf

Jaspers S., & Steen, T. (2018). Co-creatie van duurzame resultaten in de tijdelijke invulling van leegstaande gebouwen en terreinen. Onderzoek naar tijdelijke invullingen in de stad Gent. Leuven University Press.

Roe, J., & McCay, L. (2021). Restorative cities: Urban design for mental health and wellbeing. Bloomsbury Visual Arts.

Rose, N., & Fitzgerald, D. (2022). The urban brain: Mental health in the vital city. Princeton University Press.

URBACT. (2018). Inspiring a temporary use roadmap – The story of Ghent (Belgium). In URBACT III, Cities in Action – Stories of Change (pp. 46–47). https://urbact.eu/sites/default/files/2022-10/urbact-stories_of_change-web.pdf

This chapter is based on field research, document analysis and three interviews conducted in 2022: Marie Vanderghote, Broei coordinator and founder of the initiative YART.BE launched in the garden of Devil Castle; Bert Villa, ConstructLab member, founder of the ConstructLab team in Belgium; Emma Tytgadt, Equal Opportunities, Welfare, Participation, Community Work and Public Green Spaces.

Café
Estúdio
16

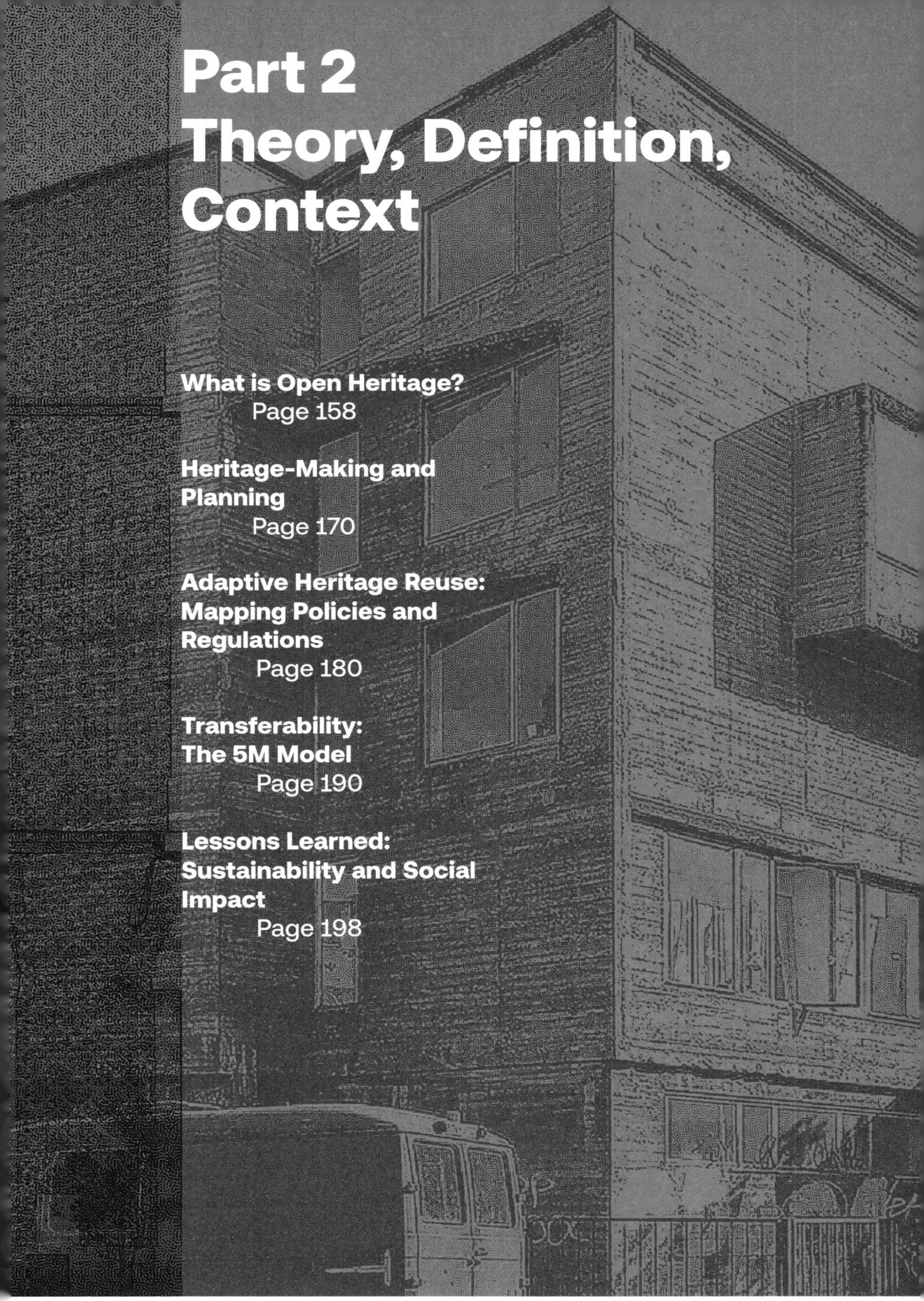

Part 2 Theory, Definition, Context

The second part of the book seeks to connect the experiences and results of the OpenHeritage project to academic discourses. What is Open Heritage? serves as an opening and defining chapter, whereas Social Impact and Sustainability offers conclusions and further challenges for research and practice. The three intervening chapters highlight heritage-making and planning, policies for adaptive heritage reuse (AHR), and transferability, which are three important and specific fields of knowledge gained through the OpenHeritage project.

The chapter *What is Open Heritage?* examines what it means to open up the definition and discourse about heritage. It seeks to understand how the process of openness can be played out, how the redefinition of heritage can be engineered at a local level, and what are the direct consequences – both positive and negative – of this process. The analysis considers how openness can become related to questions of community identity, empowerment, and inclusion. Finally, it reflects on this process as an alternative means of managing adaptive reuse, either as part of the already established processes of listing, conservation, planning, and design, or as a process of its own, keeping in mind its advantages and constraints.

The process of openness, however, is subject to numerous constraints. This is discussed in the three subsequent chapters: *Heritage-Making and Planning* explores how forms of planning support accompany the processes of reuse, and adaptive reuse in particular. References to collaborative planning or communicative planning can show how planning has historically adopted an openness to bottom-up contributions.

Adaptive Heritage Reuse: Mapping Policies and Regulations shows how national governance arrangements are supportive in specific policies, regulations, mechanisms, or their structural integration, and in understanding potential barriers or obstacles to be tackled.

Transferability: The 5M Model provides an overview of models for AHR and their conditions of application. The results show which strategies, best practices, or AHR approaches are transferable to other projects and contexts.

While the adaptive reuse of heritage buildings has become a mainstream practice in many European cities and beyond, the impacts of such projects have, until recently, been poorly defined. The concluding chapter in this section, *Sustainability and Social Impact*, examines different approaches for estimating the social impact of community-driven heritage reuse projects, bringing together impact assessment considerations and methodologies from the OpenHeritage case studies. The issue of social impact is closely connected with the social, economic, and environmental sustainability of heritage reuse initiatives. This concluding chapter therefore argues for a more strategic role of community-driven heritage reuse in EU policies, which should also be reflected in investment and development priorities.

What is Open Heritage?

By Heike Oevermann and Hanna Szemző

The term 'open heritage' was conceived within the OpenHeritage project and its meaning is closely tied to processes and debates within the field of heritage studies. The development of *open heritage* as a *conceptual approach* to heritage management occurred incrementally, where the *project's title* was turned into something more meaningful for both theory and practice. The title itself – Organizing (O), Promoting (P), and Enabling (EN) Heritage (HE) Reuse (R) through Inclusion (I), Technology (T), Access (A), Governance (G), and Empowerment (E), which led to the abbreviation OpenHeritage – acknowledged both the growing importance of bottom-up adaptive heritage reuse (AHR) practices for buildings, sites, and communities, but also the difficulties prevalent in dominant approaches to heritage management. The understanding of open heritage here differs greatly from some previous uses, which typically refer to defining and discussing databases, archives, and accessibility of museums; relate to ongoing digitisation debates in the broad cultural heritage field that includes books, documents, objects, monuments, etc.; and also raise the demand for open-source solutions and open access issues.

The current definition of open heritage builds on a new conceptualisation of heritage management, bringing a holistic element to it, relying strongly on the local community, and focusing on the notion of openness. It addresses these issues through a three-fold integration approach, combining: (1) communities/stakeholders, (2) resources, and (3) territorial/regional integration within one concept. In a way, it seeks to reorient heritage to become more productively engaged with today's compelling social, economic, political, and environmental issues, and to be adaptive to inevitable further change. It does so by developing a new theoretical model and innovative practical frameworks for more inclusive and deliberative forms of adaptive heritage reuse. Such open approaches are not yet dominant, but numerous local, community-led, or countercultural projects worldwide already successfully demonstrate alternative trajectories of development in response to both local issues and global challenges. The cases included in this book share such characteristics, and some were also key sites in experimenting with this new concept for heritage management.

The adaptive reuse of built heritage as well as its significance for communities was introduced in the international field of heritage conservation by the Venice Charter (ICOMOS, 1964), although it was not the central statement within the Charter. An important turning point in this regard was the European Faro Convention (Council of Europe, 2005), which brought focus to local communities and defined cultural heritage as: 'a group of resources inherited from the past which people identify, independently of ownership, as a reflection and expression of their constantly evolving values, beliefs, knowledge and traditions. It includes all aspects of the environment resulting from the interaction between people and places through time'. (Art. 2)

Developing the project

The starting point of the OpenHeritage project was thus strongly influenced by the Faro Convention (Council of Europe, 2005), giving weight to the involvement and self-determination of local communities. However, the project also reckoned with the existing shortcomings of heritage management, where mainstream management practices often made the adaptive reuse of cultural heritage sites complex endeavours, leaving many valuable sites unattended, especially those situated in marginal, peri-urban, or rural areas. The reasons behind the difficulties were manifold, but the constraints included institutional and regulatory factors, lack of capacities, inadequate financing, and even challenges caused by trends that support more traditional heritage sites (such as castles and churches) while overlooking others (such as postwar and post-modern architecture). We find much evidence of upcoming (but not yet mainstream) trends within engaged digital campaigns such as #SOSBrutalism or www.moderne-regional.de, which respond to the demolition of numerous young historic buildings.

The need to rethink existing participation patterns and trajectories was also viewed as an important cornerstone in the project's conceptual development. OpenHeritage acknowledged early on that. The spread of participatory practices and citizen involvement in other fields such as urban development has undoubtedly challenged classic notions of conservation, leading to slow-paced change (Waterton & Watson, 2010). In recent years the type of heritage management that is regarded as an exclusive task of governments at the local, regional, national, or inter-/trans- national scales has been questioned. In parallel, the role of the public sphere – as solely equipped to maintain the legacy of physical artefacts and intangible attributes for future generations – has been debated. However, while there has been a radical shift in the level and extent to which stakeholders and communities are involved in heritage management, the resulting processes often represented only a few select perspectives and narratives, and so their efficacy remained questionable (van Knippenberg et al., 2022).

As a result, and building on extensive work in the project's six Cooperative Heritage Labs and 16 Observatory Cases, a new conceptual underpinning of heritage management was forged, using the parallel presence of three separate pillars of: community and stakeholder integration, resource integration, and regional integration. This created a holistic and transversal model for the management of adaptive heritage reuse while also adding a new focus to heritage research. In this sense, the OpenHeritage project differed from recent AHR research and activities that discuss and extend the architectural and planning perspective (Plevoets & Cleempoel, 2019; Wong & Berger, 2021). Rather, the focus is related to discourses on participation, and social and political questions of power and sustainability, leading to the development of the particular concept. Sustainability was crucial to the project, which adopted the straightforward formulation from the 1987 United Nations Brundtland Commission: 'meeting the needs of the present without compromising the ability of future generations to meet their own needs' (Brundtland, 1987).

Conceptualising open heritage

Research was strongly informed by the work of Laurajane Smith (2006), Rodney Harrison (2013), and other scholars who understand heritage not simply as a physical object or something defined exclusively by heritage authorities, but as a complex assemblage of interconnected elements – including buildings, places, objects, knowledge, ideas, and practices – that accompany a heritage object. These elements have symbolic and/or practical importance for local communities and others, and are essential to defining and maintaining the heritage's significance. Thus, without these contextual elements a heritage object is incomplete. Contextual elements might be the natural environment; its classification due to architecture; the various groups involved with a site; knowledge of a site's social history and broader meanings; or others. Consequently, merely conserving the physical elements or appearance of a site is insufficient to secure it for the future as a heritage item, since its significance is limited unless sufficient provisions are made to maintain the entire assemblage (Sadowy et al., 2022). Thus, the roles of local communities, their definitions and relationships with heritage, and their activities in looking after it, are themselves crucial elements of the heritage itself.

Different to Harrison (2010, p. 11), we do not argue that official heritage listing of an object, building, or landscape mostly effects the perception and importance for society, although that may occur; we argue that the communities are crucial. Communities or 'heritage communities' is a blurry concept that requires definition. The term is often used to imply a simplistic dualism between dominant groups versus marginalised people, or authorised discourses versus subaltern voices. The main argument is that identifying, valuing, and using heritage are practices reserved for experts, such as authorities and culturally educated groups – thus marginalising other actors. In consequence, there is a demand for these marginalised actors to be actively included in heritage activities (Waterton & Smith, 2010; Waterton & Watson, 2013). Intensifying the argument, Rodwell (2019) argues that not only authorities but also heritage communities are often dominated by educated elites. Responding to (but not solving) this dilemma, we follow the understanding of Waterton and Smith (2010) that community-building is based on non-consensual actions and process that (re)construct identities and bond together – geographically, virtually, imaginatively. That leads on the one hand to an understanding of heritage as a conflictive issue between diverse groups, including residents, entrepreneurs (including those that are socially motivated), representatives of various institutions, NGOs, and activists, among others. On the other hand, the process of bonding allows all involved parties to be understood as experts – whether in using the heritage, in caretaking activities, or other roles – and eschews the binary scheme in favour of a multi-faceted group as a heritage community, incorporating a plurality of perceptions, approaches, and values of the same heritage. Such an approach still necessitates leadership, but nevertheless allows for a flexible decision-making system. In open heritage the awareness and engagement of groups of people towards heritage is what makes them heritage communities. Going beyond this, open heritage asks whether and how heritage has the emancipatory potential to empower communities that are engaging in bottom-up processes.

Another difference from Smith and Harrison is the integration of governance and policies, and of alternative financing in these processes of planning and adaptation, which highly influence heritage making. We understand these issues as part of the open heritage concept – even more, as factors that enable or hinder collaboration. Furthermore, regional integration – the third pillar of the OpenHeritage project – brings together heritage conservation and urban and regional development planning. This leads to an understanding of heritage and sites as part of planning programmes and strategies for urban transformation and development (Oevermann & Mieg, 2015). The literature on heritage planning includes much discussion of policies and governance (cf. Labadi & Logan, 2016) or on planning principles and processes (cf. Kalman & Létourneau, 2015); however, it does not explicitly analyse how marginalised heritage sites can be valorised in the long term, through communities and for communities. In contrast, our focus on community-driven approaches and projects strengthens to discover endogenous potentials given by people and places in cities and regions, which is important for achieving transformation that is both sustainable and innovative (cf. Mieg, 2012; Vázquez-Barquero, 2002).

The particular role of openness

As a result of all these considerations, we argue for an open definition of what constitutes heritage: not limited to formally designated, listed, or 'landmark' assets but also encompassing disparate buildings, complexes, and spaces that have symbolic or practical significance for local or trans-local heritage communities. This notion of openness became a cornerstone of the project work, influencing all aspects of the research and activities. It supported questioning the dominant narratives, the integration of novel viewpoints, and defining heritage in a more democratic way: seeing heritage not as a static thing but as a process that includes interpreting and presenting the past, but also understanding and influencing the future (Fava et al., 2021; Veldpaus & Szemző, 2021).

We follow the concept of 'heritage from below', as we agree that: 'Heritage is about more than visitors, audience and consumption. (...) It is about people (...)' (Robertson, 2012, p. 1) and their activities and articulations. However, different from Robertson, we do not focus on the notion that heritage is inherited through generations and their known practices; in contrast, many AHR activities are newly generated specifically in response to new challenges that result from the deterioration of heritage assets. Heritage has empowering potential if communities are taken seriously, in the sense that plural values become part of identifying and conserving heritage. This is reflected in familiar concepts such as already named history from below (Robertson, 2012), discussions on power and class (West, 2010), or the framing of a critical industrial culture in the context of local-global relationships of heritage (Meier & Steiner, 2018). Next to AHR practices, activities such as community inventories (Kiepke & Meier, 2019) that collect and document (potential) heritage represent further forms of community engagement and empowerment.

This co-production of heritage knowledge through citizen-, community-, or stakeholder-engagement can lead to new developments, as it can contrast with dominant or authorised positions, differentiate from common assumptions, or simply add knowledge to already established understandings and uses of heritage. Oral history can also inform the historic dimensions of heritage and even substitute lost heritage through citizens' narrations and digital tools. Additionally, different forms of knowledge can be integrated and – despite the challenges of such work – achieve consensus.

The project's Cooperative Heritage Labs served to study some of these complexities, to understand the processes and experiment with solutions. The Rome Collaboratory grappled with a set of economic, spatial, and social challenges while focusing on what heritage can bring to the local communities. The Lab aimed to build an inclusive business model to support the economic and social development of three neighbourhoods (Centocelle, Alessandrino and Torre Spaccata) that – from a cultural, archaeological, and social perspective – form a heritage district. The Lab worked hard to redefine the social position of the area, challenge existing narratives, and create a consensus-based perception about how to relate to being Roman and what it means to have a local/neighbourhood identity in the peripheries of a globally known touristic destination. Public art (Fig. 1) was created through a participatory process and might become a recognised visual remembrance in and of the district.

Fig. 1
Public artwork in Torre Spaccata

Fig. 2
OpenHeritage meeting at
Hof Prädikow

Openness also engages with the economic and social role of cultural heritage, which is seen as an activator and enabler of development by and for the local community, producing benefits in the local context. This requires new heritage management strategies and the application of novel economic models (Mérai et al., 2022). Thus, open heritage starts from the assumption that although abandoned or underused official and potential cultural heritage sites may be perceived by the public and private sectors as posing significant challenges, they also represent major opportunities for community cohesion, social integration, innovative bottom-up economic activities, and employment creation.

Openness also has a very procedural quality, meaning a flexible and open management process, supporting diverse projects that need tailored approaches (in terms of actors, policies, funding, etc.) to deliver their specific objectives. It thus includes an open discussion about such basic questions as what constitutes conservation, who is involved in the process, who can finance it, what types of interventions are allowed and how are they maintained. This aligns with the general view, during recent decades, of AHR projects as a source of experimentation to adequately respond to new challenges. These have included changing conceptions of how communities should be involved, as well as increasing environmental awareness, which have supported policy changes in this area (Lanz & Pendlebury, 2022).

Openness also focuses on the creation of complex – even challenging – partnerships, where participation is not limited, which are not necessarily expert-led, and are inclusive. It recognises that heritage conservation and management efforts are often inefficient and unsustainable without the integrated application of interdisciplinary knowledge, multi-stakeholder cooperation, and community involvement (Morel et al., 2022). Thus, its point of departure is the possibility of empowering the community in the process of redeveloping cultural heritage sites, both locally and on a wider scale, based on the concepts of heritage community and participatory culture. Inclusive governance also means incorporating a coalition of stakeholders into the reuse and maintenance process, the integration of resources, and exploring innovative financial and economic business models. Their collective knowledge can help identify appropriate (often novel) mechanisms for the conservation, reuse, and ongoing maintenance of heritage assets (many of which require unique and sensitive reuse solutions). Partnerships for co-designing and co-managing AHR projects support broader community outreach and contribute to a sense of empowerment, ownership, and belonging. They are foundational for the socially sustainable management of heritage sites and may also foster deeper understanding of the meanings and values locally attributed to heritage. Partnerships also enable the sharing of risks and responsibilities, and can foster greater resonance with the aims and methods of reuse projects among affected communities. Heritage may thereby become a catalyst for socially and economically sustainable development, where greater local input to reuse projects can facilitate closer integration with the local economy and better target local needs. In combination, these factors can contribute to stronger and more resilient outcomes (Mérai et al., 2021).

The OpenHeritage Lab at Hof Prädikow (Fig. 2), has been working towards establishing a co-housing community in a former manorial complex outside Berlin. The site was partially protected but profoundly neglected since the closure of its liquor factory following the dissolution of the former East Germany (GDR: German Democratic Republic). While various uses were envisioned, the site mostly remained unoccupied and slowly declined until *Stiftung trias* purchased the plot and leased it to a self-organised group in search of new housing and lifestyle opportunities in the region. The realisation of this costly reuse project was made possible by a broad support network, including membership in a housing cooperative, close cooperation with various foundations, support from federal ministries, and active dialogue with local villagers and regional authorities.

The work has helped the project association to develop long-lasting connections with local villagers and regional networks such as 'Netzwerk Zukunftsorte' through meetings and workshops, generating not only regional but national and international attention. Importantly, the open heritage concept also acknowledges that affected parties can reside beyond the immediate locality.

The concept of heritage communities in the introduced projects implies fostering attachment and engagement. This is in line with the findings that heritage conservation efforts based on grassroots community engagement are much more likely to endure, as the community is more likely to remain engaged and motivated to participate over the long term (Harrison, 2013; Macdonald, 2013; Perkin, 2010).

Partnerships may also be a source of conflict, for example due to differing stakeholder interests. Resolving such differences requires specifying project-specific expectations, clearly defined roles and responsibilities, and expectations of accountability among all parties. Partnerships require great flexibility and adaptability, and may also require types of training and experience (e.g., in participatory decision-making processes) that are uncommon within the traditional planning and heritage fields (Mérai et al., 2021).

Open heritage also considers AHR projects as presenting opportunities to create commons with regard to community and territory. Experience in the fields of community engagement and heritage acknowledges urban commons as an approach to citizens' self-organising, comprising three key aspects: the common and shared resource; the commoning institutions and rules that regulate the care, management, and use of the resource; and the community of commoners. AHR projects become commons insofar as communities articulate a shared interest and organise around various issues (e.g., the provision and management of affordable housing, public transport infrastructure, health care, education, or promotion for employment and local business opportunities) while simultaneously addressing the needs and concerns of the neighbouring area. Similarly, heritage conservation becomes a common when communities define a heritage object or site of interest, and subsequently appropriate and care for it (Kip & Oevermann, 2022).

AHR projects as commons might have roots in specific management of tangible assets, whereas in other cases it is intangible heritage that forms the basis for commoning processes around places. One such example involves London's first community land trust (CLT), established in the former St Clements psychiatric hospital, in the Mile End area. The CLT provides affordable housing, allowing long-term residents – who would otherwise be priced out – to remain in the area, countering the tendencies of displacement and lack of affordable housing. Similarly, the former church complex of the Convento delle Cappuccinelle, situated in a very dense neighbourhood of Naples' historical centre, which was repurposed and renamed ('Scugnizzo Liberato') and was partly self-restored by the occupants. Working on the commons principle, it now hosts mutual activities (such as language courses, after-school activities, sports, dance, and theatre) and spaces for co-working, and art & craft labs. Naples municipal government, the current owner of the complex, decided to support the occupant group and recognised – through a public resolution – the social value of the activities hosted in the complex, giving the occupants the possibility of remaining and running the structure through self-management.

Finally, openness also means a lack of precise borders, so open heritage is rather a place than a building or a site with exact limits, where conservation interventions or conservation areas end. This goes against and enlarges the understanding of heritage with a territorial dimension (cf. Bandarin & van Oers, 2012), where the surroundings of the individual object, extending to the wide-ranging references of an urban and cultural landscape, were understood as heritage sites.

All in all, in relation to historic cultural and/or urban landscapes, it is already clear that heritage conservation needs heritage management and the management of dynamic processes: 'das Bewahren [ist] nicht statisch und kein Beharren auf einem – logisch unmöglichen – Status Quo (...), sondern das Bemühen, einen dynamischen Prozess mitzusteuern' [Translation: 'Conservation is not static and does not mean insisting on a – logically impossible – status quo, but rather striving to co-manage a dynamic process'] (Meier, 2010, p. 37). Open heritage builds on this understanding of a holistic approach to planning processes, namely to think of heritage conservation and territorial developments in combination.

Framing open heritage

While, so far, there might not be a precise definition of open heritage, general objectives have been identified, where each case brings complex challenges requiring unique collaborations and solutions. The buildings, actors, practices, and policies invoked as part of open heritage processes cannot be neatly delineated across all cases. Indeed, in seeking innovative solutions within a changing world, open heritage requires – as a defining principle – greater flexibility for individual reflection and action than can be offered by a fixed definition; instead, open heritage is dynamic, and sometimes nebulous.

However, this lack of rigidity does not mean that the open heritage approach itself is uncertain or vague. On the contrary, we can clearly state what it represents: a framework for broader understandings of heritage, which leverages inclusive and even commoning processes to co-produce and co-design adaptive (socially, environmentally, and economically), sustainable and relevant AHR outcomes for both heritage places and their communities, including territorial and resource integration. The exact composition and importance of such factors invariably differs between cases and also over time, as present-day reuse solutions may themselves require (re)adaptation to future needs. Therefore, given the need to respond to as-yet unidentified and uncertain futures, so must the scope of the open heritage concept and associated practices broaden to incorporate new locally and globally important considerations.

This requires, firstly, broadening stakeholder constellations, empowering communities, and co-developing innovative solutions (financial, political, legal, etc.) to multiple complex societal and environmental challenges. The various changes (physical, social, cultural, and/or economic) resulting from AHR must be relevant and beneficial for the communities in which they are situated and beyond. In seeking to address the shortcomings often seen in AHR concepts and practices, open heritage differs in its openness to both the more theoretical understandings of what constitutes heritage (and its meanings) and also the practical approaches employed in realising the evolving objectives of AHR.

This also means that AHR should not simply focus on the physical characteristics of a site, but should instead ensure that a repurposed site becomes widely regarded as a place made by people and of the broadest practicable constituencies. Open heritage thereby necessitates the involvement of diverse stakeholder constituencies in defining the meaning/value for them of specific heritage assets, and also their participation in shaping subsequent AHR processes and outcomes. We can state that open heritage seeks to reorient heritage to engage with today's compelling challenges, and to be adaptive to inevitable further change. Such open approaches are not yet dominant, but numerous local, community-led, or countercultural projects worldwide already successfully demonstrate alternative development trajectories in response to both local issues and global challenges (Pendlebury &

Dimension of Openness	May Include
Stakeholder integration	– disparate buildings – sites at city peripheries – neglected / underused sites – difficult / uncomfortable / contested heritage – non-touristic sites – sites with vague territorial / ownership limitations – intangible heritage
Community-driven and people-related heritage activities	– recognition as local / community heritage – heritage from below – community inventories – commoning processes – neighbourhoods – civic organisations – facing class / gender barriers – facing gentrification / touristification
Flexible approaches in management	– use of interdisciplinary knowledge – support of multi-stakeholder cooperation – community-building / integration – co-creation with locals and externals – community self-management – dynamic and responsive – related to sustainable urban / regional development – social entrepreneurship – governance of the commons
Flexible approaches in financing	– inclusive business models – cooperative business models – community land trust – funding by non-profit organisations – municipal ownership – self-restoration – co-working – public-private-people partnerships – financial regulation of the commons

Fig. 3
Dimensions of openness.

Veldpaus, 2022). Beyond formal listing or designation, open heritage cares about building heritage, and responds to climate change and demands for participation by putting people at the centre.

All these terms – AHR, community, resource, and territorial integration – gain extreme relevance in the context of sustainability and climate change. First: regarding the Paris agreement on climate action in 2015/2016, the most important argument is that more maintenance and conservation leads to less tabula rasa planning and reduces CO_2 emissions from the construction sector, as demonstrated by many calculations on circular economies (cf. Hassler & Kohler, 2004). Secondly, understanding built structures as spatial resources means that they can be reactivated and adapted to changing uses and needs. Since the 1990s there has been an ongoing debate – starting with the discussion on industrial remains (Hassler, 1996; Hauser, 2001) – that even abandoned structures and sites are not waste, but a resource. With the slogan of 'Reduce, Reuse, Recycle' (Petzet & Heilmeyer, 2012), inherited built structures and architecture were understood in a broader field as a resource; and, as one example, led to theoretically considering differentiation and diversification in heritage evaluation and practices of 1960s and 1970s buildings, beyond institutionalised processes of heritage authorities (Scheuermann, 2017). In consequence, built environments are partly conserved, spatial identities kept, and energy consumption reduced (Oevermann & Mieg, 2016). However, it seems that the practices of real estate markets, developers, and construction companies, together with corresponding policies, still follow the path of demolition and new construction.

A third argument includes an educational element. Heritage is about the local and traditional knowledge of use, repair, and adaptation. Recently this quite common approach is also incorporated in responses to climate change (Morel et al., 2022). As Giovanni Boccardi, Chief of the UNESCO Emergency Preparedness and Response Unit, states when discussing climate change as one of the greatest challenges facing human civilisation: 'The most significant change that may be required, however, is the redefinition of the purpose of what we call heritage and of its role in society (...) Which of the things we call heritage would contribute to our resilience against the disruptions of the Anthropocene and which, on the contrary, would add to our vulnerability.' (Boccardi, 2015, p. 95). Heritage means historic building techniques from which we can learn to adapt buildings to a warming planet without installing energy-consuming air-conditioning systems, as one example.

Open heritage tries to bring together different sets of knowledge through integrating communities, resources, and territorial aspects.

List of References

Bandarin, F., & van Oers, R. (2012). *The historic urban landscape*. John Wiley & Sons.

Boccardi, G. (2015). From mitigation to adaptation: A new heritage paradigm for the Anthropocene. In M-T. Albert (Ed.), *Perceptions of sustainability in heritage studies* (pp. 87–98). De Gruyter.

Council of Europe. (2005). *Convention on the value of cultural heritage for society* (Faro Convention). https://www.coe.int/en/web/culture-and-heritage/faro-convention

Brundtland, G. H. (Ed.). (1987). *Our common future*. Report of the World Commission on Environment and Development. United Nations / Oxford University Press.

Fava, F. et al. (2021). *Finalized report on European adaptive reuse management practices* (OpenHeritage, Deliverable 3.6). OpenHeritage. https://openheritage.eu/wp-content/uploads/2021/05/Finalized-Report-on-European-Adaptive-Reuse-Management-Practices.pdf

Harrison, R. (2013). *Heritage: Critical approaches*. Routledge.

Harrison, R. (2010). *Understanding the politics of heritage*. Manchester University Press.

Hassler, U. (1996). *Das Denkmal als Altlast? Auf dem Weg in die Reparaturgesellschaft*. International Council on Monuments and Sites.

Hassler, U., & Kohler, N. (2004). *Das Verschwinden der Bauten des Industriezeitalters*. Ernst Wasmuth Verlag.

Hauser, S. (2001). *Metamorphosen des Abfalls. Konzepte für Industrieareale*. Campus Verlag.

ICOMOS. (1964). *International charter for the conservation and restoration of monuments and sites* (The Venice Charter). International Council on Monuments and Sites. https://www.icomos.org/en/participer/179-articles-en-francais/ressources/charters-and-standards/157-the-venice-charter

Kalman, H., & Létourneau, M. (2020). *Heritage planning* (2nd ed). Routledge.

Kiepke, T., & Meier, H.-R. (2019). Documenting modernity. In H. Oevermann & E. Gantner (Eds.), *Securing urban heritage: Agents, access, and securitization* (pp. 98–110). Routledge.

Kip, M., & Oevermann, H. (2022). Neighbourhood revitalisation and heritage conservation through adaptive reuse: Assessing instruments for commoning. *The Historic Environment: Policy & Practice*, 13(2).

Labadi, S., & Logan, W. (2016). *Urban heritage, development and sustainability*. Routledge.

Lanz, F., & Pendlebury, J. (2022) Adaptive reuse: A critical review. *The Journal of Architecture*, 27(2–3), 441–462. https://doi.org/10.1080/13602365.2022.2105381

Macdonald, S. (2013). Memorylands: Heritage and Identity in Europe Today. Routledge.

Meier, H-R. (2010). Abgrenzungen I. Städtebauliche Denkmalpflege und Kulturlandschaftspflege. In B. Franz & A. Hubel (Hrsg.), *Historische Kulturlandschaft und Denkmalpflege. Definition, Abgrenzung, Bewertung, Elemente, Umgang (= Veröffentlichung des Arbeitskreises Theorie und Lehre der Denkmalpflege e.V, Bd. 19)* (pp. 30–40). Holzminden.

Meier, H.-R., & Steiner, M. (2018). Monument-patrimony-heritage. In S. Bogner, B. Franz, H.-R. Meier, & M. Steiner (Eds.), *Monument-patrimony-heritage. Industrial heritage and the horizons of terminology* (pp. 16–37). Holzminden.

Mérai, D., Miah, J., Nasya, B., & Szemző, H. (2021) *Collaborative heritage reuse: Enabling strong partnerships* (Policy Brief #02). OpenHeritage. https://openheritage.eu/wp-content/uploads/2021/03/Policy-Brief-2.pdf

Mérai, D., Veldpaus, L., Pendlebury, J., & Kip, M. (2022). The governance context for adaptive heritage reuse: A review and typology of fifteen European countries. The Historic Environment: Policy & Practice, 13(4), 526–546. https://doi.org/10.1080/17567505.2022.2153201

Mieg, H. A. (2012). Sustainability and innovation in urban development: Concept and case. *Sustainable Development*, 20(4), 251–263. https://doi.org/10.1002/sd.471

Mieg, H. A. (2022). The responsibility of science: An Introduction. In H. A. Mieg (Ed.), *The responsibility of science* (pp. 1–8). Springer. https://link.springer.com/book/10.1007/978-3-030-91597-1

Morel, H., Megarry, W., Potts, A., Hosagrahar, J., Roberts, D. C., Arikan, Y., Brondizio, E., Cassar, M., Flato, G., Forgesson, S., Jigyasu, R., Masson-Delmote, V., Oumarou Ibrahim, H., Pörtner, H.-O., Sengupta, S., Sherpa, P.-D., & Veillon, R. (2022). *Global research and action agenda on culture, heritage and climate change*. International Council on Monuments and Sites / International Co-sponsored Meeting on Culture, Heritage and Climate Change. https://openarchive.icomos.org/id/eprint/2716/

Oevermann, H., Erek, A., Hein, C., Horan, C., Krasznahorkai, K., Gøtzsche Lange, I. S., Manahasa, E., Martin, M., Menezes, M., Nikšič, M., Polko, P., Szekely, J., Tappert, S., & Tuominen, P. (2022). Heritage requires citizens' knowledge: The COST place-making action and responsible research. In H. A. Mieg (Ed.), *The responsibility of science* (pp. 233–255). Springer. https://link.springer.com/book/10.1007/978-3-030-91597-1

Oevermann, H., & Mieg, H. A. (2015). *Industrial heritage sites in transformation*. Routledge.

OpenHeritage. (2022). *OpenHeritage: The project*. OpenHeritage. https://openheritage.eu/oh-project/.

Pendlebury, J., & Veldpaus, L. (2022). *Adaptive reuse: Definition*. OpenHeritage. https://openheritage.eu/adaptive-reuse/

Perkin, C. (2010). Beyond the rhetoric: Negotiating the politics and realising the potential of community-driven heritage engagement. *International Journal of Heritage Studies, 16*(1–2), 107–122.

Petzet, M., & Heilmeyer, F. (Eds.). (2012). *Reduce, reuse, recycle. Ressource Architektur (architecture as resource)*. German contribution to the 13th International Architecture Exhibition, Venice Biennale. Hatje Cantz.

Plevoets, B., & Van Cleempoel, K. (2019). *Adaptive reuse of the built heritage*. Routledge.

Robertson, I. J.M. (2012). Introduction: Heritage from below. In I. J. M. Robertson (Ed.), *Heritage from below*. Routledge.

Rodwell, D. (2019). Urban heritage, communities, and environmental sustainability. In H. Oevermann & E. Gantner (Eds.), *Securing urban heritage: Agents, access, and securitization*. Routledge.

Sadowy, K., Szemző, H., Brodowicz, D. P., & Czeredys, M. (2022). *Open heritage: Definition*. OpenHeritage. https://openheritage.eu/open-heritage/

Scheuermann, I. (2017). Denkmal, Erinnerungsort, Location oder Was? Zur Bewertung von Bauten der 1960er und 1970er Jahre. In F. Eckardt, H.-R. Meier, I. Scheurmann, & W. Sonne. *Welche Denkmale welcher Moderne? Zum Umgang mit Bauten der 1960er und 1970er Jahre* (pp. 62–81). Jovis.

Smith, L. (2006). *Uses of heritage*. Routledge.

Stilgoe, J., Owen, R., & Macnaghten, P. (2013). Developing a framework of responsible innovation. *Research Policy, 42*(9), 1568–1580.

Vázquez-Barquero, A. (2002). *Endogenous development: Networking, innovation, institutions and cities*. Routledge.

Veldpaus L. & Szemző H. (2021). Heritage as a matter of care, and conservation as caring for the matter. In A. Gabauer, S. Knierbein, N. Cohen, H. Lebuhn, K. Trogal, T. Viderman, & T. Haas (Eds.), *Care and the city. Encounters with urban studies* (pp. 194–203). Routledge.

van Knippenberg, K., Boonstra, B., & Boelens, L. (2022). Communities, heritage and planning: Towards a co-evolutionary heritage approach. *Planning Theory & Practice, 23*(1), 26–42. https://doi.org/10.1080/14649357.2021.1998584

Waterton, E., & Smith, L. (2010). The recognition and misrecognition of community heritage. *International Journal of Heritage Studies*, 16(1–2), 4–15.

Waterton, E., & Watson, S. (2010). Heritage and community engagement. *International Journal of Heritage Studies, 16*(1–2), 1–3. https://doi.org/10.1080/13527250903441655

Waterton, E. & Watson, S. (2013). *Heritage and community engagement: Collaboration or contestation?* Routledge.

West, S. (2010) Heritage and class. In R. Harrison (Ed.), *Understanding the politics of heritage* (pp. 270–303). Manchester University Press.

Wong, L., & Berger, M. (2021). *Interventions and adaptive reuse: A decade of responsible practice*. Birkhäuser.

We are grateful to Dave Morris for reviewing early drafts of this chapter.

Heritage-Making and Planning

By Giovanni Caudo

What is the relationship between planning and the processes of open heritage and adaptive heritage reuse? Can we identify useful references in planning theory? Are there other issues that can be seen as constitutive of planning and, at the same time, consistent with open heritage (OH) practices, even if we consider regulatory and normative issues as crucial? Are there features that can help the formation of new professionals and contribute to defining a coherent posture between planning and OH?

What are the theoretical references, and what contribution can be derived for planning theories, from observing the adaptive reuse practices promoted and the ways in which they unfold? This chapter attempts to answer these questions, with the conviction that the OpenHeritage research findings provide an important incentive to renew planning processes as well as planning theories, and to contribute to the governance of heritage transformation processes in the sense called for by OH, i.e., with the direct participation of communities.

Collaborative planning

A path already described in the literature reframes the urban planning project as a process requiring different skills and attitudes than in the past. The change of epoch mentioned above, and the theorisation of the city as the outcome of continuous and repeated adaptation processes within a complex system, pose important challenges to the planner's action. Thus, it is interesting to find that in planning theory these conditions were already felt in 1997, with an initial systematisation found in Patsy Healey's text, *Collaborative Planning: Shaping Places in Fragmented Societies* (Healey, 1997). Healey's work was, meanwhile, a systematisation of the evolution of how the planner confronted reality and the forces entering the planning arena. The structural plans of the 1960s and the process of negotiated implementation of the 1980s had already greatly affected the concept of the plan, but which nevertheless still referred to a comprehensive (holistic) vision of the city. Planning practices had shown the importance of the forces driving change, which were no longer ascribable to top-down action. It had to be recognised that local actions could not be interpreted within the logic of mere implementations of national policies. Based on these premises, collaborative planning is characterised by certain assumptions, which are summarised below in the words of Healey herself:

'The project that became Collaborative Planning was thus inspired first by the perception of planning as an interactive process. Second, I understood planning as a governance activity occurring in complex and dynamic institutional environments, shaped by wider economic, social and environmental forces that structure, but do not determine, specific interactions. By governance, I meant the processes by which societies, and social groups, manage their collective affairs. There are, of course, many modes in which such governance can occur. Third, my focus was on planning and policy initiatives concerned with maintaining and enhancing the qualities of places and territories. Finally, my project was also motivated by a moral commitment to social justice, especially as realised in the fine grain of daily life experiences in the context of culturally diverse values about local environments and ways of life. This meant a concern not merely with the justness of material outcomes, but also with the processes through which policies about resource allocation and regulation are articulated and implemented. As David Harvey states in *Social Justice and the City*, social justice has a dimension of both outcome and process, a just outcome justly arrived at.' (Healey, 2003, p. 104)

Over time, there have been several critical comments on the model Healey describes: the lack of a clear reference to context, the powers exercised in the arena of the plan, and about lacking a description of society. Such criticism allowed clarification of the contents and principles that inspired Collaborative Planning. Within the communicative theory, the planner's primary function is to listen to people's stories and assist in forging a consensus among differing viewpoints. Rather than providing technocratic leadership, the planner is an experiential learner, at most providing information to participants but primarily being sensitive to points of convergence. Leadership consists not of bringing stakeholders around to a particular planning content but of getting people to agree, and providing assurances that, whatever the position of participants within the social-economic hierarchy, no group's interest will dominate (Fainstein, 2000).

Bruno Latour was one of the first to call for an epochal change, in his text *Politics of Nature* (Latour, 2000), an epoch in which the separation between subjects and objects has been overcome. The scenario has gradually emerged that no longer lives from the separation between things and people, and has also lost its usual order, programmes, and results: the concept of the collective is changing. There is no longer, on one side, the social and political world and, on the other, the world of objects of profitability. What was considered the normal order of things has disappeared. Latour illustrates how the collective is changing as the relationship between nature and society evolves, a model that envisages two separate 'chambers': nature versus society, a split in two. The new collective, as Latour describes it, is based on the extension (inclusion) of the collective to all human and non-human members who inhabit the context.

The adoption of a greater sensitivity to what has been called the participatory revolution, which was immediately followed by that of communication and, finally, community with the affirmation of Community Planning. This development is described and partly anticipated by concepts (Watson & Gibson, 1995) that have developed around postmodern city and space concepts. In this context, it is interesting to recall feminist thinking as it has contributed to changing the planning attitude: understanding that has developed a different way of thinking about space and thus heritage. Elizabeth Grosz writes:

> "Metaphors of spatiality are central to post-structuralist feminist thought. The concept of Chora is part of a concept of space already developed by Derrida, Kristeva and (indirectly) Luce Irigaray. Chora is the Platonic space between being and becoming or the space in which place happens."
> Grosz, 1995, p. 111

This describes a space in which many masculine features are absent, and the feminine characters are present instead, resulting in a reconceptualisation of space and spatiality. It is a return to the origin, to the constitutive character of space, to be in a relationship. The theoretical basis for much of this discussion was developed in the 1960s by the French theorist Henri Lefebvre, who defined space as being constituted by social relations rather than, as had been the case until the 1960s, by its territorial, physical, and demographic characteristics. Under this reading, space ceased to be a container of buildings, population, and production. However, it became a constituent of the relations of production and reproduction, and a contributing source of inequality and – by implication – injustice. Using a definition of the city as constituted by social relations led to a new critical urban scholarship (Zukin, 1980).

The emergence of heritage

The concept of open heritage and explicitly the practices described in the research of the project align with a phase of profound developments that affect both the concept of space and, thus, of heritage and planning. A radical change that has to do with the centrality of relationships. The subjectification of each object affects the planning processes and, at the same time, the interpretation of reality. In this space of change, the environment takes the form of coexistence, of *throwntogetherness*, of all things being together (Massey, 2005), interconnected and therefore in a constant and conflictual process of constituting the social that holds together the human and the non-human. Thus, a new ontology has gradually emerged by which we describe the social context of our practices and actions, an ontology that no longer lives within the boundaries of the human and excludes the rest; now, the 'social' includes everything. The consequence of the 'relational turn' imagines the city as a field of forces that compete and combine; it is the workings of relationships that produce, build, and transform the city today. A combination that puts into play space, the physicality of life, and the symbolism that cannot be ignored in the interweaving of relationships. For Patsy Healey (Salet et al., 2015, p. 253), 'the symbolic-cultural dimension is often underdeveloped in many of today's strategies of city-regional integration, in two ways: either it is absent – and city-regional governance is considered a technocratic exercise, therefore, lacking fundamental legitimacy of a feeling of belonging by the inhabitants – or it is strongly driven by an urban, core-centric vision that symbolically recognises the city region on behalf of the hinterland. Only few cases, among those presented by the OpenHeritage research project, have successfully built on existing cultural perceptions. Among them, the Scugnizzo Liberato (Fig. 1), developed in the City of Naples as part of the network of commons, draws on the idea of redemption of the city's most vulnerable residents, and particularly those who inhabited the old convent.* In this respect, the title of the project, which literally means 'released scugnizzo', is self-explanatory. In use from the 19th century, the term *scugnizzo* refers to a smart street-child who is used to scraping a living by not entirely honest means, representing a condition that remains very common in Naples' working-class districts. In naming the project Scugnizzo Liberato, the community wished to shed light on the potential of heritage regeneration to reverberate in larger contexts, significantly impacting on the lives of local people.

The challenge of conceptualising urban agglomerations in spatial terms has inspired the imaginations of generations of planners, urbanists, and utopian dreamers. However, it is quite a different challenge to generate conceptions and vocabularies that relate to the dynamics of a specific urban complex and reso-

Fig. 1
Scugnizzo Liberato, Naples

nate with what matters to those inhabiting and moving through and around an urban area (Salet et al., 2015). All too often, generalised and abstract planning imaginaries have been imposed on an emerging urban agglomeration, justifying regulatory regimes (e.g., green belt designations) or investment programmes (e.g., for new settlements) that may bear little relation to emerging urban dynamics and, as the planning history literature teaches, may have serious adverse consequences.

Out of this set of interconnections emerges the practice of heritage-making (Khanna, 2016), a set of thoughts and practices that involve not only humans but also non-human sensibilities and capacities, processes of construction and transformation that have their timing and modes of intervention and are no longer confined to the sphere of rationality but include subjective aspects, even psychophysical, and are driven by desires and aspirations that connect subjects into forms of active communities. From the intersection of desires, the power of community, and the transformation of what exists, heritage emerges, and the processes of adaptive reuse take place within it.

The '*cum*': Heritage-making and adaptive reuse

Heritage-making is a product of urban transformation. Heritage is a 'construction' and reveals the relationships between subjects and space, the built environment, and its use. Consequently, the ideal view of the city – as an oeuvre or an artwork – has lost its importance as proposed by the perspective view. The city is already given and inhabited, and the planner's gaze must deal with interconnected spaces, times, uses, and daily practices.

Heritage-making is a way of shaping the future. Creating heritage is dynamic; it is not just about preserving what already exists, as in urban planning, where limiting land use is a static dimension. It is no longer a linear sequence of scales or dimensions, from the architectural object to the city to the territory. Today, everything is together, the project is interscalar, and the interrelations between physical and phenomenological aspects are its characteristic features.

We register new protagonists in the encounters between objects, subjects, and uses that broaden the meaning of heritage and put the concept of cultural heritage in tension, the latter no longer determined only by institutions, by rules, but by encounters with subjects and their desires. In a projective sense, heritage is not only the set of particular episodes recorded in official histories with didactic and instructive value, but also a presence whose circulation and multi-cultural characteristics are recognised.

In the process of heritage-making, the protagonists are the citizens, the desires of citizens and people; when the 'already built' meets these desires, it becomes an inheritance and opens the possibility of improving our lives, our condition, and the world around us. The place is given in a double sense: towards others and the physical world, including us. It is the suffix with (the Latin *cum*) that gives place meaning. The cum is a collection of things and people, an intrinsic action brought into play by existential factors. Construction (*cum-instructīo*) means to accumulate things, to arrange, to create an order. Place emerges in the interrelation between existences and the 'world of things' that people have in common: urban planners can thus engage in its formulation (Caudo & Pietropaoli, 2021).

Adaptive reuse and planning

The adaptive reuse of heritage, including cultural heritage, activated by local communities, establishes itself as an alternative and increasingly widespread intervention over institutional and top-down processes. The evolved built environment has imposed itself as the current territory of the urban planning discipline, called upon to deal with a territory that is already entirely inhabited and permeated by that heritage that is the legacy of a past that has a different form and duration. A territory full of a world of commonalities that opens before us, a world created by the artifices that man has put into the world to live together.

The world we inhabit is now built, we have filled it with things, and in some cases we have saturated it (Caudo & Pietropaoli, 2021). The new, which we still must build, is hidden in what is already there. In transitioning from *tabula rasa* to *tabula plena*, the discipline (urban planning) faces a profound need for innovation, both conceptually and operationally, starting from the gaze directed at the things that make up our shared world. In this context, local communities are taking action to advance heritage reuse and transformation by adopting innovation practices on several fronts, whether social, financial, territorial, or governmental.

As for the case of ExRotaprint, Berlin, Germany (Fig. 2), Largo Residências, Lisbon, Portugal and LaFábrika detodalavida, Los Santos de Maimona, Spain, the engagement of highly diverse actors – from social foundations to municipalities and international networks – becomes a prerequisite to rearrange not only heritage assets but also territorial portions, affected by very diverse problematics such as gentrification and/or touristification in Berlin and Lisbon, or industrial abandonment in the case of Los Santos de Maimona.

Confronted with such realities, what does the planner do? In the restitution of practices and especially about regional integration and governance processes, forms of collaboration and even co-planning are repeatedly referred to. In this context, we would like to focus on the work of the planner and the theoretical and practical knowledge he or she uses in the heritage reuse processes promoted by local communities.

The prefix co- ('*cum*') seems to assert itself as a mode of working that puts the planner in a particular position within the arena of the actors of transformation and, in any case, in a fruitful relationship with the community and all the other actors who together construct the possibility of the project taking shape and then unfolding all its possibilities. We shift our attention from place to interaction. In that case, the reference to '*cum*' (together with others) becomes necessary precisely because it implies a relationship

Fig. 2
ExRotaprint, Berlin

between '*sem*' (one) and '*multi*' (many) and because it is closely linked to generative intentionality based on the construction and dissemination of fruitful interactions. The interactions determine the planning activities (collaborative planning, co-design, co-planning) and the object of planning, i.e., the web of relationships that each initiative forms with its ecosystem (collaborative city, cooperative city).

Assemblage and the role of planners

How does the role of the planner change in this heritage-making scenario? What place does (s)he occupy? What do planners do? The planner is an active part of a process that moves from rationality as a presupposition to the construction of a 'collective rationality' that creates new intentions and possibilities when old practices and attitudes are abandoned in favour of a new attitude. The urban planner's task is not neutral. It is not a matter of facilitating and seeking compromises but rather of applying, in the arena of decision-making, a technical knowledge based on the

Collaborative Planning	Assemblage	Heritage-Making	Adaptive Reuse Planning	Innovation
Planning as an interactive (revolutionarily) participatory process	Concatenation of spatial, material, and immaterial objects or forces (a configuration)	Interconnected intervention and reconstruction (The new, which we still must build, is hidden in what is already there)	Planning based on engaged local collective rationality	Transformation of a complex constellation (people, things, places...), creating new functions
Healey (1997), Fainstein (2000)	Giardini (2017), Livesey (2010)	Khanna (2016), Caudo & Pietropaoli (2021)	ExRotaprint (Berlin, Germany); Largo Residências (Lisbon, Portugal); LaFábrika detodalavida (Los Santos de Maimona, Spain)	Latour (2000), Dovey (2012)

Fig. 3
Concepts of heritage making

knowledge of territories and the territorial impact of initiatives, on the ability to uncover values and critical aspects, contained in the layers of the existing city and potentially present in actions of reuse and change, and last but not least, to restore within the normative corpus of laws and regulatory instruments that substantial connection with the collective interest that is otherwise depotentiated or circumvented by a purely formalistic application.

The planner's role is inevitably dependent on the description of the city. When the city is seen as a 'complex adaptive assemblage' (Dovey, 2012, p. 5) rather than a product of rational programmatic action, the planner's way of working, their training, and the knowledge they bring to their work inevitably change. The concept of assemblage accompanies the planner's reappropriation of the spatial dimension of the city. It engages with the evidence of a fragmented, broken urban reality, often made of waste. In the action of the planner, the assemblage takes the form of concatenation in the sense that there is a close correlation with the spatial and material dimensions of the territory: 'Assemblage implies the identification of the forces, the dynamics that constitute the space of their unfolding, as, on the other hand, they are only visible from the space they reconstitute. Indeed, the notion gives a materialistic and not only spatial indication, focusing on the processes, imbalances and rebalances through which they are substantiated.' (Giardini, 2017, p. 4).

The planner's operation in terms of assemblage has a precise methodological charge and positions the planner's action in a neo-materialist position: (s)he understands the production of knowledge as an exploration of the force fields, the heterogeneity of processes, and the unforeseen interrelations of the context in which (s)he acts and to whose production (s)he contributes. The result is the disarticulation of the consequential and ordered vertical logic, originally the organisational logic that presided over the planner's actions, in favour of a horizontal action, the 'stitching' of the parts. The rational, orderly, and vertical sequence that refers to the image of the tree is contrasted with multiple contexts – that of the rhizome: with nodes, non-calculable directions, new connections, the concatenation outlines a 'constellation of objects, bodies, expressions, qualities, and territories that are assembled for variable periods to create new functions' and that configure a range of forces as expressed through heterogeneous entities such as behaviours, organisations, spatiality, and ecologies (Livesey, 2010, p. 18).

The considerations on the role of the planner give rise to two reflections on the orientation of the planner's work, which still contains its own specificity and an aura of authority of the planner, which has to do with the reading of reality, its interpretation, and its recovery, no longer analytical but immersed in the perspective of the project. Today, the project is the main instrument of knowledge/interpretation/transformation (all together) of reality.

The planner's work is produced in reconstructing (recognising) the urban force to leverage for transformation. A force with a coalitional character and heterogeneous in terms of the subjects and interests involved. One can understand how the outcomes of the action are open, and do not depend on the combination of the recognised elements but rather on the character of an operativity that can be combinatory and disjunctive, even adaptive. The other operative dimension sees the planner as the operator of this assemblage (concatenation) but also as one of the subjects in a complex and differentiated network (or rather rhizome) that includes immaterial aspects and echoes of facts that are extraneous to the specific context (Fig. 3).

The interpretation of the word adaptive derives from the complexity of the systems, which corresponds to the definition by Dovey: 'Complex adaptive systems theory is an attempt to understand the dynamics of complex systems in which the behaviour of the system depends on unpredictable interactions between the parts.' (Dovey, 2012, p. 18). Thus, it involves iterative and dynamic mutual adaptations with different temporalities, where the single body of factors and elements has been replaced by an articulated complex of parts that are independent but interdependent and therefore individually responsive to external pressures, self-organising but at the same time determining changes in the field of action of the system itself. The reciprocity of influences cannot be (completely) determined *a priori*, and the resulting arrangement cannot be predicted. Each state of change can only be recognised in its outcome at the end and requires a high degree of control during its unfolding. Being bottom-up and/or experimental, all OpenHeritage case studies (including Observatory cases and Heritage Labs) show processual characteristics. When it comes to informal tactics of adaptation though, this becomes particularly evident, since material transformation goes hand in hand with reinforced capacities in terms of collaborations, economies, or even general recognition. Among the examples, the reference is especially to experiences located in Southern and Eastern Europe: the abovementioned Scugnizzo Liberato, Largo Residências, LaFábrika detodalavida, but also the Jewish District (Budapest, Hungary), Halele Carol (Bucharest, Romania), Stará Tržnica (Bratislava, Slovakia). Needless to say, the factor of time is considered not only as a functional element (duration) towards a final configuration but also as a component of unpredictability that fully aligns with the spirit of complex adaptive systems theory.

In the action of assembly, the concept of place, as already mentioned, is about *cum* (Latin) and how place happens precisely in the relationship between people and space. Assemblage is a theory that rethinks place in terms of a complex and adaptive process:

'An assemblage is a whole that is formed from the interconnectivity and flows between constituent parts – a socio-spatial cluster of interconnections between parts wherein the identities and functions of parts and wholes emerge from the flows among them. It is not a systematic set of pre-determined parts that are organised to work in a particular way, yet it is 'a whole of some sort that expresses some identity and claims a territory' (cf. Wise, 2005, 77). The assemblage is at once material and representational and defies any reduction to essence, to textual analysis or to materiality.' (Dovey, 2012, p. 4)

For most citizens, the area they inhabit exists more in the mind as a collection of locales with attributes and ways of getting about. Alternatively, it may be valued as a political and cultural entity with which they associate. However, when some proposal is made to change the character of a specific locale or to disrupt people's ways of getting about, citizens are likely to engage in a vigorous struggle over a development proposal. Furthermore, they may campaign to 'save' a locale from losing once-valued qualities. In such struggles, people may 'call up' a broader conception of the urban complex of which a place is a part. Moreover, it is not only the more affluent who defend locales which are essential to them (Salet et al., 2015).

Reinventing places

The scenario described in the abovementioned case studies shows the relevance of involving stakeholders in the heritage recognition, reuse, and adaptation processes. The theoretical framework of collaborative planning seems to provide a way of acting that has a more systematic character and responds more incisively to the needs of urban transformation processes. Transparency of processes, achieving greater social justice, and combating inequalities are some goals that can be pursued. The risk of pursuing only critical but selective, atomistic transformation practices could be reduced in favour of a comprehensive vision of transformation actions, giving more relevance and diffusion to adaptive reuse practices, to the point that they become a specific modality in urban transformation processes. Discerning by now the importance of understanding the complexity and diversity of the arena in which the urban transformation process takes place, both in the processes of adaptive reuse and in the definition of the theoretical framework of planning, it is necessary to ensure with conviction that this approach does not degenerate into selective analyses of specific episodes and with results limited to single situations.

At the end of this examination, stimulated by the initial questions, a significant encounter leads to a renewed planning practice with existing theoretical frameworks that can still be put into practice. An innovation that also concerns the formation of new personalities as protagonists of urban transformation processes, better able to 'play' the game of complexity, both in recognition of place, of space, and in the role of connector that brings about change. The fallout of the processes of interaction and recognition of power and agency of what constitutes urban power must then ultimately be re-read within the space in which we live and constitute ourselves as a body and thus as a place.

In the practices of adaptive reuse of heritage, the people are at the centre, but how to use resources to protect them; how to create an inclusive and socially cohesive environment? How to manage memories and identity; create innovation (education, arts, and research); create work and prosperity. Reinventing places in the body of the city can happen anywhere. Reinventing can happen by creating the conditions for making places; and this is what awaits the urban planner: a shift from the more material and architectural aspects to those of community involvement, to those of an economic nature, and even the spillover onto the territorial context in the context of planning actions that refer to collaborative planning to have a broader and more integrated action. The description of the city as a complex system in which to act through assembly practices is a description that is at the same time capable of direct reference to operational practices. The operative practices that, as said, include the description of the existing and that are developed horizontally, according to the needs of a process open to the community, find in collaborative planning not only a theoretical reference but a concrete instrument of operativity in the processes that concern heritage and that we can synthesise as heritage-making processes. In this operative perspective and considering that the planner acts in a context characterised by a *tabula plena*, the city is already built, the reference to the adaptive reuse processes of heritage does not appear as one of the actions or one of the operative contexts but rather as the primary reference context of his/her action.

List of References

Caudo, G., & Pietropaoli, M. (2021). *Riabitare il mondo*. Quodlibet.

Dovey, K. (2012). Informal urbanism and complex adaptive assemblage. *International Development Planning Review*, 34 (3) 371–390. https://doi.org/.3828/idpr.2012.23

Fainstein, S. S. (2000). New directions in planning theory. *Urban Affairs Review*. https://doi.org/.1177/107808740003500401

Giardini, F. (2017). Assemblaggio, una mappatura. *Politics. Rivista di Studi Politici, 7*(1), 1–13.

Grosz, E. (1995). *Space, time and perversion*. Routledge.

Healey, P. (1997). *Collaborative planning: Shaping places in fragmented societies*. Macmillan.

Healey, P. (2003). Collaborative planning in perspective. *Planning Theory*, 2(2), 101–123.

Khanna, P. (2016). *Connectography*. Fazi editore.

Latour, B. (2000). *Politiche della natura*. Raffaello Cortina.

Livesey, G. (2010). Assemblage. In A. Parr (Ed.), *The Deleuze dictionary* (pp. 18–19). Edinburgh University Press.

Massey, D. (2005). For space. Sage Publications.

Salet, W., Vermeulen, R., Savini, F., Dembski, S., Thierstein, A., Nears, P., Vink, B., Healey, P., Stein, U., & Schultz, H. (2015). Planning for the new European metropolis: Functions, politics, and symbols / Metropolitan regions: Functional relations between the core and the periphery / Business investment decisions and spatial planning policy / Metropolitan challenges, political responsibilities / Spatial imaginaries, urban dynamics and political community / Capacity-building in the city region: Creating common spaces / Which challenges for today's European metropolitan spaces? *Planning Theory & Practice, 16*(2), 251–275.

Watson, S., & Gibson, K. (1995). *Postmodern cities and spaces*. Blackwell.

Wise, J. M. (2005). Assemblage. In C. J. Stivale (Ed.), *Gilles Deleuze: Key concepts* (pp. 77–87). McGill-Queen's University Press.

Zukin, S. (1980). A decade of the new urban sociology. *Theory and Society, 9*, 575–601.

* For more than 50 years, the convent was used as a juvenile detention centre. This function strongly marked the identity of the place and residents' imaginary. For a full description of the case, see: https://openheritage.eu/wp-content/uploads/2020/01/D2.2_Observatory_Cases_Report.pdf

Adaptive Heritage Reuse: Mapping Policies and Regulations

By Dóra Mérai, Federica Fava, Loes Veldpaus

Adaptive heritage reuse (AHR) has seen a flourishing of interest in the last decade within the European context of this study, both as a practice, and in scholarly work as explored in detail by Lanz and Pendlebury (2022). In the broad sense, the term adaptive reuse suggests a change of use of a building or place, which requires some level of material change, while *adaptive heritage reuse* assumes a recognition of heritage values within the process of reuse (Pendlebury & Veldpaus, n.d.; Pendlebury et al., 2018). These heritage values are often formalised through designation or listing, or emerge from a more local or informal discourse. We consider both as valid, while we also recognise that the policies and regulations discussed in this chapter focus on the former. Therefore, when discussing the 'heritage system', we refer to the formalised governance structures in place for conservation, designation, and protection of heritage.

The recent surge in AHR can be understood within a wider discourse on the usefulness of heritage, and its contributions to urban regeneration. Moreover, supra-national documents, such as the Council of Europe conventions (Council of Europe, 2000, 2005) and UNESCO's Recommendation on the Historic Urban Landscape (HUL) (UNESCO, 2011), have highlighted the potential of heritage as a resource beyond its use and economic benefits, for creating social cohesion and promoting democratic engagement. The increased focus on AHR is also the result of the mainstreaming of heritage by the European Union. While the EU coordinates, supports, and supplements policies and measures around heritage and culture, it does not have legislative powers, since culture and heritage are seen as national matters. Nevertheless, the EU has been rather successful in mainstreaming heritage, through shifting perceptions regarding the societal and economic value of heritage and its role in sustainable development. The EU-led 2018 European Year of Cultural Heritage[1] advanced this discourse, emphasising the role of AHR in supporting a more inclusive, participatory, and high-quality process of urban transformation (Architects' Council of Europe, 2018; Swiss Confederation, 2018). This has also influenced further EU programmes, such as the New European Bauhaus initiative[2] and the European Green Deal[3], slowly shifting the focus from new-build to reuse, including AHR. All these policy and funding programmes are useful in mainstreaming AHR; yet, as heritage is considered a domestic matter for each EU member state, an understanding of how to make AHR easier also lies within the national context. For example, the presence (or lack) of an open and participatory understanding of heritage that facilitates AHR, is largely determined by legislation and policies at the level of individual member states. Moreover, effective integration between the planning and heritage systems was found to be crucial in making AHR less complicated. The OpenHeritage project systematically explored this policy context, and this chapter discusses some of the findings and presents a way to map the national system in order to increase the understanding of how AHR is (or can be) facilitated through the combination and integration of a range of national policy frameworks. Published overviews of national regulatory systems for heritage, conservation, and planning (Dühr et al., 2010; Nadin et al., 2018; Pickard, 2002; Stubbs & Makaš, 2011) have been taken into account, but these do not focus on adaptive heritage reuse nor make the connections – between the heritage and planning systems, or wider policy realms – necessary to understand the governance arrangements that facilitate AHR.

This chapter offers an approach to bring together the policy realms and governance arrangements that facilitate (or impede) AHR at the national level. Our aim is to sketch the governance arrangements; specifically, to identify how these arrangements support particular policies, regulations, mechanisms, or their structural integration; as well as understand potential barriers or obstacles to be tackled. We present some of the findings from mapping out these governance

arrangements in 15 European countries[4] and analysing them across all settings, focusing on how they facilitate AHR. We present this mapping of AHR within institutional frameworks, aimed at enabling a contextual understanding of the conditions in which heritage can be reused, also as an analytical framework to map additional countries.

A conceptual framework to study adaptive heritage reuse

We built on national and regional knowledge from previous research, and discussions in several workshops with researchers from the various countries and disciplines on how to capture similar data in different countries. We developed an analytical framework based on this, which we then finetuned throughout the research process. Eight research groups across Europe undertook country-based analyses, using their networks, language skills, and cultural knowledge to identify and analyse policies and interview key practitioners and stakeholders. The results were presented to be understandable by readers from other countries. We collected, structured, and analysed policies and policy practices per country considered relevant to AHR, which were then analysed as a whole and translated into more narrative country overviews (Veldpaus et al., 2019).

The analytical structure we used is represented in Fig. 2 (for a more detailed template, see Veldpaus et al., 2019). We included national, regional, and local levels, and covered various policy sectors, starting with the (urban) planning and heritage protection frameworks. In addition to a policy analysis of formal documents, such as acts, codes, and policies, mostly on a national level, we specified what the regional and local contexts mean (e.g., province, county, commune), and how regulations and responsibilities are devolved (or centralised). We also related our research to the local setting by examining the policy contexts of the case studies presented elsewhere in this volume. To fully understand the regulatory framework, we aimed to address the entire policy cycle, from formulation to implementation to feedback, including incentives and bottlenecks, as seen by practitioners at various points of the institutional system as well as working in AHR initiatives. We therefore undertook informative interviews with key experts engaged in the (daily) practice of AHR, to further understand the reality on the ground. This gave us access to experience of 'the system', e.g., how do governance levels relate or work together, and identified other relevant policy areas to be examined. It also provided us with a better understanding of the different ways in which national and local experts understand AHR and how they relate it to heritage, visualising aspects that might remain obscured in a textual representation.

As Fig. 2 shows, our focus was on heritage and planning legislation, policy, and regulations on one side, and on financing and funding structures on the other. Governance arrangements showed that these domains provide the formal context for most decisions on whether AHR can happen or not. There are, however, many other legislative, policy, and regulatory realms that are potentially relevant, such as environmental sustainability, culture and the creative sector, and community and civic engagement. Specific policy or funding programmes can also play a significant role in making AHR possible.

Based on the 15 national overviews, we undertook further thematic analysis to consider the institutional, cultural, and semantic factors that facilitate AHR (Veldpaus et al., 2019). A comparative analysis based on the approaches across Europe was also used to generate country-groupings where AHR is (1) common and facilitated, (2) supported and developing, and (3) where it is difficult. (Mérai et al., 2022).

We pay specific attention to differences in language, policy aims, and definitions across countries, and how this influences the ways in which AHR is supported or not. We also address the level of horizontal and vertical policy integration, meaning the integration of heritage and planning policy contexts, and the integration between local, regional, and national levels of governance, which we found to be a structural facilitator for AHR. Finally, we look at how local groups and communities can get involved in (or even lead) AHR projects and how they are supported.

Adaptive heritage reuse: terminology in acts and policies

Adaptive heritage reuse, despite being a common term in discourses on heritage (cf. Lanz & Pendlebury, 2022), is not included in the policy terminology of most countries we analysed. Moreover, the terms 'heritage' and 'adaptive reuse' are ascribed a variety of meanings in the literature, and our analysis demonstrated that this is also true for the institutional contexts of the 15 countries. It is essential to understand the terminology, since diverse terms also imply divergent practices, which can create confusion when trying to learn from each other's systems and approaches.

Some countries employ specific terminology, such as *herbestemming* in Dutch. However, AHR is more commonly referenced through general terminology such as restoration or regeneration. This can make it complex to unpack what are considered AHR projects in the first place, and how they are (and would want to be) supported (or not) by institutional contexts or policy programmes. Terms used to encompass adaptive reuse might include heritage restoration or rehabilitation; however, the term reuse also has several potential meanings, such as (partial) reconstruction, or reusing materials or design features rather than the actual building – which are more contentious and quite far removed from the idea of 'reuse' central to AHR. On the other hand, adaptive reuse can also relate to projects where reuse has been undertaken with little visible or material intervention. Or, in the context of activism, it may happen as temporary reuse, which is a relevant practice that does not necessarily change the building but may showcase its potential, protest against its demolition, and provide a glimpse of alternative futures. AHR as a concept may also relate to areas or archaeological sites, which can, for example, become an element in urban regeneration, recycling terminology, and feature in landscape design (cf. Rome Centocelle, Fig. 1, 3).

Adaptive heritage reuse: supportive policy frameworks

We found that AHR is already widely used as a tool in urban regeneration, solving vacancy, restricting urban sprawl, and connecting with local communities, which immediately implies that a range of policies are involved. However, all this happens very unevenly within and between countries. This influences not only where AHR can happen, but also who can undertake such projects. The research demonstrated that heritage, and its reuse – supported by policy, knowledge, and resources – can be a resource for development, engagement, branding, tourism, local and regional identity, and is becoming more popular as a sustainable means of caring for existing building stock.

The practice of AHR is rarely directly regulated. In most countries, however, it is regulated to some extent between the planning and heritage systems; and is emerging as a tool in (or result of) other policies, funding, and programmes. For example, it is used as a tool in the context of energy efficiency, greening, circularity, reducing carbon and nitrogen emissions, crisis recovery programmes with their focus on reuse to support the construction sector, participation and inclusion, local identity, and localism, stimulating people to get involved, creating places of belonging, and opening multiple perspectives on history (Fig. 3). Tourism, the arts, cultural and creative industries, youth initiatives, and wellbeing agendas were also found to stimulate AHR, as heritage is seen as an attractive setting for such sectors, connecting it to the local identity and historic character. Either way, AHR is a way to achieve policy aims.

The lack of integration between the heritage, as introduced in this chapter, and planning systems emerged as a fundamental barrier to AHR, since

Fig. 1
Archaeological heritage site, Rome Centocelle

changes of use and related material interventions usually require approval from two different departments: those deciding on planning applications, and those deciding on consent to change heritage. While planning decisions are largely devolved to local government, responsibilities for heritage decisions often lie at the regional or national level. It is much more difficult to integrate the systems for heritage and planning when key decisions in each field are made at different tiers of government. This not only impacts direct contact and conversation about cases, but the various government tiers may also differ in their priorities, staffing resources, funding, or political leadership. There is great variation in local decision-making powers concerning material changes to heritage, and the less power there is to decide on this level, the more difficult AHR appears to be. The various obstacles to AHR are thus tied to the rigidity, complexity, and contradictions between or within planning and heritage systems, and their respective authorities. This can refer to overlapping responsibilities and/or plans, and a lack of coordination and cooperation between different levels of government or competent authorities. While none of these problems are specific to adaptive reuse, they are more pronounced in projects that require the collaboration of heritage and planning systems and authorities.

Heritage, protection, and legal frameworks for conservation

Each country operates with its own definition of heritage, either formulated explicitly or implied by a range of legal and policy documents. Most countries have a *national* heritage act, setting out a system of designating, registering, and listing heritage assets at a national or sub-national level. However, some systems can be more complicated, such as in Germany where the definition is constitutionally devolved, with each of the 16 federal states having their own heritage act. In most European countries, formal definitions of heritage address wide groupings such as monuments, sites or areas, landscapes, and archaeology. These are sometimes complemented by more specific categories, such as architectural or military heritage (Hungary), industrial heritage (Romania), and 'work of recent architectural interest' (France). There are often distinct regulatory frameworks for movable versus immovable (or built) heritage, or tangible versus intangible heritage.

Influenced by international documents such as the 2003 UNESCO Convention for the Safeguarding of the Intangible Cultural Heritage, many countries have updated their regulations by including references to intangible heritage. Intangible and tangible heritage are, however, often separated in law, and protection measures are mostly focused on what is considered tangible heritage. Thus, in most legal systems, the idea of heritage as material and tangible objects prevails. Within the built heritage context, explicit references to intangible heritage tend to be limited to (traditional) uses or practices, and addressed through considering 'proper' uses, or making connections with traditional construction skills and practices.

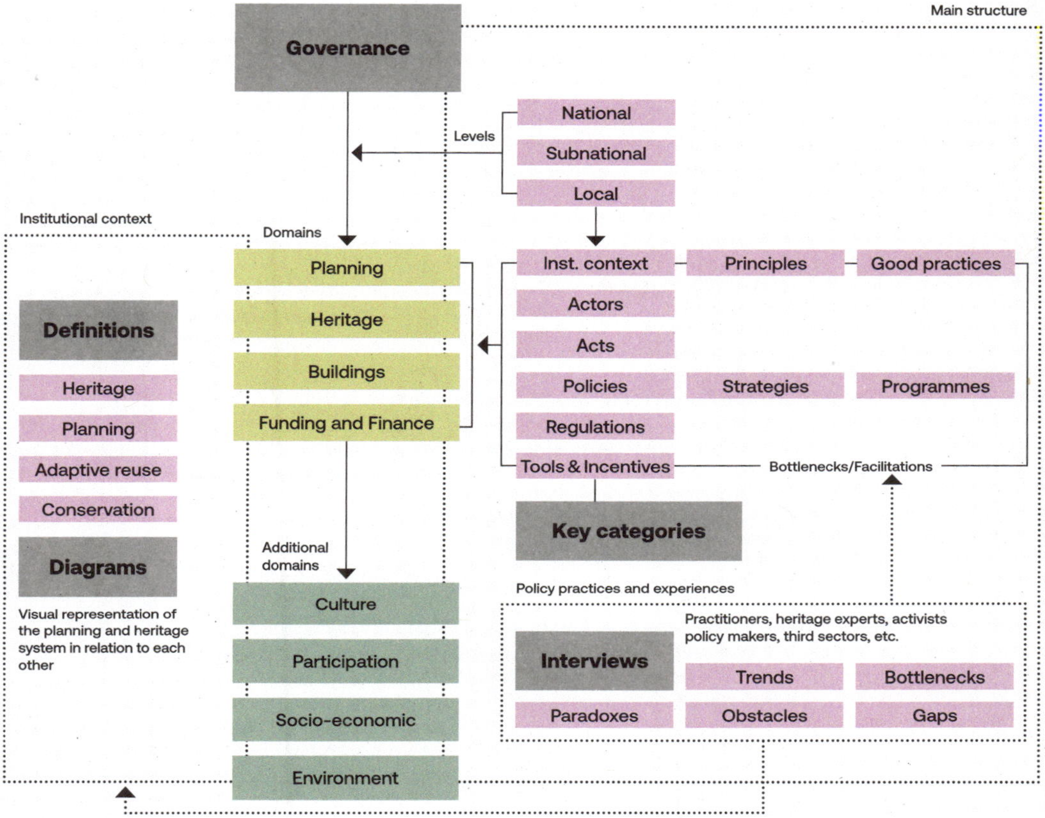

Fig. 2
Mapping governance arrangements by country

Fig. 3
Neighbourhood centre Fusolab, Rome Centocelle

Conservation practices, policy programmes, national or international cultural, heritage and (conservation) planning documents, as well as funding criteria can widen or 'stretch' the understanding of heritage compared with the legal definition. This broader concept can include more elements and aspects of the landscape, the historic environment, cultural practices, or community value through their inclusion in policy and descriptions, or even through funding requirements. In practice, concepts in (conservation) planning policy, such as 'setting' or 'character', can also widen this understanding of heritage beyond the legal definition. Most countries make a distinction between what is seen as heritage, and what is being protected: not all that is seen as heritage is protected (nor protected in an equal manner), but all sites, spaces, and practices with a protected status are defined as heritage. This 'stretching' of what is included in 'heritage' – and, relatedly, what sort of protection is deemed suitable – influences what is considered AHR, and where it can happen, as it slowly shifts perspectives on what is 'acceptable' change.

Protection is thus important. While heritage is protected in every country we looked at, there are different systems. Generally, there is protection for heritage through designation, and in some countries parts of the historic environment can also be protected via the planning system, through area-based protection. Some systems are much more nuanced and flexible than others. Two principal types of regulatory system can be distinguished based on the levels of protection: binary versus graded systems. In a binary approach (e.g., Italy), heritage assets are either protected (1) or not (0). A graded system introduces some nuance, using grades of protection (as in England), or a 'scale' of cultural significance varying from (inter)national to local interest (as in Spain, Portugal, Hungary, Romania, Sweden, the Netherlands, and England). Parts of the historic environment can also be protected through the planning systems, by the creation of conservation areas (England), areas of culture-historical value (Netherlands), or settlement images (Hungary). Graded systems ultimately allow for different levels of flexibility when it comes to change, and leave more space for discretion and negotiation per case, and thus potentially for adaptive reuse. At the same time, the discretion in the protection process might make it easier to dismiss the value of (parts of) cultural assets, as it creates space for more contentious practices, such as (partial) demolition and facadism.

Countries where AHR is difficult tend to have inflexible heritage protection systems, and AHR is easier and more common in countries where heritage protection is flexible (that is not to mean weak). A difference can also be seen in the general way countries define heritage, whether as something to care for or as something to protect from harm. Inflexible heritage legislation, however, may also be the only reason that a heritage asset has survived. A heritage designation can mean legally binding protection; however, it tends to offer only a level of protection, and can also be simply a suggestion or offer very minimal protection; how it is implemented then depends on local planning and heritage officers. Flexibility leaves space for discretion and negotiation, and thus the space for the interventions necessary for adaptive reuse. This discretion can make AHR much easier, but may also block it altogether.

Discretion can be helpful, especially at the local level, but also requires reliance on 'good faith' and support, which is not a given everywhere and not a structural solution. The discretion and flexibility to accommodate local specifics can promote adaptive reuse processes in systems where heritage or planning officers have time for or interest in supporting and exploring alternatives and options. However, it can also lead to blocking or favouring specific groups of people; and may threaten the value of cultural assets, as it also creates space for negative practices such as (partial) demolition and facadism. Discretion does not mean deregulation, and therefore clear guiding criteria are needed. Clear regulatory frameworks de-risk the process of adaptive reuse, making outcomes more predictable, especially as they are often (one-off) bottom-up processes, and since it can be complicated to navigate complex systems.

In a few countries, policies implicitly or explicitly mention that heritage can be 'put to use' for economic gain, and/or better-quality places and lives. Where there is such a preference for 'use' of heritage, as a way of protecting it, AHR is much more likely. In other countries this understanding is less direct, through stimulating heritage tourism, but this is not guaranteed to stimulate AHR. An overall tendency towards capitalising on 'cultural-historical values' is evident in all the countries studied. Following international recommendations such as HUL (UNESCO, 2011) we see a general shift towards understanding heritage as a resource for development, for engagement, and for branding, rather than solely a cultural asset significant in defining national identity and history.

Codes and regulations on adaptive heritage reuse

Building regulations and codes are also crucial in enabling AHR. They are mainly set at national, or even supra-national level, such as Eurocodes, CEN, and ISO, and function in combination with local or regional plans. However, they tend to be written either for new construction or for restoration and conservation purposes, which can make the 'in between' status of AHR complicated, unclear, and high-risk. Some countries have already made efforts to secure better integration; however, this is not a straightforward process – requiring time, money, the sharing of practices, knowledge, experiences, examples, and evaluation of pilot projects. The lack of integration between levels of governance can complicate such integration.

To support the (cultural) shift from a construction-oriented system to one favouring reuse, most countries in our study start by making non-standard solutions possible as an exception, where proposals seek to reuse listed buildings. In effect, this requires those working on projects to present 'in practice and on the ground' solutions. For example, legal requirements on fire safety and energy efficiency may clash with the demands of heritage protection, thereby requiring experts in all fields to collaborate towards creative solutions. Such challenges may be implemented in different ways. In some cases, the legal framework already provides for exceptions (e.g., exempting heritage protection projects from certain energy performance requirements). In other situations, specifically designated 'regeneration areas' may have greater flexibility in dealing with protection and/or other regulations, but these remain predominantly case-by-case scenarios. To enable more fitting solutions, some countries also offer additional grant funding or (low-interest) loans. This requires exceptions, and (temporary) proportional or flexible criteria, which can then lead to further integration or the rewriting of building regulations and codes.

Administrative innovation, by developing alternative models of public procurement and tendering, can also support AHR (Fava, 2022). Similarly to regulatory systems, procurement and tendering processes often presume new construction, and display little understanding of circularity or recycling in their criteria, let alone local identity or memory. Refocusing these, to include sustainability and social criteria, has already been taken up to some extent through the *2022 Action Plan on Public Procurement*. However, this could be extended by revising the European Public Tender Criteria for the construction industry and could be piloted through a New European Bauhaus Lab.

The complexity of the abovementioned administrative aspects has also been found to impede the accessibility and possibilities for AHR, especially for those actors who are interested in AHR for a 'one-off' project, e.g., for their own future use, as stimulated through other policies. For example, social policies may fund organisations to reuse vacant property in particular neighbourhoods, or provide economic stimuli for reuse by SMEs in the cultural and creative industries; however, countering such initiatives, countries have introduced pre-application fees (e.g., England), costly guarantees (e.g., Italy), or tenders based on principles of 'low expenditure' or 'construction efficiency' (e.g., Portugal and Spain). These are counter-productive, especially for innovation and risk-taking actors. Thus, revising the way that public tenders and procurement processes and criteria are set up, as well as which assets and funding are granted, might facilitate a significant step forward in designing a context that is more open and accessible and thus potentially more participative. This concerns not only the initial phase of the process but also the evaluation framework through which projects are assessed and thus supported in the implementation phase.

Participation in adaptive heritage reuse

Since the 2008 financial crisis, more attention has been paid to facilitating community initiatives and participation, if only in an attempt to compensate for the effects of austerity policies in local government. This often goes hand in hand with mechanisms of asset transfer – meaning to sell, lease, or gift unprofitable government-owned heritage assets to local community groups, or to third sector organisations (NGOs) such as heritage trusts. This accelerated the general trend towards democratising heritage, where community engagement became an increasingly important theme in supra-national heritage planning approaches over the past decades (cf. Council of Europe, 2000, 2005; UNESCO, 2011).

Most of the countries we looked at have some projects, funding, and thematic programmes to stimulate engagement within their heritage and planning systems. Genuine participation and clear policy guidance on this, however, remain complicated and limited. In countries where the state and/or expert-oriented approach still prevails, community initiatives are less promoted, and in some cases are actively discouraged through creating bureaucratic structures that make it difficult to formalise and organise.

Where we found community involvement in AHR to be a priority – especially in the form of supporting bottom-up temporary use projects – the support is mostly project-based, and concentrated in the initial phase of the process, namely: awareness raising, providing information, or decision-making. Communities are more often left to their own devices in the subsequent phases of construction (for example by DIY practices), developing management and governance structures, and long-term implementation and maintenance. This significantly weakens the resilience and sustainability of community-based AHR.

Temporal factors are important for both community engagement and adaptive reuse. AHR often starts off as a trial, temporary, or meanwhile use for an old building, which can be difficult if the 'temporary change of use' is not regulated. Enabling temporary uses and temporary changes of use makes community action more feasible. The need to allow for temporary or partial use, and/or temporary changes in the use of heritage buildings is not limited to land-use or use-class regulations. The regulatory framework should also allow the waiving or proportionate application of any levies or taxes placed on this new temporary use(r). Market pressures can be an important factor when granting exceptions and permissions for (temporary) change of use, while bottom-up local initiatives may struggle to receive similar benefits.

Concluding remarks

Policy analysis as part of the OpenHeritage project aimed to understand the wider regulatory environments surrounding AHR proposals. Clarifying these national contexts also means we could explore the potentials and problems for the transferability of certain practices and approaches between countries. The goal was to understand which factors support AHR and which allow projects to successfully navigate systems that are less supportive of AHR. The comparative analysis allowed us to develop a general understanding of what a policy environment that is favourable to AHR looks like. The results served as the basis for policy briefs at local, national, and EU levels, and were also utilised in an analysis of the European (and in particular EU context) to develop a policy road map for Europe (Veldpaus et al., 2023). The conceptual framework employed to identify and explore the policies relevant for AHR in the 15 EU member states can be applied to map the policy context in other countries, while the overview of trends offered in this paper aims to present policy practices for AHR, as well as a context for future analyses.

The wider European comparative analysis demonstrated that governance systems that support AHR are those where the planning and heritage domains are integrated. Besides focusing on the conservation and restoration of heritage by reuse, AHR can explicitly be applied as a 'tool' in wider policy areas, either to deliver policy aims by using AHR, for example to increase sustainability, greening, circularity, or to stimulate AHR through funding the reuse old buildings for social and cultural initiatives as one possibility. Such an integrative approach benefits all domains, but it requires cooperation at the level of institutions and procedures. This must go hand in hand with changing standards and regulatory frameworks (building codes, fiscal, procurement, and tendering regulations) to be more focused on supporting heritage, reuse, and circular economies rather than favouring new construction.

Finally, there is a broad range of other organisations that can play a crucial role in promoting and supporting AHR, such as national heritage knowledge centres, and college and university degree programmes, as well as national professional bodies and accrediting institutes, which define the content of, for example, architecture and planning degrees. This may encompass training days, workshops, specific or additional certification or accreditation, discussion platforms, and other activities that support knowledge building and awareness raising around adaptive reuse, in a context of urban transformation and regeneration.

List of References

Architects' Council of Europe (2018). *Leeuwarden declaration – Adaptive re-use of the built heritage: Preserving and enhancing the values of our built heritage for future generations.* https://www.ace-cae.eu/uploads/tx_jidocumentsview/LEEUWARDEN_STATEMENT_FINAL_EN-NEW.pdf

Council of Europe. (2000). *European landscape convention.* https://www.coe.int/en/web/conventions/full-list?module=treaty-detail&treatynum=176

Council of Europe. (2005). *Convention on the value of cultural heritage for society*. https://rm.coe.int/1680083746

Dühr, S., Colomb, C., & Nadin, V. (2010). *European spatial planning and territorial cooperation*. Routledge. https://doi.org/10.4324/9780203895290

Fava, F. (2022). Commoning adaptive heritage reuse as a driver of social innovation: Naples and the Scugnizzo Liberato case study. *Sustainability, 14*(1), Article 1. https://doi.org/10.3390/su14010191

Lanz, F., & Pendlebury, J. (2022). Adaptive reuse: A critical review. *The Journal of Architecture, 27*(2–3), 441–462. https://doi.org/10.1080/13602365.2022.2105381

Mérai, D., Veldpaus, L., Pendlebury, J., & Kip, M. (2022). The governance context for adaptive heritage reuse: A review and typology of fifteen European countries. *The Historic Environment: Policy & Practice, 13*(4), 526–546. https://doi.org/10.1080/17567505.2022.2153201

Nadin, V. et al, (2018). *COMPASS – Comparative analysis of territorial governance and spatial planning systems in Europe. Applied Research 2016-2018: Final Report*. ESPON & TU Delft. https://www.espon.eu/planning-systems

Pendlebury, J., & Veldpaus, L. (n.d.). *Adaptive reuse*. OpenHeritage. https://openheritage.eu/adaptive-reuse/

Pendlebury, J., Wang, Y.-W., & Law, A. (2017). Re-using 'uncomfortable heritage': The case of the 1933 building, Shanghai. *International Journal of Heritage Studies, 24*(3), 211–229. https://doi.org/10.1080/13527258.2017.1362580

Pickard, R. (2002). A comparative review of policy for the protection of the architectural heritage of Europe. *International Journal of Heritage Studies, 8*(4), 349–363. https://doi.org/10.1080/1352725022000037191e

Stubbs, J. H., & Makaš, E. G. (2011). *Architectural conservation in Europe and the Americas*. Wiley.

Swiss Confederation (2018). *Davos declaration. Towards a high-quality Baukultur for Europe*. https://davosdeclaration2018.ch/davos-declaration-2018/

UNESCO (2011). *Recommendation on the historic urban landscape*. United Nations Educational, Scientific and Cultural Organization. https://whc.unesco.org/en/hul/

Veldpaus, L., Fava, F., & Brodowicz, D. (2019). *Mapping of current heritage re-use policies and regulations in Europe: Complex policy overview of adaptive heritage re-use* (OpenHeritage deliverable 1.2). OpenHeritage. https://openheritage.eu/wp-content/uploads/2020/01/D1.2_Mapping_current_policies_regulations.pdf

Veldpaus, L. Iossifidis M., Mason, A. & Hofman, M. W. (2023). *A roadmap for the EU and Europe: Integrating adaptive heritage reuse in wider EU policies, programmes and practices* (Policy Brief #04). OpenHeritage. https://openheritage.eu/policy-briefs/

1 For more details, see: https://culture.ec.europa.eu/cultural-heritage/eu-policy-for-cultural-heritage/european-year-of-cultural-heritage-2018.

2 See the online platform at: https://new-european-bauhaus.europa.eu.

3 For more details, see: https://commission.europa.eu/strategy-and-policy/priorities-2019-2024/european-green-deal_en.

4 Austria, Belgium, England, France, Germany, Hungary, Italy, Poland, Portugal, Romania, Slovakia, Spain, Sweden, the Netherlands, Ukraine.

Transferability: The 5M Model

By Harald A. Mieg

Open heritage requires a discussion about the transferability of measures and experiences. In a relatively new field like adaptive heritage reuse (AHR), we need to learn from each other to advance ourselves and our projects. AHR measures may be seen as social innovations whose scopes and effectiveness we have yet to explore, but which can serve not only cultural heritage but also sustainable urban development (cf. Mieg, 2022; Mieg & Töpfer, 2013). In concrete terms, we might ask: can the collaborative reuse of a former convent in Naples by small business owners and cultural projects (project Scugnizzo Liberato) be implemented similarly in Budapest or Warsaw? What underlies the successful spread of the ruin bars concept that started in Budapest? And how does this differ from the hype surrounding *LaFábrika detodalavida* (The Factory of a Lifetime, Fig. 1), a participatory cultural space located in an abandoned cement factory in a rural region of western Spain, which is promoted by an architect network as a model for similar projects in Spain?

In planning as in AHR, it is common to use cases from other cities or countries as a guide. However, there is a general problem with case studies: if they are too specific, the case may not appear transferable to broader contexts. Therefore, we often use *models*, which are somewhat abstracted from the cases they represent but can still serve as general examples. One can say that the more specific or important the local context, the less opportunity there is for transferability. Thus, if one focuses solely on the authenticity of a given case, there is no scope for transferability to other settings; or only low transferability, for example, when national differences become important.

What are the preconditions for transferability? We often gain a strong experience of transferability when we meet people with similar professional backgrounds and personally share concrete cases with them. This was also true for OpenHeritage. Beyond personal exchange, there are other means of transfer, such as texts, programmes, tools, and different goals, e.g., informing vs. co-creation. These aspects of transfer are contextualised through the 5M model of transferability.

The 5M model is based on five dimensions:

1 meaning,
2 models,
3 mechanisms,
4 means, and
5 moment.

The 5M model aims to clarify:
What is the purpose of the transfer (meaning), what exactly is being transferred (models), under what conditions (mechanisms), through which channels (means), and when (moment)? This chapter summarises the 5M model. It provides a general approach to the issue of transferability and its role in open heritage and AHR.

Meaning of transfer

What is transfer? Usually, we distinguish transfers according to the effect that we want to achieve, e.g., to inform someone, or enable them to reproduce our achievements. Or does transfer mean to simply export in the sense of selling some kind of technology? Accordingly, we can distinguish at least five objectives and forms of transfer:

Information
The goal of informing is to impart knowledge. Classic information channels include written texts, such as books or brochures, as well as seminars and information events; or news on radio, television, or social media. Recently, special online formats have also been added, such as YouTube videos or webinars. OpenHeritage used all of these formats.

Capacity building
Capacity building goes beyond information. The goal is for others (the transfer recipients) not only to know and understand something, but to be empowered to take action themselves. In OpenHeritage, training events (by Eutropian) provided capacity building for professionals.

Inspiration
Inspiration should not so much impart knowledge, but motivate people to do something. For this, feelings, values, or attractive ideas must be addressed. In OpenHeritage, videos about the AHR cases showed an inspiring effect.

Co-creation
Co-creation means close collaboration, with the goal of creating something together. Co-creation can involve significant other transfers in terms of information, capacity building, or inspiration, but – unlike the transfers mentioned so far – it requires reciprocity. In co-creation, all partners can learn. The work of the Cooperative Heritage Labs was conceived in OpenHeritage as a means of fostering co-creation among academia and the community linked to a particular heritage site.

Implementation
Implementation is meant here as a counterpart to co-creation. In implementation, a particular approach that is successful in one place is also adopted elsewhere. Implementation can also be understood as export. Largo Residências, one of the OpenHeritage case studies, had to relocate to another property in Lisbon, where they re-implemented their business and AHR model.

These forms of transfer can be reminiscent of Arnstein's (1969) ladder of participation, which distinguishes different levels of citizen participation in planning, ranging from passive recipients of information to citizen control. Arnstein was concerned with participation in the exercising of power. In that context, transfer in the form of export could be seen as non-participation and manipulation. However, the above classification should first be seen independently of power issues. For example, in the Largo Residências project, transfer in the form of re-implementation is an expression of self-determination rather than of powerlessness.

Models of transfer

Models have a medium degree of abstractness. In the context of OpenHeritage, models represent typical combinations of good practices and policies for AHR. Therefore, models are sufficiently abstract to be applied to different settings. At the same time, they can be represented by concrete examples and are thus sufficiently specific to be of practical use. This is well illustrated by ownership models, which play a major role in open heritage. Cooperatives are one such AHR ownership model. Cooperatives may be represented abstractly, for example by their characteristic values, legal structures, and organisational concepts, but can also be made tangible through practical examples from different countries.

Fig. 1
LaFábrika detodalavida, (LFDTV), Los Santos de Maimona

In the context of OpenHeritage, we can distinguish three types of model: first, *thematic models*, those concerning issues such as the ownership of a property; second, *models of good practices*, e.g., successful strategies for initiating AHR and making it heard in the city, or forms of inclusive urban policy that enable the embedding of AHR projects in the urban community; and third, *model cases*, i.e., specific projects or cities that can be considered as role models for AHR, such as Stará Tržnica, the old market hall in Bratislava. Fig. 2 and 3 show the OpenHeritage models sorted by two factors: first, ownership models; second, general strategies or specific cases as models. The large number of different ownership models demonstrates the great importance of ownership issues for AHR.

Mechanisms of transfer

Part of OpenHeritage's mission was to identify 'mechanisms that promote the transferability of good practices and policies, but also those that hinder it'. The impact of political mechanisms is obvious, for example in the political value given to historic preservation and cultural heritage, including that heritage that is uncomfortable or difficult for political or historical reasons, whether funding is made available for it, or a legal framework has been established, etc. Such mechanisms can also be found in communication at the local level, as the success of a planning project may depend on how local stakeholders feel about it and whether they can be involved. In OpenHeritage, we identified five mechanisms:

Ownership Models

CLT: Community Land Trust	Cooperative	NPO: Non-profit Organisation	Private	Regulation of the Commons	Municipal Ownership
A CLT is a model of community-led development, where local non-profit organisations hold land, and develop and manage homes and other assets important to their communities (e.g., London CLT)	A cooperative is democratically owned by its members; it is autonomous and self-organised. Cooperatives have existed in Europe since the Middle Ages	In this model, a non-profit organisation acquires a property and leases it on condition that its subsequent functions are not merely profit-driven (e.g., Stiftung trias, www.stiftung-trias.de)	In this model, a private investor with a social agenda provides a property that they already own or have acquired (e.g., Jam Factory, Lviv)	In Italy, the ownership model of the commons is based on constitutionally granted access to 'common goods' for 'civic use' (Art. 43 of the Italian Constitution; cf. URBACT, 2018)	Municipal ownership can be an element of a city's strategic land use planning. The actual site management can vary greatly depending on the property, context, and stakeholders (e.g., Praga Lab)

Fig. 2
Models of adaptive heritage reuse: ownership models

Strategies and Cases

Heritage Strategies	Governance of Inclusion	Flexibility	AHR Tactics	Cases as Models	Disintegrated Models
Obtain formal heritage status Preservation by using Raise awareness Connect heritage with people Align with socio-economic values Amplify the heritage links 'Mainstream' heritage Explore multiple layers and voices Different understandings of heritage	Setting up an open, participatory process Designing space to be accessible Ensuring affordable housing Empowering marginalised groups Strategies of sharing power Politics and policies to support inclusive processes	Flexibility in AHR increases gradually with: Adaptability Diversification The creation of ecosystems (Szemző et al., 2022)	1 Problematisation: e.g., informal meetings 2 Interessement: e.g., capturing local knowledge 3 Enrolment: e.g., structuring the decision-making process 4 Mobilisation of allies: e.g., creating a network of projects	Two sites, two cities: 1 Szimpla Kert, Budapest: the potential of the place! (https://ruinbarsbudapest.com/szimpla-kert-ruin-bar/) 2 Stará Tržnica, Bratislava: you need a business model 3 Naples: regulate commons 4 Lisbon: an active, integrated strategy	Examples: Touristification (e.g., Berger & Pickering, 2018) Gentrification (e.g., De Cesari & Dimova, 2019) Heritagisation (Bessière, 2013) Commodification (Goulding, 2000) Musealisation (e.g., Macdonald, 2013) However, open heritage requires community integration

Fig. 3
Models of adaptive heritage reuse: strategies and cases

Stakeholder Integration stands for the social function. This is about conditions of community-building and communication in a community – in short, the cooperation of local actors.

Governance stands for the political function. This is about political framework conditions. These may be formally regulated within a political system, but may also consist of the informal exercise of power.

Project management refers to the specific organisation and management of a particular AHR project (tasks, time, people, resources ...).

Contract options stand for the range and effectiveness of legal arrangements to contract appropriately for a specific AHR case.

Funding stands for financing and securing resources for an AHR project (cf. Patti & Polyák, 2017).

As OpenHeritage has shown, all five mechanisms matter. If one mechanism becomes too dominant, such as the funding aspect in the case of heritage 'touristification' (cf. Berger & Pickering, 2018) or gentrification (cf. De Cesari & Dimova, 2019), then heritage reuse can lead to a disintegrated model (Fig. 2). To understand the extent to which mechanisms are considered, an AHR traffic light system was proposed. For each type of mechanism, four categories of conditions that affect AHR can be identified:

1. *Sufficient* conditions (success factors): highly recommended to do / to have / to use;
2. *Necessary* conditions: necessary to do / to have / to use;
3. *Knock-out* conditions: to avoid (a hindering factor);
4. Important *constraints*: to take into account.

Figure 4 shows the traffic light system, indicating sufficient (green), necessary (yellow), and knock-out (red) conditions. The exclamation points warn of important constraints.

The mechanisms can overlap or be somewhat mutually dependent. To better identify the five mechanisms, functions were specified such as political or financial ones to which the mechanisms contribute. As an example, consider the mechanism of stakeholder integration. It is listed first in Fig. 4 because open heritage is an approach that understands heritage in relation to a community for which a heritage object has meaning. This mechanism concerns a social function, i.e., it is about how actors (people and organisations) refer to each other in a place. From there, community is defined as a group of actors based on networks of shared interests and often a shared history associated with the place. The four 'social' conditions mentioned are:

Highly recommended (green)

Early involvement of key stakeholders. This is important to gain both information and support for an AHR project and to avoid blocking by key stakeholders at a later stage.

Necessary (yellow)

Community integration/building. An AHR project needs to make a positive connection to its local setting. Sometimes it can be useful to use the AHR project as a catalyst for neighbourhood development or in community-building (cf. Pendlebury et al., 2004). Community-building is a guiding requirement of open heritage.

To avoid (red)

Lack of social trust. Without trust, local collaboration cannot be developed.

Important constraints (to take into account!)

Shared values. Shared values provide a good foundation for motivation and collaboration in planning (cf. Oevermann & Mieg, 2021). Opposing values can have an unfavourable impact on AHR projects.

It is important to note that this list of mechanisms is by no means exhaustive. One obvious additional consideration for heritage is the spatial dimension (Oevermann & Mieg, 2015). How large is the heritage object, where is it located, how is it accessible, etc? For AHR, it makes a big difference whether the heritage is a single building or an entire neighbourhood; whether it is located in an urban or rural context. It is easier to transform a single building than an entire neighbourhood; and easier to define and activate a community for a heritage site in a city than for an archaeological site in the countryside. These are all issues that arise in land use planning and are also familiar to architects, for example. In this sense, a heritage site can have a specific potential of place – as in the case of Budapest's '*ruin bars*'. The mechanism of spatial dynamics would suggest, for example, that the path-dependency of development in a place should be taken into account: there is always a local history that is reflected in the spatial conditions and is not easily changed.

Means of transfer

We can distinguish three forms in which knowledge can be embodied and thus transmitted in our societies (cf. Abbott, 1991). First, people, who may be experts or else persons with relevant knowledge, e.g., about urban history. Second, tools or goods, which can include texts, guidelines, tools, or computer programs. Third, organisations such as companies or organised networks (cf. UNESCO or ICLEI). To give a simple example: if we want to eat something, we can ask a person with appropriate expertise to prepare something, this is knowledge through people; alternatively, we may prepare something ourselves, by consulting a cookbook or online tutorials, this is knowledge through tools; thirdly, we could go to a restaurant or fast food outlet: here, no one needs culinary knowledge, but through appropriate process organisation we get a meal, this is knowledge through organisation.

OpenHeritage was a research network and also embedded in a network of heritage projects in Europe including URBACT, CLIC, Interreg, ICLEI, and others. This involves exchange and transfers in all the above-mentioned ways: firstly, personally; secondly, via materials that are produced; and thirdly, via organisations that endure beyond individual projects, such

Mechanism	Function		Conditions
Stakeholder Integration	Social	🟢	early engagement of key stakeholders
		🟡	community integration/building
		🔴	lack of social trust
		❗	shared values
Governance	Political	🟢	support by local authorities
		🟡	multi-level governance
		🔴	lack of transparency
		❗	power relations
Project Management	Managerial	🟢	(social) entrepreneurship
		🟡	team building & timing
		🔴	incompetence
		❗	intermediaries, potential of the place
Contract Options	Legal	🟢	long-term contract security
		🟡	ownership / partnership model
		🔴	insufficient legal system
		❗	contract options may limit funding options
Funding	Financial	🟢	business model
		🟡	sustainable funding
		🔴	corruption
		❗	non-financial resources (resource integration)

Fig. 4
Mechanisms, functions, and mechanism-specific conditions

Legend
- 🟢 highly recommended to do / to have / to use
- 🟡 necessary to do / to have / to use
- 🔴 to avoid (hindering mechanism)
- ❗ important constraint (to take into account)

as ICLEI or Eutropian GmbH, but also the universities involved such as Roma Tre University.

If we take into account that transfer has different meanings and can involve different means, then we could examine, for a specific target audience: what means are useful for transferring AHR-relevant results from OpenHeritage, and for what purpose, in other words what is the meaning of transfer? Example means may include videos presenting OpenHeritage Observatory Cases or training offered by Eutropian, Vienna. The videos, which are means of transfer, can serve as inspiration (meaning of transfer) for civil society organisations (target audience) in other cities. The training offered by Eutropian (means of transfer) served as capacity building (meaning of transfer) for future AHR professionals (target audience). Thus, the appropriate means of transfer depends not only on the target audience but also on the meaning of the transfer (Mieg, 2023).

Moment of transfer

Time is an important factor in planning and therefore also for the transfer and transferability of AHR. Planning looks to the future, aiming to achieve an optimal (or improved, at least) state. The prospects for successful transfer can change over time in response to shifting legal, political, or financial conditions.

We should distinguish at least two conceptions of time, namely *chronos* and *kairos*, both of which are relevant to AHR projects and transfer (cf. Jaques, 1982; Mieg, 2005). *Chronos* means a specific time as measured by a clock, whereas *kairos* means an appropriate time or occasion. The distinction can be grasped if we ask when a meeting should begin. Going by chronos, we should start at the exact scheduled time, whereas according to kairos the meeting would start when everyone is present. Project planning follows – at least in the framework – the chronos logic, often resulting in a sequence of about five phases:

1. Initiation
2. Planning, preparation
3. Implementation, execution
4. Maintaining: monitoring, controlling
5. Concluding and follow-up

As a rule, work is synchronised and coordinated chronologically over time. But when it comes to skilful communication – especially in political contexts – then kairos, i.e., the good opportunity, plays a much more important role. The so-called AHR tactics provide a good example of how kairos can be used for the purpose of AHR (Mieg, 2023).

In planning, a third aspect is important: momentum. *Momentum* refers to what state or phase a project or system such as a team, a district, or a city is in. It concerns issues such as maturity, which can make it necessary to take a next challenging step – otherwise, the motivation of those involved will be lost or development will not move forward. For the OpenHeritage Cooperative Heritage Labs, three phases were distinguished, termed: 'enthusiastic beginners', 'committed intermediates', and 'experienced professionals'. This categorisation refers to different levels of maturity and professionalisation of the Labs, which determine different next steps in an AHR project. At various phases, the 'enthusiastic beginners' can benefit from project management support, and the 'committed intermediates' can consider hiring staff, whereas it may be useful for the 'experienced professionals' to examine new funding models.

Conclusion

The OpenHeritage project has provided numerous insights into the transferability of AHR measures. The 5M model developed on this basis is primarily aimed at professionals who do not shy away from the analytical approach of AHR, acting as facilitators in translating the ideas of a measure into concrete practice and making appropriate recommendations to municipalities or civic organisations.

It is therefore not surprising that one of the main findings, although not necessarily new, is that transferability is greatly enhanced by knowledge exchange among professional European networks. This concerns specific urban development networks such as URBACT or ICLEI, but also exchanges among professionals such as planners or architects (cf. Mieg & Oevermann, 2021). An important means of transfer is through people, new AHR professionals, whether in the context of urban development planning or AHR funding. The following is a brief overview of our key findings on transferability from the perspective of the 5M model.

Means

Transfer through people is of primary importance – most often professionals – as previously described. Reports and other materials are less important, since these must still be interpreted to become transferable.

Meaning

Capacity building becomes a priority. The ability to develop some form of business model proved to be important for AHR projects. OpenHeritage has developed its own guide on this for AHR projects. In the case of 'ruin bars' (Budapest) or Largo Residências (Lisbon), the AHR model is closely linked to a business model anyway. This makes a project economically viable and more easily transferable.

Model

Surprisingly, the type of ownership model seems critical to many things that may or may not be possible in an AHR project. The most important recommendation is to clarify ownership issues in a timely manner. Unresolved ownership or even a change in ownership can make a project impossible or quickly end it.

Mechanisms

The political aspect comes first. The national differences in AHR are enormous (cf. Mérai et al., 2022) and are associated with different legal traditions; consequently, we find, for example, cooperatives in German-speaking countries, whereas Italy employs legal regulation of commons. In particular, it is important for politics to create long-term contractual security. This not only affects the possibility of private investment, but in unfavourable cases can also hinder the functioning of social entrepreneurs. In some countries, such as Poland and Hungary, long-term contractual security is not necessarily in place.

Moment

Targeted project management with clear scheduling helps with the implementation of AHR measures and thus with their transferability.

Transferability is a property of both a model and a target location (Mieg, 2023, p. 72). What matters is whether the five mechanisms mentioned are adequately addressed in a place. From an open heritage perspective, this means specifically whether AHR is associated with some form of community-building. After all, it is the understanding of a community that makes a building or site a heritage asset. And it is only through a community that heritage is preserved. Professionals, as OpenHeritage also shows, can play an important role as facilitators to support an AHR project.

List of References

Abbott, A. (1991). The future of professions: Occupation and expertise in the age of organization. *Research in the Sociology of Organizations, 8*(1), 17–42.

Arnstein, S. R. (1969). A ladder of citizen participation. *Journal of the American Planning Association, 35*(4), 216–224.

Berger, S., & Pickering, P. (2018). Regions of heavy industry and their heritage–between identity politics and 'touristification': Where to next? In C. Wicke, S. Berger & J. Golombek (Eds.), *Industrial heritage and regional identities* (pp. 214–235). Routledge.

Bessière, J. (2013). 'Heritagisation', a challenge for tourism promotion and regional development: An example of food heritage. *Journal of Heritage Tourism, 8*(4), 275–291.

De Cesari, C., & Dimova, R. (2019). Heritage, gentrification, participation: Remaking urban landscapes in the name of culture and historic preservation. *International Journal of Heritage Studies, 25*(9), 863–869.

Goulding, C. (2000) The Commodification of the past, postmodern pastiche, and the search for authentic experiences at contemporary heritage attractions. *European Journal of Marketing, 34*, 835–853. https://doi.org/10.1108/03090560010331298

Jaques, E. (1982). *The form of time*. Crane Russak.

Macdonald, S. (2013). *Memorylands: Heritage and identity in Europe today*. Routledge.

Mérai, D., Veldpaus, L., Pendlebury, J., & Kip, M. (2022). The governance context for adaptive heritage reuse: A review and typology of fifteen European countries. *The Historic Environment: Policy & Practice, 13*(4), 526–546. https://doi.org/10.1080/17567505.2022.2153201

Mieg, H. A. (2005). Die Form der Zeit: Elemente einer Wirtschaftspsychologie der Zeit [The form of time: Elements of an economic psychology of time]. *Wirtschaftspsychologie, 7*(3), 5–21.

Mieg, H. A. (Ed.). (2022). Social innovation in sustainable urban development. *Sustainability* (Special Issue). https://doi.org/10.3390/books978-3-0365-4174-7

Mieg, H. A. (2023). *Transferability matrix* (OpenHeritage Deliverable 3.7, revised version).

Mieg, H. A., & Oevermann, H. (2021). Architects in Europe: Models of professionalization and potential implications for the planning profession. *disP - The Planning Review, 57*(1), 6–17. https://doi.org/10.1080/02513625.2021.1945817

Mieg, H. A., & Töpfer, K. (Eds.). (2013). *Institutional and social innovation for sustainable urban development*. Earthscan.

Oevermann, H., & Mieg, H. A. (Eds.). (2014). *Industrial heritage sites in transformation: Clash of discourses*. Routledge.

Oevermann, H., & Mieg, H. A. (2021). Urban development planning and world cultural heritage: Two perspectives of planning practice dealing with industrial heritage. *Planning Practice & Research* (CPPR), 36(4), 430–441. https://doi.org/10.1080/02697459.2021.1874639

Patti, D., & Polyák, L. (Eds.). (2017). *Funding the cooperative city*. Cooperative City Books.

Pendlebury, J., Townshend, T., & Gilroy, R. (2004). The conservation of English cultural built heritage: A force for social inclusion? *International Journal of Heritage Studies, 10*(1), 11–31.

Szemző, H., Mosquera, J., Polyák, L., & Hayes, L. (2022). Flexibility and adaptation: Creating a strategy for resilience. *Sustainability, 14*, 2688. https://doi.org/10.3390/su14052688

URBACT (2018). *Transferability study. Civic eState: Pooling the urban commons as civic patrimony*. http://www.civicestate.eu/wp-content/uploads/2021/05/Civic_eState_Transferability_Study-1.pdf

Lessons Learned: Sustainability and Social Impact

By Hanna Szemző, Levente Polyák, Daniella Patti, Jorge Mosquera

In the past decades, adaptive heritage reuse has become a widespread phenomenon in Europe and beyond. Recognising the value of heritage buildings, many local, regional, and national authorities created policies to protect these assets and, by prohibiting their demolition, incentivised their respectful renovation and use. Beautifully renovated heritage buildings are converted into lofts, office buildings, and exhibition spaces that connect the past of these spaces with contemporary life and needs. However, many of the venues created through adaptive heritage reuse are not accessible to a broader public: they might be restricted to a selected clientele, able to afford the luxury of living, working, shopping, or visiting exhibitions in converted heritage spaces.

From its conception, the OpenHeritage project has put a strong focus on the notions of accessibility, inclusiveness, and social impact. Instead of admiring architectural marvels, the OpenHeritage partnership determined to explore the dynamics of community-driven heritage reuse, in order to understand the importance of heritage spaces

as key assets for communities. Seen from the perspective of accessibility, inclusiveness, and social impact, heritage buildings carry symbolic value that puts them at the centre of social imagination and the life of local communities. Initiatives that build on this symbolic value often succeed in mobilising local resources – from volunteering to skills and financial support – in order to create activities, structures, or institutions that address local needs and desires. Another shared characteristic of these community-driven initiatives is that – in contrast to profit-oriented, large-scale adaptive heritage reuse projects executed by traditional real estate developers or even public authorities – these initiatives often define their purpose as generating 'profit' for their local users, in the form of community building, care, sociability, and services. The inclusive aspect of community-driven development projects also supports their sustainability and resilience.

OpenHeritage addressed such community-driven adaptive heritage reuse initiatives at various stages, engaging with them both as practices to study (and replicate) but also using them as living labs. Thus, OpenHeritage researchers studied a series of Observatory Cases – good practices considered as pioneering or exemplary in their ways of experimenting with innovative governance, financial, or territorial integration models, as well as with new forms of community engagement and social impact. The consortium also led or supported Cooperative Heritage Labs aiming to achieve more sustainable organisational and business models, as well as a better outreach and a more consolidated social impact.

Researching the social impact of community-driven heritage reuse initiatives required an approach that was sufficiently sensitive to the nuances of social engagement and community involvement. Aiming to develop methods for 'research with a purpose', OpenHeritage partners created a long-lasting dialogue with Observatory Case and Cooperative Heritage Lab operators, offering a counterbalance to the traditional relationships between academia and social initiatives that are often based on models of knowledge-extraction. OpenHeritage also claimed a position in support of the community dimension of adaptive heritage reuse. Identifying themselves as activist researchers, OpenHeritage partners engaged with various advocacy activities at the levels of local municipalities as well as EU institutions.

OpenHeritage intentionally avoided imposing any preconceived notion of social impact on the studied Cases and the supported Labs. The project sought to avoid classic monitoring and evaluation methodologies, instead emphasising local activism, valuing and supporting local processes, and utilising the resulting lessons to develop management and business models reflective of its approach. Thus, researchers invited the protagonists of their examinations to share their concepts of impact and sustainability. The dialogues conducted with these initiatives allowed the OpenHeritage consortium to explore a variety of visions and methods to assess the impacts of initiatives.

The current chapter reflects on the social impact observed and achieved during the project. In the following pages, we examine the connection between social impact and sustainability through the OpenHeritage experience, building on its findings and highlighting various concrete cases. The examples are from selected Observatory Cases and include all the Labs. They emphasise various ways in which social impact can be achieved. The chapter concludes by considering the future – more specifically, investments for social impact – highlighting the opportunities that these could offer for adaptive reuse processes.

Sustainability

While both the academic and policy discourses have increasingly focused on sustainability, this gained additional importance through the crises (and perceptions thereof) experienced since the start of the millennium. As a result, on various levels, public and private sector strategies have increasingly addressed how social, economic, and environmental sustainability can be achieved, with a growing body of literature also examining the role of cultural sustainability (Ottaviani et al., 2023).

To achieve sustainability, partnership-building has become a key issue, as put forward by the United Nations 2030 Agenda for Sustainable Development (2015), which outlines actions 'for people, planet and prosperity'. In this sense, bottom-up adaptive reuse projects that rely on local and trans-local partnerships are key in creating such a sustainable framework at the local level. Adaptive heritage reuse initiatives have become key elements in advancing processes that are crucial to securing sustainability in various fields. They are singularly equipped to redefine and repurpose sites, and recreate public spaces in a cooperative manner. They can also become grounds where contested and emerging territorial identities can be discussed, and where a common understanding for local development can be established. While empowering civil society, these reuse experiments can provide a place to try out novel economic arrangements, to engage more vulnerable population segments in economic activities, and to test inclusive approaches to the distribution of possible roles and responsibilities of various partners, thereby establishing new partnership arrangements (Patti & Polyák, 2017).

The Observatory Cases and Cooperative Heritage Labs have demonstrated various ways in which adaptive heritage reuse can correspond to the UN Sustainable Development Goals (SDGs). All Cases and Labs have contributed to SDG11 (Sustainable Cities and Communities) through the adaptive reuse of vacant buildings, which represents a responsible approach to land and resource use compared with demolition and new construction. The community-led nature of these processes also supported the communities themselves around these adaptive reuse initiatives. Similarly, many initiatives have given important emphasis to transversal concepts such as building multi-stakeholder partnerships (see SDG17: Partnerships for the Goals) and gender equality (see SDG5) through the adaptation of inclusive approaches and/or feminist principles of leadership and governance. Fig. 1 provides an overview of the topics addressed by Cases and Labs and their links to the SDGs.

Social impact in OpenHeritage

The social impact of adaptive reuse projects can be leveraged by local communities that are active in the care and reuse of public assets. Impact evaluation mechanisms can be promoted either by joint action between local communities and public administration, when such a mechanism is part of a broader public policy, or by single communities, supported by a group of expert evaluators, in order to enhance their action and stimulate public response in support of reuse processes.

To maximise local impact, OpenHeritage mobilised various methods and tools built around its three distinctive pillars, namely (as detailed in previous chapters): community/stakeholder integration, regional integration, and resource integration. Community integration meant the creation of a socially inclusive process of adaptive heritage reuse, built on a multi-actor partnership with partners engaged on equal footing. The use of digital space was regarded as a possibility to further enhance this process (Dias & Schulbaum, 2022). In this setting, the concepts of heritage community and local identity were linked with participatory mechanisms and new governance models that take into consideration the concept of commons and other innovations in the field of urban development.

Resource integration focused on creating an inclusive business model, concentrating on the economic empowerment of affected communities, including the marginalised members of the local community (de Roo & Novy-Huy, 2022). Here, the main line of development was the creation of a model that allows community members to profit from the adaptive reuse processes. Finally, regional integration focused on the territorial scope, highlighting the need to incorporate the local adaptive reuse projects into a larger regional framework, in order to support cooperation among various actors working in different fields, sectors, and tiers of government (Szemző et al., 2022).

Topics addressed	Decent Work and Economic Growth	Gender Equality	Good Health and Wellbeing	Partner-ships for the Goals	Quality Education	Reduced Inequalities	Responsi-ble Con-sumption and Pro-duction	Sustainable Cities and Communi-ties
Related to	**SDG8**	**SDG5**	**SDG3**	**SDG17**	**SDG4**	**SDG10**	**SDG12**	**SDG11**
Hof Prädikow Prötzel, Germany		●	●	●			●	●
Praga, Warsaw	●	●		●		●	●	●
Glasshill, Pomáz, Hungary		●		●	●		●	●
High Street, Sunderland UK	●	●		●		●		●
Rome Collaboratory, Centocelle, Torre Spaccata and Alessandrino, Rome	●	●	●	●		●		●
Marquês de Abrantes, Lisbon		●	●	●		●		●
Largo Residências, Lisbon	●	●	●	●	●	●	●	●
LaFábrika detodalavida Los Santos de Maimona, Spain		●		●				●
Cascina Roccafranca, Turin	●	●	●	●	●	●	●	●
Scugnizzo Liberato, Naples	●	●	●	●	●	●		●
London CLT, London		●		●		●		●
ExRotaprint, Berlin	●	●		●	●	●		●
Jam Factory, Lviv		●		●				●
Färgfabriken, Stockholm		●		●	●			●
Stará Tržnica, Bratislava	●	●	●	●	●		●	●

Fig. 1
SDG Topics addressed in Labs and Observatory Cases.

Fig. 2
On the roof of Scugnizzo Liberato

There was no rigid impact assessment system in place in OpenHeritage. However, both Lab and Observatory experiences were translated into a comprehensible narrative, conveying these from the perspective of an activist researcher. The reports were detailed, encompassed a wide range of issues, and could be regarded as detailed qualitative impact assessments.

Learning from the Observatory Cases

The Observatory Cases were explored through site visits, interviews, and surveys, with special focus on their governance and financial models, heritage interpretation, and territorial integration (Fig. 2). Part of the case studies focused on the different ways in which these initiatives conceived and measured their social impacts. There is an important difference in how the studied initiatives approach their impact. Some organisations analyse the demographic components of their visitors and activities, whereas others utilise metrics to assess economic impact or look at newly created services (Polyák et al., 2019).

The impact of Cascina Roccafranca, for instance, as explored in Part 1 of this book, is realised at a variety of levels. The foundation running the venue invests significant energy in better understanding its reception and impact on the territory. Cascina Roccafranca periodically surveys the community's perception of the organisations, and regularly invites members and participants to attend public assemblies in order to evaluate ongoing projects and discuss possible improvements. For example, the project La Cascina si ripensa (The Cascina rethinks itself) called on Cascina's members to evaluate its work over the year. As part of the Rete delle Case del Quartiere, Cascina Roccafranca regularly evaluates its social impact, collecting data on people entering the premises, activities, events, the state of its partner associations, and its economic revenue.

Cascina Roccafranca developed a concise methodology to study the impact of the organisation as well as that of the various initiatives it hosts. Every one or two years, the management publishes a social impact report that quantifies the activities undertaken in the venue. Keeping track of its visitors (50,000 annually) allows the Cascina to better understand their geographical movements (in 2021–22, 51% were from the immediate surroundings of Mirafiori Nord) and demographics (in 2021–22, 20% aged <6 years, 12% aged 7–14, 9% aged 15–30, 44% aged 31–65, and 14% aged >65), enabling programmers to better target their services and events. In its various buildings, Cascina Roccafranca hosts hundreds of activities per year, mainly organised by the foundation running the venue and resident organisations, filling the service gaps for the area's residents.

Another strong element of Cascina Roccafranca's social impact is applied through the social and solidarity economy actors hosted on-site. Cascina Roccafranca regularly works with cooperatives that promote the integration of isolated women, children, disadvantaged youth, and people with disabilities. The flexibility of these organisations enables them to address local residents with specific needs and to reinvest their revenues in employment and local benefits. Another important factor in Cascina Roccafranca is volunteering: in 2021–22, organisations based on-site engaged 127 volunteers who worked more than 17,000 hours, equivalent to 12 full-time employees.

Another Observatory Case, Stará Tržnica in Bratislava, understood its social impact mainly in economic, architectural, and urbanistic terms. Under fully market circumstances, the Old Market Hall Alliance could rent its spaces for €16–20,000 more per month. By keeping its rents lower, the Alliance significantly subsidises tenants whose presence is important for the market or that have a strong social, environmental, or educational dimension. The difference between market versus subsidised rents corresponds to the Alliance's social investment. While the rent-to-investment scheme defined by the agreement with the municipality invests €10,000 per month in the public property, the activities on-site also provide work for around 90–100 people, as another important factor in the organisation's impact. From an urbanistic perspective, the growing number of visitors passing by the building (40,000 per day) has a strong impact on the surrounding area: small businesses have benefited from increasing footfall, and the small investments in public space made the market area more accessible and attractive.

In the case of Largo Residências, impact is measured qualitatively, with a focus on the social relations and services it created. In its ten years of activity in Lisbon's Intendente neighbourhood, Largo developed a presence with a strong social impact, especially in its business model, forms of employment, community engagement, and advocacy.

Understanding the power and threats represented by tourism, Largo has created an economic model that allows monetary streams related to tourism to be channelled into local cultural and social activities, thus reversing the tide of the extractive tourism economy. Based on revenues from its cafeteria and hotel, Largo created stable employment opportunities for some of the most vulnerable individuals in the neighbourhood, some of whom were never previously in formal employment. Until the termination of its contract on Largo Intendente in 2021, Largo Residências employed 15 workers, 30% of whom came from highly vulnerable backgrounds, and 80–90% of whom were from the neighbourhood. This employment policy helped marginalised individuals in consolidating their lives and finding new opportunities once the economic activities that assured their livelihoods were threatened by touristification and gentrification.

Besides employment, Largo also developed a series of services to benefit local residents, ranging from cultural events to social services and legal advocacy. Cultural events giving voice to local residents allowed them to build networks and join forces around the most pressing issues, particularly touristification and gentrification. Aware of the many conflicts emerging in the Intendente neighbourhood, Largo developed a legal assistance service for residents facing eviction, empowering them in their fight against profit-seeking landlords and inactive authorities. With its detailed knowledge of everyday life in inner-Lisbon neighbourhoods, Largo also prepared legal proposals related to housing and to protect older citizens from exploitation and fraud.

Action-taking: Cooperative Heritage Labs

Quite contrary to the Observatory Cases, the six Cooperative Heritage Labs were not only observed, but were places to try out new ideas. To serve this experimentation better, the Labs were chosen to be representative of very different circumstances and contexts. Their individual foci also differed: some worked on large neighbourhoods, others on smaller building complexes or archaeological sites. Although five of the six Labs were already operational when the project started (except for the Lab in Praga, Warsaw, which was established as result of the project), OpenHeritage influenced how they operated on a daily basis, including their most important goals.

While the specific Lab objectives differed, on a general level it was always an important aim to support long-term sustainability and exert a strong local impact by increasing their role as part of the local discourse about identity, heritage, and memory, by enlarging their locally embedded networks and by making community members the real 'owners' of these sites. Nevertheless, what the local community exactly entailed, and who and how was included, also formed part of the challenges tackled during the experimentation (Szemző & Tönkő, 2022).

At all the locations, probably the most significant local impact was that project activities contributed to rediscovering the importance of intangible heritage in the daily lives of many. They also introduced new ideas about what constitutes local heritage and brought forgotten elements of local heritage to the surface. In this respect, the Pomáz Lab changed remarkably during the project. Pomáz, a village outside Budapest, serves as one of the capital's suburbs. It is losing its original architectural structure and facing challenges from a rapidly increasing population. The Lab's work not only contributed to the conceptualisation of local heritage, but also produced a tangible increase in the sense of belonging among locals. As part of its activities, the Lab created a Local Heritage Inventory with the local community, relying on the help of an online platform and a participative methodology. The activities also opened the way for a public discourse on exploring heritage and various means of maximising inclusivity.

The experience in Pomáz demonstrated that community- and stakeholder-integration activities can deliver tangible local impacts, also enhancing sustainability. Here, a new governance model was established, also as a result of the main stakeholder, the Central European University, moving to Vienna. Inviting local and a regional civic organisation as key partners (i.e., the Friends of Pomáz Association and the Community Archaeology Association) allowed the Lab not only to survive but to involve people more; work with local schools and organisations became more structured, including the delivery of concrete pedagogical toolkits.

The Lisbon Lab, which occupied Palácio Marquês de Abrantes (a former aristocratic building, situated today in the vicinity of an industrial area) also benefited from exploring the attachments and memories of local residents. The initial plan for the palace was to establish a mixed-use site, but the lack of affordable housing led to a rearrangement of the goals during the project. Despite this adjustment, the overall aim of the Lab – as an anchor to support a wider and sustainable urban and social development process in the area – was reinforced.

While reaching this decision was far from straightforward, collaborating with a local association and opening a designated office on-site had a strong local impact, allowing people to have a voice and influence the outcome of the renovation. It also significantly changed the access to local heritage. Through this engagement, the City Municipality of Lisbon – the project partner and developer – recognised that residential memories are deeply tied to the building and still play an important role in the lives of many. This was a quintessential realisation, also influencing the approach to planning the refurbishment.

The increasing role of local awareness was also a significant impact of the Rome Collaboratory (which includes the neighbouring districts of Centocelle, Torre Spaccata and Alessandrino). This is a physical and increasingly digital urban Lab that agglomerates territorial actors. Its main goal has been to incubate NGOs, community and neighbourhood enterprises; to find collaborative solutions for the community care of the tangible and intangible heritage of the area; and to create institutions and services that are capable of triggering processes of community-based economic development, using heritage as a tool. The Lab activities also stimulated discussions about individual and collective memories and about building collective identities. Initiatives included guided tours around the district and the Centocelle Park that were developed in partnerships with local associations, where participants could share their own stories. Additionally, a Living Memory Exhibition served as an occasion to co-design a series of murals in the neighbourhood. Another of the main local impacts was increased institutional embeddedness, an important milestone reached by the Lab's adherence to the Faro Convention Network.

In the complex site of the Praga Lab (consisting of the Praga North neighbourhood in Warsaw), the formation of a stakeholder group helped to generate interest in saving and reconceptualising the working-class heritage of the area, and rebranding it. The Lab focused on interpreting the concept of work, on understanding its place in Praga, and understanding modern Praga through work. This helped to place previously abandoned sites on the mental map of residents and policy makers, while the creation of the Made in Praga brand reached out to artists active in the neighbourhood and promoted their work. The Lab's

Fig. 3
Open Heritage event at Hof Prädikow

activities also focused on a former industrial complex that had been vacant for ten years, a former bakery. The ensuing heightened interest fostered discussion about the building and contributed to its listing as a monument. There has also been tangible interest from users with various perspectives, with three potential tenants hoping to rent the site.

Another important local impact of the project was the strengthened regional cooperation. One of the best examples of successful and meaningful regional cooperation comes from the Sunderland Lab, where activities focused on returning three buildings (built in the 1790s, situated now on the edge of Sunderland city centre) to long-term sustainable uses that benefit the neighbours and wider local community. The Lab could build on a strong partnership with Historic England in the framework of its High Street Heritage Action Zones (HAZ) programme. The partnership brought together public entities, trusts, and charities, and resulted in a cooperation programme that set an example for many subsequent initiatives. It helped to create a supportive policy context for the renewal of Sunderland High Street and conservation area, catalysed the wider area and, most importantly, empowered social actors in the long-term engagement and the building of trust with local communities.

Similarly, in the Hof Prädikow Lab (Fig. 3), OpenHeritage supported the project group in establishing connections with villagers and increasing its embeddedness within the wider region. While the overall aim of the Lab was to create a co-housing on the site of an abandoned manor house in Brandenburg, inhabited by people coming overwhelmingly from Berlin, in order to make the project sustainable, it was essential to connect it better to its direct environment. Activities thus aimed at fostering relations between the villagers and the co-housing residents, among others by supporting learning about locals' memories of the site. A new association 'Netzwerk Zukunftsorte' (Future Places Network) was also established, which connects similar initiatives in Brandenburg, working to make such initiatives 'future-proof' and sustainable. Today, Hof Prädikow is highly appreciated by officials and people living in the area alike.

Finally, the local impact of the Labs was also felt through the acceleration of local economic development, by bringing in more funds, amassing various resources (both financial and non-financial) that support the economic empowerment of local communities. While resource integration was a very important priority for all Labs, they managed to pull in grants and financial support to varying extents. In Hof Prädikow this was very successful, since the project group received some targeted state funding (from a federal ministry), which was then combined with public support for rural regeneration and heritage conservation. Additional community initiatives on-site were financed by the Bosch Stiftung (foundation). The complexity of the project required the help of Stiftung trias, which had purchased then leased the site. Finally, for the project to be successful, the co-housing members also put in their money and work, the latter meaning both do-it-yourself activities and working together on different programmes with the villagers.

Investment for social impact

OpenHeritage has made an attempt to explore how sustainability and social impact are approached and analysed within initiatives for adaptive reuse of heritage. These engagements with social impact and sustainability are also representative of the consortium's broader ambition to support the recognition and increase the legitimacy of community-driven adaptive heritage reuse projects as contributors to more resilient neighbourhoods and cities in Europe.

There are, however, many obstacles that prevent community-driven adaptive reuse initiatives from becoming mainstream. Despite the above-mentioned attempts to define their social (and economic) impact, as well as their key role in European cities overcoming the successive economic, refugee, health, and energy crises, these initiatives remain more the exception than the rule in adaptive heritage reuse and in urban regeneration in general.

The reasons for this marginalisation are manifold, and include a non-supportive environment, rigid governance arrangements, actors' lack of skills and time, and – very importantly – lack of funding. While demonstrably more stable and sustainable than many profit-driven property development mechanisms that are highly sensitive to the dynamics of financial markets, community-driven adaptive reuse initiatives rarely have access to financing options. The atypical partnerships they represent, the collective legal forms they use, the peculiar buildings they occupy, or the strong presence of volunteering and other in-kind contributions make many initiatives unattractive to traditional financial institutions. Similarly, while promoting social innovation, inclusion, and sustainability through targeted research and development funding, community-driven adaptive reuse initiatives have been largely ignored in the attribution of larger Structural Funds targeting infrastructure development.

Fortunately, a new generation of ethical finance organisations, such as Stiftung trias and Stiftung Edith Maryon, have financed property regeneration projects that have strong social and environmental impacts, providing various forms of revolving funds that allow the multiplication and upscaling of community-driven adaptive reuse initiatives across Central Europe. If the EU were ready to also apply its innovation criteria to broader development funding, this logic could be taken up by various public investment and development banks, in order to adapt their funding streams to these needs. Heritage buildings are unique assets that allow communities to build identities and find anchors to their activities and social networks. In their uniqueness, heritage buildings need more than standard design, finance, and development solutions. Instead, they need site-specific approaches, mobilising distributed knowledge, and a variety of relationships and knowledge that people can maintain through these spaces.

List of References

Dias, T., & Schulbaum, O. (2022). *Replicable model of heritage points to support the adaptive reuse of heritage assets*. OpenHeritage Deliverable 5.3. https://openheritage.eu/wp-content/uploads/2022/12/Replicable-model-of-Heritage-Points-to-support-the-adaptive-reuse-of-heritage-assets.pdf

de Roo, J., & Novy-Huy, R. (2022). *Inclusive business models: How to build an inclusive business model around your adaptive heritage reuse project?* (OpenHeritage Deliverable 5.6). OpenHeritage. https://openheritage.eu/wp-content/uploads/2022/11/Inclusive-business-models-for-sustainable-heritage-reuse-processes.pdf

Ottaviani, D., Demiröz, M., Szemző, H., & De Luca, C. (2023). Adapting methods and tools for participatory heritage-based tourism planning to embrace the four pillars of sustainability. *Sustainability, 15*(6), 4741. https://doi.org/10.3390/su15064741

Patti, D., & Polyák, L. (Eds.). (2017). *Funding the cooperative city: Community finance and the economy of civic spaces*. Cooperative City Books. https://cooperativecity.org/wp-content/uploads/2017/11/Funding-the-Cooperative-City_Community-Finance-and-the-Economy-of-Civic-Spaces.pdf

Polyák, L., Patti, D., Nasya, B., Fava, F., Cannella, F., Caudo, G., Tönkő, A., Szemző, H., Mérai, D., Kulikov, V., Cwik, A., Schulbaum, O., Nadesan, N., Tomescu, A., Sklokina, I., van Knippenberg, K., & Boonstra, B. (2019). *Individual report on the observatory cases* (OpenHeritage Deliverable 2.2). OpenHeritage. https://openheritage.eu/wp-content/uploads/2020/01/D2.2_Observatory_Cases_Report.pdf

Szemző, H., & Tönkő, A. (2022). *Evaluation of the cooperative heritage labs* (OpenHeritage Deliverable 4.6). OpenHeritage. https://openheritage.eu/wp-content/uploads/2021/07/Updated-Local-Action-Plans-of-the-Cooperative-Heritage-Labs.pdf

Szemző, H., Tönkő, A., Fava, F., & van Gils, H. (2022). *Roadmap to enhance regional cooperation* (OpenHeritage Deliverable D5.7). OpenHeritage. https://openheritage.eu/wp-content/uploads/2023/03/Roadmap-to-enhance-regional-cooperation.pdf

United Nations (2015). *Transforming our world: The 2030 agenda for sustainable development*. UN General Assembly. https://sdgs.un.org/sites/default/files/publications/21252030%20Agenda%20for%20Sustainable%20Development%20web.pdf

Appendix:
About the Authors
Acknowledgements
Illustration Credits

Imprint

About the Authors

Sophie Bod

Sophie Bod is a communication expert with extensive campaigning experience in the arts and non-profit sector. Working with several UK cultural institutions, NGOs, and some of the UK's largest charities, her tasks focused on advocacy, research, digital and offline campaigns to mobilise and engage various target groups, and the development and delivery of key communication messages. Currently, her work focuses on architecture, culture, and non-profit campaigns. She is co-editor of *Cooperative City Magazine*.

Dominika P. Brodowicz

Dominika P. Brodowicz gained her PhD from Dublin Institute of Technology, and is an assistant professor at Warsaw School of Economics. Her areas of specialisation include tangible and intangible urban heritage, green and smart cities, and social responsibility of real estate investors. She has a successful record of grants, including from the US State Department, ZEIT-Stiftung, and the Kościuszko Foundation, and she headed the Cooperative Heritage Lab in the OpenHeritage project (OW SARP, Horizon 2020 programme).

Giovanni Caudo

Giovanni Caudo is a full professor of urban planning at the Architecture Department, Roma Tre University, where he is responsible for the master's degree in Urban Design. His research interests concern the contemporary urban condition studied through living forms, the new housing issue, and the reuse of heritage. He was councillor for urban planning of Rome Capital, and is currently a city councillor and president of the Rome Capital Commission for implementing the National Recovery Plan.

Federica Fava

Federica Fava is an assistant professor, currently at Roma Tre University. Her research focuses mainly on temporary architecture and planning, cultural urban tools, and participation. She has specific experience in applying urban innovation and regeneration practices to heritage and cities (both historical and otherwise).

Andrea Giuliano

Andrea Giuliano is a human rights activist primarily focusing on SOGIESC issues, access to sport, and urban justice. He is a research assistant at Eutropian and project assistant for Erasmus+ projects within the framework of AiCS (Associazione Italiana Cultura Sport)-LGBTI+ Sector.

Lukács Hayes

Lukács Hayes is a researcher and consultant at Eutropian. He holds a bachelor's degree in Sociology and Social Policy from the Corvinus University of Budapest and a master's degree in Political Science from Central European University (Budapest campus). Lukács has experience as a freelance consultant, researcher, and project manager at various public and private organisations, and joined Eutropian in 2021.

Martin Hulse

Martin Hulse is an experienced heritage practitioner working in northeast England. He has operated in the public, private, and third sectors, and his passion is the delivery of urban regeneration using heritage at risk as a catalyst for change. He currently leads the Tyne & Wear Building Preservation Trust.

Volodymyr Kulikov

Volodymyr Kulikov is a historian holding the position of visiting assistant professor at the Department of Slavic and Eurasian Studies at the University of Texas at Austin. His most recent appointment was to the Cultural Heritage Studies Program of Central European University, Vienna. He specialises in the business and economic history of Eastern Europe, with a particular interest in the history of industrial enterprises and monoculture.

Ashley Mason

Ashley Mason is a research associate within the School of Architecture, Planning, and Landscape at Newcastle University, UK. Her research is engaged with paracontextual practice, collective action, and marginalised matters within architecture and urbanism, as well as with continued collaborative work building on the impacts of the Sunderland Cooperative Heritage Lab.

Dóra Mérai

Dóra Mérai is an art historian and archaeologist, and cultural heritage specialist. Formerly affiliated with the Cultural Heritage Studies Program of Central European University, Vienna, she is currently a researcher at the University of Texas at Austin. Her research and publications span the intersection of cultural heritage studies, memory studies, visual and material culture studies, social history, and urban studies.

Harald A. Mieg

Harald A. Mieg serves as honorary professor of Metropolitan Studies at Humboldt-Universität zu Berlin and president of the Berlin Society for the Study of Science. From 2005 to 2010 he established the Georg-Simmel Center for Metropolitan Studies at Humboldt-Universität. He has authored a series of books and articles on professionalisation, urban planning, and higher education and co-authored *Industrial Heritage Sites in Transformation*.

Jorge Mosquera

Jorge Mosquera is an architect and urban researcher based in Vienna. With expertise in urban regeneration and social innovation, he is currently a PhD candidate in planning and public policies at IUAV University of Venice. As a member of the Eutropian team, Jorge is involved in research and dissemination of EU-funded projects related to urban governance and social sustainability. The primary focus of his research is the interplay between community-led initiatives and local governmental bodies concerning policy making and spatial planning.

Heike Oevermann

Heike Oevermann is full professor for Heritage Conservation and Built Heritage Use, including reuse and adaptation, at Vienna University of Technology. She studied Architecture and World Heritage, practised as an architect, and completed her doctorate on the transformation of the Zeche Zollverein World Heritage site (TU Berlin) and her habilitation on adaptive heritage reuse of industrial architecture in European cities (Bauhaus Universität Weimar). She was interim professor at Otto-Friedrich Universität, Bamberg and is guest professor at the Oslo School of Architecture and Design, Norway. Her publications include *Industrial Heritage Sites in Transformation* (2014), *Securing Urban Heritage* (2019), and *Urban Textile Mills: Conservation and Conversion* (2021).

Giovanni Pagano

Giovanni Pagano is a spatial planner and environmental researcher whose research interests mainly revolve around sustainable urban development and the spatial, socio-ecological characteristics of urban foodscapes, such as urban farms, community gardens, and food markets. He actively participates in a range of local, national, and international partnerships, aiming to better understand (and thereby change) the food system. His other interests reside in governance and justice, having conducted studies with social movements and bottom-up initiatives, and more recently analysing the emergence and evolution of urban food strategies. Engagement is also central to his research work, being involved in participatory-action research with civil society organisations and public institutions, and advocating local initiatives.

Daniela Patti

Daniela Patti is an Italian-British architect and urban planner. Her recent project and research work focus on the relationship between cultural heritage and urban governance in relationship to local community development, peri-urban landscape promotion and revitalisation of local food markets by tackling urban poverty and reducing social inequalities. She is co-founder of Eutropian; regularly works with URBACT, the European Urban Initiative, and other international programmes; and has worked for the City of Rome Planning Department. Daniela studied in Rome, London, and Porto, and holds a PhD in urbanism from the Vienna University of Technology.

John Pendlebury

John Pendlebury is professor of Urban Conservation at Newcastle University. He teaches and researches on issues of heritage, conservation, development, planning, and governance. His principal publications include *Conservation in the Age of Consensus* (2009) and the edited collections *Valuing Historic Environments* (2009, with Lisanne Gibson) and *Alternative Visions of Post-War Reconstruction: Creating the Modern Townscape* (2015, with Erdem Erten and Peter Larkham). His most recent book (2021, with Jules Brown) is *Conserving the Historic Environment*.

Levente Polyák

Levente Polyák is an urban planner, researcher, community advocate, and policy adviser. With his organisation Eutropian, he co-edits *Cooperative City Magazine* and helps public administrations and citizen initiatives across Europe create new partnerships, cooperation processes, learning trajectories, and knowledge exchange around themes of spatial development, social inclusion, and environmental sustainability. He is co-author of the books *Funding the Cooperative City* (2017), *Il rilancio dei mercati* (2019), and *The Power of Civic Ecosystems* (2021).

Katarzyna Sadowy

Katarzyna Sadowy is an interdisciplinary researcher in urban studies, working as an academic and practitioner. She graduated from the Faculty of Architecture at Warsaw University of Technology, and Warsaw School of Economics where she is an assistant professor. She is a co-creator of such municipal programmes as 'Warsaw Local Centres Network' (15-minute city). Her main topics of interest encompass urban evolution, the role of work, heritage, and architecture in creating more sustainable and just cities. She led the Polish team in the OpenHeritage project.

Iryna Sklokina

Iryna Sklokina is a historian, PhD (2014), and research associate at the Center for Urban History in Lviv, where her research is focused on Soviet and industrial heritage, museums and memory cultures, and the company towns of Donbas. She participated in several projects focused on cultural heritage and regionalism, including 'OpenHeritage', 'Un/Archiving Post/Industry: Engaging Heritage and Developing Cultural Infrastructures', and 'Region, Nation and Beyond. An Interdisciplinary and Transcultural Reconceptualization of Ukraine'.

Hanna Szemző

Hanna Szemző is a sociologist, and one of the managing directors of Metropolitan Research Institute, a privately owned think tank in Budapest. She has over 20 years' experience in research and consultancy in the fields of urban regeneration, social inclusion, demography, welfare, residential energy efficiency, and governance analysis. Recently, she has been concentrating on issues around adaptive heritage reuse, community engagement, and urban governance. She was one of the coordinators of the OpenHeritage project.

Andrea Tönkő

Andrea Tönkő is an economist, and has more than 20 years of research and consultancy experience in the areas of territorial development, intergovernmental financial relations, and financing public services. She has conducted widespread research on these themes and project-managed several international programmes. She was also one of the coordinators of the OpenHeritage project.

Hanne van Gils

Hanne van Gils studied architecture and urban planning. She gained experience as an architect, working on the scale of both the building and the city. The communications agency DIFT was an introduction to terms such as USPs, automation, and customer journeys. At Endeavour, she often works on heritage reuse projects, diverse research projects, neighbourhood development plans, and space for youth. In addition to her work as a researcher, she also enjoys creating light-hearted illustrations. The OpenHeritage project brought together her experience with city making, regional development, architecture, and civic initiatives.

Loes Veldpaus

Loes Veldpaus is based at Newcastle University (UK), where she is a senior lecturer in architecture and urban planning and co-director of the Centre for Heritage. She has a background in architecture, urban planning, and heritage studies, and researches and teaches across and between those areas, with a focus on what (re)making and (re)using heritage, both materially and conceptually, means and does in the wider processes of urban governance.

Acknowledgements

This book started on a sunny afternoon in Ghent, in late May, 2022. Then only an idea, it was completed in less than a year. The help of many people and institutions has been indispensable in achieving this.

For the OpenHeritage project, the European Union provided funding through its Horizon 2020 research and innovation programme under grant agreement No. 776766. This not only made research possible, but enabled the collaboration across 11 countries and 16 partners. We would like to thank the European Research Executive Agency for its support in this complicated yet nurturing process. We are especially indebted to Ugo Guarnacci, who was the main project officer during this period, supporting the project as it developed and showing a great deal of flexibility when we faced difficulties. We would also like to thank Emanuela de Menna, who took on the responsibility of guiding OpenHeritage through its final months.

The diversity of the consortium was key to the success of OpenHeritage. The multi-disciplinary background allowed us to see problems from different perspectives and to arrive at novel concepts and solutions. Although the current volume does not include contributions from every consortium member, their work and knowledge have been instrumental in realising this book. Thus, we would like to thank Joep de Roo, Rolf Novy-Huy, Christian Darr, Christian Iaione, Elena de Nictolis, Maria Cristina Pangallozzi, Alessandro Piperno, József Laszlovszky, Maciej Czeredys, Natalia Daca, Alina Tomescu, Sofia Dyak, Taras Nazaruk, Monica Alfredo, Celina Adriano, Rui Neves, Miguel Brito, Miranda Iossifidis, Karim van Knippenberg, Luuk Boelens, Olga Krajewska, Cristina Garzillo, Bahanur Nasya, Yilmaz Vurucu, Olivier Schulbaum, Tayrine Dias, Nadia Nadesan, Julia and Mathieu Baudier, and Iván Tosics for the great discussions, the results achieved, and the questions asked. Some changed positions during the project but, nevertheless, helped us significantly. We are grateful for the opportunity to have collaborated with Beitske Boonstra, Markus Kip, Jasmin Miah, Ania Rok, Ivan Vergés and Stephania Xydia.

Dave Morris was our proofreader and supported us in enhancing our texts. Johannes Paintner was responsible for drawing the case study maps (using data extracted from OpenStreetMap.org) and helped to select and manage images; Nina Armberger assisted with image post-production and communication on copyright issues.

We would like to thank all authors and institutions for contributing, as well as our team. Finally, we thank Birkhäuser Verlag, and especially Baharak Tajbakhsh, for their ideas and professional assistance in realising this publication.

Illustration Credits

Introduction
1, 2 Eutropian (cc)
3 Eutropian (cc)

Enabling Collaboration: Policies and Governance
1 van Gils
2, 3 Eutropian (cc)

Cascina Roccafranca, Turin, Italy
1 Editors, Map data from OpenStreetMap. openstreetmap.org/copyright (2023)
2 Cascina Roccafranca
3, 4, 5 Eutropian (cc)

High Street, Sunderland, UK
1 Editors, Map data from OpenStreetMap. openstreetmap.org/copyright (2023)
2, 3, 4, 5 Veldpaus

London CLT, UK
1 Editors, Map data from OpenStreetMap. openstreetmap.org/copyright (2023)
2, 3, 4, 5 Eutropian (cc)

Enabling Collaboration: Financing Projects
1 van Gils
2, 3 Eutropian (cc)

Färgfabriken, Stockholm, Sweden
1 Editors, Map data from OpenStreetMap. openstreetmap.org/copyright (2023)
2, 3, 4, 5 Eutropian (cc)

Stará Tržnica, Bratislava, Slovakia
1 Editors, Map data from OpenStreetMap. openstreetmap.org/copyright (2023)
2 Stará Tržnica
3, 4, 5 Eutropian (cc)

Jam Factory, Lviv, Ukraine
1 Editors, Map data from OpenStreetMap. openstreetmap.org/copyright (2023)
2 Paliy
3 Open Source: Narodowe Archiwum Cyfrowe, 1-U-3584-6
4 Ivanova
5 Yemets
6 Collection of Jam Factory

Enabling Collaboration: Supporting Regional Integration
1 van Gils
2 Allemeersch
3 Eutropian (cc)

Largo Residências, Lisbon, Portugal
1 Editors, Map data from OpenStreetMap. openstreetmap.org/copyright (2023)
2, 3, 4, 5 Eutropian (cc)

Praga Lab, Warsaw, Poland
1 Editors, Map data from OpenStreetMap.
openstreetmap.org/copyright (2023)
2 Pindor for OW SARP
3 Zaczyn for OW SARP
4 Bilska for OW SARP
5 Pindor, Open Source

Broei, Ghent, Belgium
1 Editors, Map data from OpenStreetMap.
openstreetmap.org/copyright (2023)
2 Allemeersch
3, 5 Eutropian (cc)
4 Villa

What is Open Heritage?
1, 2 Oevermann
3 Oevermann, Szemző

Heritage-Making and Planning
1, 2 Eutropian (cc)
3 Caudo, Editors

Adaptive Reuse
1 Oevermann
2 Fava, Mérai, Veldpaus
3 Eutropian (cc)

Transferability
1 Eutropian (cc)
2, 3 Mieg
4 van Gils

Lessons Learned
1 Szemző, Polyák, Patti, Mosquera
2, 3 Eutropian (cc)

Imprint

Editors
Heike Oevermann, Levente Polyák, Hanna Szemző, Harald A. Mieg

Copy editing
Dave Morris

Proofreading
Julia Dawson

Project management
Baharak Tajbakhsh, Regina Herr

Production
Bettina R. Algieri

Layout, cover design and typesetting
HE&AD Büro für Gestaltung,
Roman Heinrich, Ronald Adolf

Paper
Enviro Polar, 115 g/m^2

Printing
Grafisches Centrum Cuno GmbH & Co. KG, Calbe

Library of Congress Control Number
2023939417

Bibliographic information published by the German National Library
The German National Library lists this publication in the Deutsche Nationalbibliografie; detailed bibliographic data are available on the Internet at http://dnb.dnb.de.

ISBN 978-3-0356-2680-3
e-ISBN (PDF) 978-3-0356-2682-7
DOI: https://doi.org/10.1515/9783035626827

P.O. Box 44, 4009 Basel, Switzerland
Part of Walter de Gruyter GmbH, Berlin/Boston

The book is published open access at www.degruyter.com.

9 8 7 6 5 4 3 2 1
www.birkhauser.com

MIX
Paper from responsible sources
FSC® C043106
www.fsc.org

Carbon neutral
Print product
ClimatePartner.com/13493-2307-1011